AF662579

METAPHYSICAL ASPECTS OF BUDDHISM

METAPHYSICAL ASPECTS OF BUDDHISM

Suraj Vashishth

CYBER TECH PUBLICATIONS
4264/3, Ansari Road, Daryaganj, New Delhi-110002 (India)
Ph.: 011-23244078, 011-43559448 Fax: 011-23280028
E-Mail: cyberpublicationsdelhi@yahoo.com
Website: www.cybertechpublications.com

METAPHYSICAL ASPECTS OF BUDDHISM

Suraj Vashishth

© Reserved

First Edition 2011

All rights reserved. No part of this publication may be reproduced, stored in a retrieval system or transmitted, in any form or by any means, electronic, mechanical, photo copying, recording or otherwise, without the prior permission of the publisher.

Published by :

G.S. Rawat for **Cyber Tech Publications**
4264/3, Ansari Road, Daryaganj, New Delhi-110002 (India)
Ph.: 011-23244078, 011-43559448 Fax: 011-23280028
E-Mail: cyberpublicationsdelhi@yahoo.com
Website: www.cybertechpublications.com

Printed at: Asian Offset Printers, Delhi-53

CONTENTS

Preface

1. Introduction 1
2. The Further Teaching 23
3. What the Buddha Taught and Abhidhamma Thought 40
4. Sabhåva and Buddhist Doctrinal Thought 100
5. Individuals Revisiting the Abhidhamma Dhamma Theory 149
6. Causation as the Handmaid of Metaphysics 217

Bibliography 278

Index 279

Preface

When the first Hindoo missionaries arrived at the capital of China and were admitted to see the emperor, it was, the Buddhists tell us, in the last month of the year A.D. 68, and the 30th day of that month. By imperial command they were entertained in a building called Pe-ma sï, "Office of the white horses;" so named because they had ridden on white horses on their way from Cabul. The two Brahmans enjoyed the imperial favour, and one of the books they translated has remained popular to the present time. Thirteen years before these men reached China, the first missionaries of Christianity crossed the Ægean Sea and entered Europe. Instead of being received, however, with the smiles of those in power and enjoying imperial hospitality, they were publicly whipped and imprisoned by the magistrates of a Roman colony, and ignominiously dismissed.

Buddhism covered China with monasteries and images; Christianity covered Europe with churches and charitable institutions. A hundred authors have written on the history of the spread of Christianity in the various countries of Europe. Very few have ever studied the history of Buddhism as it has spread through China, and taught its doctrines in every part of that empire. There is room for new information on the entrance, progress, and characteristics of Chinese belief in the religion founded by Shakyamuni. Especially is there a need for facts on the history of Buddhism, because it is that one among the world's religions which has acquired the greatest multitude of adherents, and has also above any other carried out most systematically the monastic institute. Isaac Taylor drew attention in his Ancient Christianity to the knowledge of Hindoo monasticism possessed by Clement of Alexandria, and traced the origin of the monasticism of Christianity to that of India. Buddhism never became the State religion of China. It has grown side by side with the State religion, and obtained only the partial faith of the people. In this it differed from Christianity, which in Europe took the place of the old State religions of the various countries, after first vanquishing them all. Such is the ideal of Buddha. Let it be compared with that of the Christian Saviour. Let the result of the teaching of Shakyamuni on the Chinese be compared with that of the teaching of Christ on Europe.

—*Author*

1

Introduction

The Buddha's teaching, the *Dhamma,* is presented in the *Sutta-pitaka* of the Pali Canon as a path to the solution of the fundamental problem of human existence, namely, *dukkha,* customarily translated as 'suffering' or 'unsatisfactoriness'. In the *Nikayas* the processes that bring about the cessation of *dukkha* are conceived of primarily in terms of spiritual practice and development – such as *bhavana* (literally 'bringing into being', rendered as 'development'), *brahmacariya* ('the holy life'), *magga* (path) or *patipada* (way) – thus reflecting an interest in the workings and salvific capability of one's bodily, speech and mental acts. Although the Buddha's message does contain doctrinal concepts and theoretical statements on the nature of *dukkha,* its cause, its cessation and the way to its cessation, these statements function as guidelines for comprehending Buddhist thought and do not amount to a systematic theory. The attempt to ground the Buddha's scattered teachings in an inclusive theory was introduced later on with the advance of the subsequent Abhidharma/Abhidhamma tradition: a doctrinal movement in Buddhist thought and exegesis that gradually developed during the first centuries after the Buddha's *mahaparinibbana* in tandem with distinctive theoretical and practical interests, resulting in an independent branch of inquiry and literary genre, as documented in the third basket of the Pali Canon, the *Abhidhamma-pitaka.*

While the *Nikayas* present the Buddha's teachings as addressed to specific audiences at specific times and locations, the Abhidhamma seeks to describe the structure underlying the Buddha's *Dhamma* fully, in ultimate terms that apply in all circumstances. In this sense it marks the attempt to establish

Buddhist thought as a comprehensive philosophy. Since the Buddha's teaching is primarily concerned with lived, sentient experience, the Abhidhamma's philosophical rendering of the *Dhamma* attempts to provide a systematic and comprehensive account of the constitution of that experience. It does so by explicating the nature of all types of physical and mental events that make up one's conscious world, as well as that of their relationships and interrelationships of causal conditioning. Physical and mental events, the ultimate terms used by the Abhidhamma in its philosophical enterprise, are known as *dharma/dhamma* (hereafter *dharmas/dhammas*), and hence the overarching inquiry involving both the analysis of all types of *dhamma* and their synthesis into a unified structure by means of their manifold relationships is referred to as the '*dhamma* theory'. But what exactly is a *dhamma* as opposed to *dhammas*? How did the *dhamma* theory proceed from its Nikaya-based origins and why? What role did early Buddhist tradition's apprehension of the concept of *dhamma* play in the formation of the Abhidhamma? What kind of a philosophical system is it that founds itself upon the concept of *dhamma,* and what are the sote-riological implications of this concept for the ensuing philosophical system? Is not the Abhidhamma understanding of the concept of *dhamma* at odds with the Buddha's teaching? Ye t might not it be misleading to qualify Abhidhamma thought as 'Buddhist ontology'? In this study I have undertaken to answer these questions.

The present monograph seeks to analyse and provide a philosophically adequate account of the doctrinal transition from the earliest strata of Buddhist thought to the Abhidhamma, thus rendering the Buddha's philosophical position more explicit and locating the Abhidhamma in relation to its origins. The underlying question taken up here is: 'How does the Buddha's experientially oriented and pragmatic teaching become in the Abhidhamma a systematic philosophy?' What I show is that this doctrinal transition results from early Buddhist tradition's shifting construal of conscious experience, and is best understood in terms of a change in epistemological orientation and metaphysical outlook. Before we begin reconstructing the making of early Buddhism as a philosophical tradition, though, a preliminary terminological elucidation is necessary in order to locate the subsequent discussion within the realm of philosophy.

First we must attend to the intricacy of the laden concepts of metaphysics and ontology. What is distinctive of philosophical inquiry is the attempt to understand the relation between human thought and the world. This project is constitutive of metaphysics, which is, in its broadest interpretation, the attempt to arrive by rational means at a comprehensive picture of the world. Metaphysics is the most general and abstract part of philosophy, dealing with the features of reality, what ultimately exists and what it is that distinguishes and makes that possible. Western philosophy at its very beginnings with the Pre-Socratics was metaphysical in its nature, but it was Plato's theory of Forms (or Ideas) that clarified the distinction of metaphysics from physics. The term 'metaphysics' originated as a title referring to some of Aristotle's treatises which followed his works on physics in the catalogue of their edition produced by Andronicus of Rhodes in the second half of the first century BCE. These treatises are heterogeneous: they are concerned with being, both as such and in respect of various categories of it (foremost of which is substance), as well as with other matters coterminous with later metaphysical theories. The general picture of the world which forms the content of a metaphysical system, though, ought to be distinguished from the detailed account of what there is in that world. In contemporary philosophy metaphysics customarily concerns the study of being *qua* being, being in itself, prior to and regardless of the extension or categories of being and the reality of the world. As Umberto Eco observes,

> [W]hether what we call the outside World, or the Universe, is or is not, or whether it is the effect of a malign spirit, does not in any way affect the primary evidence that there is "something" somewhere (even if it were no more than a *res cogitans* that realized it was cogitating).

Metaphysics thus aims at the intension of being *per se*, the question 'What is the nature of being?' which may be designated 'the definition question'.

Being *per se*, however, is unthinkable unless it is organized within a system of entities: entities are the way in which being is revealed to us. The science of actual being, being as embodied in entities, is the subject matter of ontology. Ontology, understood as a branch of metaphysics, captures the question of the extension of being, or 'the population question', that is, 'What are the beings?', or 'What does exist?' In a derivative, additional sense, 'ontology' is used to refer to the set of things the existence of which is acknowledged by a particular theory or system of thought. It is in this sense that one speaks of a metaphysical system as having a particular ontology, such as an ontology of material substances or of events. Metaphysical problems go beyond the realm of ontology; they concern our con-strual of encountered phenomena and features of our life other than the question of what there is. For instance, questions of how mind and mental phenomena are possible in a world of matter, of how values and norms can agree with scientific facts, as well as issues regarding space and time, change and identity through time, God, the nature of personal identity or immortality.

While it is not uncommon for Western philosophical systems to begin with metaphysical presuppositions and secondarily to generate epistemological criteria by which to verify the particular ontology resultant from those presuppositions, it is occasionally possible to find the reversed situation, wherein the solutions a certain system offers to the abovementioned metaphysical questions derive from epistemological assumptions regarding what is comprehensible or knowable, and the ways in which this is so. Here one must first make such decisions as to which primitive notions the philosophical system will build upon, whether the things spoken of within the system will be restricted in certain ways, or what the limitations of its referential terms are. Metaphysical worldviews and specific ontologies have indeed resulted from epistemological constraints. For instance, it might be argued that Descartes's metaphysics is founded on epistemological grounds, for his dualism of mind and body as discrete substances is based on the claim that we have a clearer and more distinct idea of our minds than of our bodies. It is Kant's *Critique of Pure Reason*, though, which exem-plarily illustrates the idea of a metaphysics as subject to epistemological constraints, for its primary concern is with the possibility of metaphysics understood as philosophical knowledge that transcends the bounds of sense experience. Rejecting what he considered the speculative metaphysics handed down by the Rationalists, yet being concerned, as the Empiricists had been, with the boundaries of human understanding, Kant's transcendental idealism, unlike traditional metaphysics, sidesteps the trap of using reason beyond its appropriate limits. His critique of the limitations of human understanding and of what is necessary about it forms a watershed in the history of metaphysics, but is certainly reckoned as metaphysics.

In the Indian arena philosophical systems ordinarily commence with episte-mological rather than with metaphysical or ontological assumptions. A primary concern of classical Indian philosophers is with the nature of right cognition (*prama/pramaja*) and its means, and only once they have established the criteria for means of valid knowledge do they make metaphysical, ontological or ethical claims. Although the Indian concept of *pramaja* does not neatly overlap with the Western epistemologists' standard characterization of knowledge as justified true belief, the study of the nature of *pramaja*, its scope, basis, reliability, etc., corresponds for the most part to what is meant by 'epistemology' and may safely be rendered 'Indian epistemology'. Different schools hold conflicting views on the nature of right cognition: the Naiyayikas, for instance, accept four *pramaja*s, namely, perception (*pratyaksa*), inference (*anumana*), analogy (*upamana*) and verbal testimony (*fabda*), whereas Buddhist epistemologists, having conceived of *pramaja* as valid cognition itself rather than a means to it, recognize the validity of perception and inference alone. Notwithstanding their different positions, Buddhist and non-Buddhist philosophers alike partake in the general apprehension of epistemology as setting off philosophizing. What does distinguish Buddhist thought, however, is that, having recognized that lived experience is unsatisfactory, it locates the cause of *dukkha* in our lack of insight into the dynamics of cognition, and its prescribed soteriological solution is therefore to gain insight into the conditions of our cognitive apparatus. For early Buddhism epistemology is not only the foundation, but also the most urgent endeavour.

A distinction should thus be drawn – especially when dealing with classical Indian philosophy – between criteria normally used in confirming perceptual claims that depend on the use of our sense faculties, by which what exists in some sector of the world is ascertained (claims such as 'x is to be found in the room'), and those ontological criteria by which we claim to ascertain what there really is in the world. Criteria of this second sort inevitably infect those of the first, but they may be distinguished from whatever is admitted to be true by those criteria of the first sort. Hence different ontologies, namely, different accounts of what exists in actuality, may result from whatever is said to be true about things as identified in a particular domain. This also means that it may be possible to endorse an epistemology while remaining neutral on any particular metaphysical position, or even while shunning ontology altogether. We will see in Chapter that such is the case of the Buddha's doctrinal and philosophical legacy.

The Buddha, as he is portrayed in the *Nikayas,* rejects purely theoretical questions known as the undeclared or indeterminate (*avyakata*) questions – those that are to be set aside on the grounds that they are not conducive to *nibbana* – and the *Dhamma* is accordingly presented as a therapeutic way of life rather than a system in the traditional sense. The Buddha's interest is in gaining insight into the conditions of sentient experience in *saμsara,* namely, in experience as lived, not in its foundation in reality, and he suspends all views regarding the nature of such reality, of the person and his or her relation to the environment, and of the ontological status of the encountered world. His teaching is therefore portrayed as pragmatic, empirically focused, concerning itself with the cessation of *dukkha* and to that end emphasizing issues of cognition, psychology, epistemology and soteriology – characteristics that show family resemblance to some of the motifs of Western phenomenology. Two other 'phenomenological features' could be added to the above list: the first is the Buddha's challenge of the representationalist model of knowledge and of the innocent correspondence of thought, word and world; the second is his emphasis on the intentional structure of consciousness. This emphasis is already present in the earliest stratum of Buddhist epistemology in the taxonomies of the twelve *ayatana*s and the eighteen *dhatu*s, and is retained in the Abhidhamma analysis of *citta.* In accordance with all these motifs, various scholars have offered a phenom-enological reading of Buddhist thought, claiming that the Abhidhamma in particular is a 'phenomenological psychology' dealing with conscious reality or the world as given in experience; a 'metapsychology' of which the primary objects of investigation are the various concepts and categories of consciousness.

This is not the proper venue for addressing the question as to what order of phenomenology Buddhism is, if any, though one should note that this characterization raises a potential for ambiguity in the distinction between phenomenological attention to the constituents of experience *qua* the contents that present themselves in consciousness (suspending the question of the existence of the intentional object) and introspective attention to the flow of experience itself, that is, to its status as a process or a sequence of events, etc. Moreover, before we can sweepingly endow Buddhism as a whole with a phenomenological orientation, we must be clear about what a *dhamma* is, but this is one of the most complex and disputable issues in Buddhist thought. As we shall see in Chapter , along with its doctrinal development Buddhist tradition itself was shifting its con-strual of the concept of *dhamma*, so that for the Abhidhammikas this concept meant something quite different from what it had originally signified for the Buddha's immediate community. What I do wish to stress here – and is decisively part of early Buddhist self-portrayal – is, first, that the Buddha's teaching founds itself upon the observation that there is something fundamentally wrong with the human condition as lived, and, second, that it comprises an account of how conscious experience arises and of how the dissatisfaction involved in this experience can be removed. In the sense of its concern with one's lived experience rather than with the foundation of this experience in reality the Buddha's teaching may broadly be qualified as phenomenological.

The first centuries after the Buddha's *parinibbana*, however, witnessed the rise of the Abhidhamma that, subject to the contemporary doctrinal and social conditions, undertook to supplement the principles scattered throughout the Buddha's discourses with a comprehensive, unified theory. But it is the Abhidhamma's very concern with one's lived experience – the object and so-called phenomenological orientation of the Buddha's teaching – that has been the subject of a longstanding dispute in modern scholarship.

Educated in the historical and philosophical tradition of the nineteenth century and inspired by New Testament scholarship, the European establishers of the tradition of Buddhist studies, whose interpretation of the Pali Buddhist tradition provided the grounding for a more sophisticated understanding of Pali Buddhism in the future, tended to present Nikaya Buddhism as centred on an ethical doctrine that was gradually distorted by the Buddhist 'church' and by the Abhidhamma 'scholastics'. This portrayal gave rise to the view of the Abhidhamma as a divergent conceptual framework, often contrary to the Buddha's intentions, that brought about the ossification of the 'original' teaching, misconceived it and, to a large extent, lost touch with it. Even more recently acclaimed scholarly works show traces of this heritage and tend to support the view that the Abhidhamma systematization resulted in scholasticism and detachment from lived experience. Erich Frauwallner, for instance, characterizes the Abhidhamma method as '"formal "or "formalistic" scholasticism', meaning that its sole aim was to preserve the Buddha's teaching and illuminate it from different angles. This method, Frauwallner argues, degenerated into artificiality and senseless exaggeration, and replaced genuine thought with redundant, extended *matikas*. Moreover, 'this degeneration was probably at its worst in the Pali school, which confined itself exclusively to the transmitted doctrinal material and never really developed any original thought of its own.' More specifically, other Buddhologists opine that while the Buddha refrained from making any ontological assumptions about the grounds of sentient experience in a mind-independent world, the Abhidhamma introduced ontology into its system, so that the *dhammas* emerged as primary elements to which everything else is reducible, their categorization as a categorial theory describing what really exists. 'Ontology began to creep back into Buddhism', Richard Gombrich has thus argued, 'when texts were compiled making lists of things the Buddha had referred to'.

The present study calls into question some of the claims of 'distortion' and 'ossification' regarding the Pali Abhidhamma elaboration on the basic principles of Buddhist thought. It shows that a close reading of the Pali treatises with attention to their subtleties and subtexts may exhibit that the Abhidhamma, at least in its canonical period, shares the concerns of the Nikaya mindset, even if it is a product of a different doctrinal-social milieu and is necessarily bound up with an ongoing process of conceptual reframing of the earliest Buddhist teachings. Since the latter are concerned with what may provisionally be called 'soteriology', or 'religious experience', or yet again 'mental cultivation of the path to awakening', Buddhism as a religious-philosophical movement– rather than a closed system in which everything is the logical consequence of initial premises – would develop as dialectic sequences of responses to its founding teachings. Must such a process of conceptual reshaping result in a distortion of the first, 'most genuine' teachings? Is the term 'scholasticism' neatly attributable to the Abhidhamma?

Does a scholastic method necessarily hinder soteriology and practical concerns with human experience? Should not the encounter with the Nikaya mindset and with the Abhidhamma doctrines broaden one's apprehension of what philosophy is and deepen one's understanding of what religion may be? With these questions in mind, let us first examine the meaning of 'scholasticism' at issue.

SCHOLASTICISM AND THE ABHIDHAMMA FROM THE PERSPECTIVE OF THE COMPARATIVE PHILOSOPHY OF RELIGION

Scholasticism as a practice, rather than a term for a medieval European philosophical movement, has been spurned by philosophers and intellectuals since the Renaissance: it has represented for modernists a vain engagement with theoretical issues and useless conceptual distinctions, and hence has become an object one should surpass. Nevertheless, intellectual practices that constitute scholasticism may have solid merit and interest. Paul Griffiths suggests that the root metaphor for scholastic intellectual practice is reading: scholastic movements establish certain relations with the texts they read, relations which imply an ontology, epistemology and ethics. The prime element in these relations is that the texts read (these are not necessarily written: they may well be orally transmitted and 'reading' is used in a figurative manner) are a stable and vastly rich resource that yields truth, meaning, suggestions and rules of conduct, and that lends itself to a continuous, ever-repeated process of interpretation. Scholastic reading is an active engagement aimed at altering the course of the readers' cognitive, affective and active life by ingesting, digesting, ruminating over and restating what is read. Hence the significance of commentary to scholastics and its position as their basic literary genre.

In his study of the dGe lugs pa Tibetan Buddhist view of language, José Ignacio Cabezón brings forward the concept of scholasticism as a primary category in comparative philosophy of religion, suggesting that the phenomenon of scholasticism ought to be more broadly construed than its parochial medieval European meaning. The scholastic method in medieval Christian Europe is known for its formal nature, its systematicity, its preoccupation with scriptures and their exegesis in commentaries, its rationalism and reliance on logic and dialectics in defence of its tenets, its penchant for lists, classifications and categorizations, and its tendency towards abstraction. Nevertheless, a broader construal of the phenomenon of scholasticism shows that many religious movements which may be classified as 'scholastic' – such as rabbinic Judaism, neo-Confucianism, certain movements within Islam, Mimaµsa Hinduism or the Indo-Tibetan Buddhist tradition – are concerned with reconciling the rational and experiential aspects of religious life. 'Over and above the mere synthesis of experience and reason', Cabezón states, 'many scholastic movements would go one step further, claiming that reasoning and systematicity, far from being incompatible with personal religious experience, are the very *prerequisites* for spiritual realization and action'.

Despite their differences, Cabezón identifies four factors that generally motivate scholastic traditions toward rationalism and systematicity. The first is the basic intelligibility of the universe: reality, for the scholastics, is accessible via rational inquiry, and though the latter may be superseded by intuitive knowledge it is nonetheless necessary. Second, scholastic movements are traditionally oriented: they have a strong sense of history and lineage, and are committed to the preservation of their tradition. To preserve a tradition means to preserve its spirit as it is expressed in experience and practice.

Insofar as these are conditioned by doctrine, to preserve a tradition means to establish a rational inquiry into its doctrinal and intellectual underpinnings. In this sense, rational inquiry is essential to the maintenance of the tradition's self-identity. Third, rational inquiry is also essential to distinguishing the tradition's outlook from its opponents' and to defending it against their intellectual criticisms. Fourth, since scholastics deal with large bodies of disparate textual material that is often contradictory, part of their task is to synthesize this material into an ordered, unified whole. In so doing, they usually tend towards textual proliferation and inclusion rather than elimination and exclusion: they prefer to elaborate on and systematize the textual material rather than to limit and ignore portions of it which may be contradictory. Scholastics often attempt to reconcile both the systematic-rational and the experiential-practical dimensions of their respective tradition, and this should naturally lead to a tension that may manifest itself in various ways. This tension, as it occurs within the conceptual framework of the Theravadin Abhidhamma, lies at the heart of the present study. In line with Cabezón's suggestion, I seek to examine this tension in the light of a broader construal of the phenomenon of scholasticism.

Moreover, the broader notion of scholasticism should include the way Indian philosophical-religious schools understand knowledge and philosophical texts. It has often been pointed out that Indian philosophy developed historically as a commentarial tradition, and that Indian learned traditions seek to restate and explicate their fundamental ideas as given at the beginning of the history of their disciplines. Eliot Deutsch has convincingly argued that this idea of philosophy as 'recovery' rather than 'discovery' is central to the traditional Indian understanding of a philosophical text. What constitutes the text in Indian thought, Deutsch claims, is the *sutra/karika* along with the ongoing exegetical work, and hence the basic unit in Indian philosophy is the 'tradition text'. A tradition text has its authoritative sources grounded in its oral transmission, its summaries and its ongoing written elaborations. The commentaries, sub-commentaries and glosses form integral parts of a continuing argument or text, and in this sense are not merely appendages to a fixed, completed work, but an ongoing, developing text. The tradition text preserves its body of ideas, seeking to expand, refine, explicate and bring greater systematic coherence to it. This kind of preservation is essentially an act of reason: a creative undertaking that innovates something through each vital engagement with the tradition text. From the philosopher-commentator's standpoint he is making new contributions to the tradition text through his creative appropriation of it, while at the same time remaining faithful to his authoritative sources. Appropriation, as opposed to mere borrowing and influence, is a creative process of retaining a content that is made one's own while reframing and reshaping it, thus revalorizing its meaning to one's own end; it is a dynamic engagement that brings about true synthesis, for what is appropriated is transformed while simultaneously transforming its appropriator-bearer. To appropriate something means to take it as part of one's own being while redefining one's self, so that the appropriated content becomes the stuff of personal identity. In this 'existentialist' sense, as Deutsch notes, knowledge is a genuine act of creation; it is karma. In the same vein, the Abhidhamma's alleged scholasticism should be apprehended more broadly, and so its following investigation will be juxtaposed with the key concepts of tradition text and appropriation.

Method and Scope

The question of how and why the Buddha's first teachings resulted in something quite different, namely, the Abhidhamma, spawns a host of subsidiary queries: is it possible to trace the distinct phases of the conceptual transition from the earliest Buddhist teaching, through the Abhidhamma literature and up to the later Theravadin commentarial tradition? What motivated the Abhidhammikas in this process of change?

Even if we are entitled to characterize the Abhidhamma as a 'scholastic' movement, does its scholastic orientation imply that it is bound to embody a complete misreading of the 'original' teaching? To what extent did the canonical Abhidhamma genuinely become 'removed in spirit' from early Buddhist teaching and why? What, then, is the place of soteriology within the Abhidhamma framework?

My inquiry into these questions is based on the Pali canonical texts, several para-canonical works and the *Atthakatha.* In what follows by 'early Abhidhamma' I mean the *Abhidhamma-pitaka,* particularly the *Dhammasangani,* the *Vibhanga* and the *Patthana.* By 'later', 'mature' or 'developed Abhidhamma' I intend what is referred to in the *Atthakatha,* the *Visuddhimagga* and two of the primary Abhidhamma manuals, - the *Abhidhammavatara* and the *Abhidhammatthasangaha.* The *Petakopadesa, Nettippakarana, Milindapañha, Buddhavamsa* and the *Patisambhidamagga* – para-canonical works whose role in the establishment of the *dhamma* theory is appraised in Chapter 3 - I regard as transitional texts that reflect the canonical Abhidhamma's formative period. Any investigation into the doctrinal development of the tradition ancestral to the Theravada must take into account the contemporary Brahmanical backdrop against which it arose and the challenges posed by its rival Buddhist schools.

Alongside the Pali sources I therefore use throughout this study such texts as the *Upanisads,* the *Nyayasutra,* the *Vaisesikasutra* and works of the grammatical *Vyakarana* literature, and also look into relevant sources that summarize the views of the Northern Sarvastivada-Vaibhasika and Sautrantika schools, as these often highlight distinctive features of the Theravadin position and clarify difficulties of interpretation.

Buddhological literature is replete with discussions of the difficulties associated with the assessment of the early phase of Buddhist literature, and a number of attempts have been made at compiling a detailed chronology of the evolution of the Pali texts. While our understanding of the texts have certainly profited from these attempts, they have not been able satisfactorily to provide a comprehensive chronological stratification either of the earliest phase of Buddhist literature as represented by the *Vinaya-pitaka* and the four primary *Nikayas* (along with certain other smaller texts associated with them), or of its second broad phase as documented in the para-canonical texts and the Abhidharma literature. I do not wish to enter the methodological, historical and philological maze surrounding this area of Buddhist studies, for my concerns in the present study are elsewhere.

Following the commonly accepted, preliminary relative chronology of the Pali sources mentioned above, I shall adopt here the view that while the later works belonging to the second broad phase of Buddhist literature contain much that is apparently new and distinctive to a particular tradition ancestral to the Theravada, they also contain a fair amount of material that is still part of the common heritage and earliest stratum of Buddhist thought as found in the *Nikayas* (and *Agamas*).

To make headway in understanding early Buddhism we might as well benefit from a stratification of the ideas and concepts contained in the Pali texts rather than of the texts alone. Thus although linguistic and historical concerns form a necessary part of this inquiry, what I have set out to do here is pursue a conceptual investigation into the development of Buddhist ideas, assuming first that Buddhism and philosophy are comparable and commensurate, and second that such an investigation must, at times, overstep the textual sources and involve philosophical reconstruction.

Reflecting on this subject, D. Seyfort Ruegg observes that in deciding whether Buddhist teaching is genuinely philosophical, much will depend on what we think philosophy is about. Representing itself as therapeutic and soteriological, Buddhism is not essentially philosophical if 'philosophy' denotes but analysis of concepts, language and meaning. As a teaching prescribing a path to the cessation of *dukkha,* Buddhism has had to develop a soteriological method that is theoretically intelligible and satisfying, and hence within its framework soteriology and epistemology are interconnected. In line with Ruegg's view, this study assumes that Buddhist thought – albeit irreducible to any single philosophy – can be meaningfully described as philosophical in the sense that philosophical thinking comprises a major part of its procedures and mindset, and that this philosophical dimension is heuristically necessary in the study of Buddhism.

Weaving Buddhology with comparative philosophy, in addition to the Buddhist and Brahmanical sources I rely on Western philosophical literature from its Greek origins up to contemporary texts pertaining to analytic philosophy, philosophy of mind and cultural criticism.

This eclecticism is intentional and methodologically motivated: here I follow Bimal Krishna Matilal's apprehension of the study of classical Indian philosophy vis-à-vis analytic philosophy as exemplifying the inseparable relation between philosophical theory and Indian thought. Drawing on a wide range of both classical Indian and Anglo-American literary sources, Matilal's work shows that through the study of such diverse literature and by giving the Indian material a genuine prospect of informing contemporary philosophical discussions, one can become immersed in the process of reinterpreting the values and the fundamental concepts of one's own culture or tradition, thus revealing its mechanisms of self-awareness and approaching a critical, deeper understanding of the culture itself, perhaps from the inside.

As for comparative philosophy, this is still in a formative stage and the 'comparative method' is far from being a completed project. Comparative studies, and such studies of Western and Indian philosophies specifically, are abundant in discussions of the problems of the comparative method and the various questions involved in it.

These include such questions as whether there is a common ground for comparing Western and Indian philosophical-religious traditions and a universal medium through which they can communicate; whether revealing similarities between the two respective traditions is possible only at the cost of obliterating their different contexts, thus of misconstruing their doctrines; whether overemphasizing each tradition's particular context does not lead one into yielding to the danger of conceptual relativism; whether we can understand, and if so to what extent, the Indian statements by drawing on Western philosophy, or what the study of Indian thought means if it leaves us without the guidance of Western terminology. This study presupposes that the questions of philosophy and their treatments by various traditions transcend considerations of time and place, and hence that there is, indeed, a basis for a cross-cultural comparison of such traditions as twentieth-century Western scholarship and early Buddhism. Still, we should bear in mind that the comparative method is not an end in itself. As Wilhelm Halbfass captures this point:

If 'comparative philosophy' is supposed to be *philosophy*, it cannot just be the comparison of *philosophies*. It cannot be the objectifying, juxtaposing, synoptic, comparative investigation of historical, anthropological data. Comparative philosophy is philosophy insofar as it aims at self-understanding. It has to be ready to bring its own standpoint, and the conditions and the horizon of comparison itself, into the process of comparison which thus assumes the reflexive, self-referring dimension which constitutes philosophy.

Cross-cultural comparisons frequently prove to have limited heuristic value. Every comparison ends with the vexing question 'So what if X and Y are similar/ different in such-and-such respects?', and comparative philosophy should be able to answer that question. This is possible if we are willing to examine our conceptual distinctions that foster the conditions of the very act of comparison. The customary guiding method in dealing with non-Western texts has been to ask to what extent these texts solve our philosophical problems. This question, however, reads into the texts those issues by which the investigator is already seized and generates answers that depend upon his or her cultural determinants.

Comparative philosophy should therefore reformulate the question and ask instead to what extent non-Western texts suggest that we should be asking different philosophical questions. 'By asking this latter question', Henry Rosemont stresses, 'comparative philosophers can hope to revitalize philosophy in general by articulating alternative conceptual frameworks, showing how, why and that they make sense; and by so doing begin to develop a new conceptual framework that embodies the insights from a multiplicity of cultures, which can assist the ongoing work of human and biological scientists to solve the puzzles of what it is to be a human being'.

We must constantly acknowledge the fact that our definitions and presuppositions may not be directly applicable to the Buddhist conceptual infrastructure. The comparative method can then turn terminological and conceptual ambiguities to its advantage by utilizing them to make sense of Buddhist thought and in its mirror to call into question our habitual categories and presuppositions that shape our approach to human experience and its relation to the environment. Comparative philosophy may thus become illuminating and innovative if it turns into a means to gaining self-awareness and novel insights into the nature of philosophy and religion *qua* thought and religion.

We are now able to describe our research topic more accurately. Although the Buddha is recorded as claiming to have no interest in purely theoretical questions because they are not conducive to ***nibbana***, this does not necessarily mean that he rejects metaphysical questions, or that in his teaching there is hardly any of what we may nowadays call a philosophy. Setting aside certain matters as unexplained itself has philosophical significance, for in philosophy, semantics and pragmatics the principle of relevance is recognized as essentially philosophical. As will be shown, despite the Buddha's silence on ontological matters he clearly had a distinctive epistemology, subject to the constraints of which there followed, if only implicitly, a particular kind of metaphysics, and indeed a radical one.

Subsequent generations continued to grapple with the Buddha's heritage and to elaborate on his teaching, teasing out from it a clearer albeit different metaphysical theory, and stratifying it with conceptual realism. This process, as we shall see throughout this book, is evidenced in the canonical Abhidhamma literature. Ye t despite the Abhidhamma's gradual movement towards reification of terms and concepts, we will see that in its early period it remained epistemologically geared, and that if a realist ontology is to be found in Theravadin thought then this is a post-canonical development derivative from the commentarial systematization of the earlier teachings.

Moreover, when dealing with the Theravadin mindset one contends with an ontology remarkably different from its customary construal in Western tradition. In the Theravadin arena ontology is bound up with what we may provisionally call psychology, and although it is concerned with what and how things really are, this reality is not necessarily external. Ontology here is grounded in a conceptual scheme that lacks the postulate of transcendence and holds a special place for the concept of *kamma,* that is, a particular kind of mentality, one's 'act of will' or intention (*cetana*). This means not only that the real is not necessarily external, but also that what something *is* could be equated with how it *acts* and what it *does*, and that the criteria of truth of ordinary judgements about what is real are rooted in one's consciousness.

Rather similar views are nowadays acceptable to Western mind and are even dominant among philosophical circles that, following such figures as Wittgenstein, Heidegger or Quine, endorse behaviouristic, pragmatic and holistic approaches to knowledge, meaning and existence. These views, though, sprang up at a very late stage in the history of Western thought and have been accompanied by a sense of philosophical crisis. They were anticipated by Kant (although he retains the picture of philosophy as an architectonic scheme providing a framework for inquiry in the form of a theory of knowledge), but gained importance as late as the nineteenth century and became dominant only in the twentieth century. The philosophical crisis they induce is connected with the rise of post-modernism, the deconstructionist criticism and the demise of foundational epistemology. These movements are regarded as offensive to the philosophical quest for commensurate truth and to rationality as a whole, because they dismiss both the idea of knowledge as an assemblage of accurate representations of an objective reality and the notion of apodictic philosophy as picking out the foundations of knowledge. Now throughout this study by 'Western philosophy' or 'Western thought' I mean the classical European tradition that dominated until the end of the eighteenth century. For this tradition epistemology as the foundational discipline of philosophy was thought to be distinct from psychology, and the idea that the world contains mind-independent entities, properties and relations was central to any ontological account of the real. Aligning this line of development in Western thought with the Theravada thought-world may clarify that what the earliest Buddhist teaching offers is a deflationary notion of knowledge (albeit such that avoids a philosophical crisis or a sense of a threatening conceptual vacuum that needs to be filled), whereas what the Abhidhamma promulgates in response to this radical position is a more commonsensical view – pragmatic at first, and later, in the post-canonical period, a representational model of knowledge and an ensuing psychological ontology.

THE DOCTRINAL TRANSITION FROM THE BUDDHA'S TEACHING TO THE ABHIDHAMMA: PRELIMINARY REMARKS

It has become widely accepted to present the history of Buddhist thought as a struggle to come to terms with an account of one's experience based on a conceptual infrastructure that does not presuppose an underlying substantial core unifying that experience. According to this portrayal, the history of Buddhist thought is the history of a continuing debate over the construction of reality and the self in substantial terms. The Buddha presents a vision of human experience as a transitory array of phenomena that are not held together by any underlying substrate. The Abhidharma's account of this experience, by contrast, is based on the notion of ultimate, self-sufficient elements, that is, *dharmas*. Madhyamaka thought is then seen as a watershed in the history of Buddhist ideas: Nagarjuna's notion of emptiness (*funyata*) demonstrates the logical impossibility of the Abhidharma ontological realism, and shows that the Buddha taught that everything was indeterminate and empty of its own-existence. Finally, the Yogacara is said to have returned to a positive account of reality, although from the perspective of idealism and based on the workings of the mind, as embodied by the idea of 'store consciousness' (*alaya-vijñana*) entertained in the works of Vasubandhu. This general portrayal illustrates that the development of Buddhist thought hinges upon a long-lasting debate regarding the tradition's notion of the term *dhamma*, its signification, and of what its true nature and its ontological status are. As Richard Gombrich has suggested, 'the development of a Buddhist ontology, perhaps contrary to the Buddha's intentions, might be traced through considering how the word *dhamma* is used'. This consideration underlies Chapter . I wish to take this idea one step further, though, and claim that the concept of *dhamma* lies at the core of a major metaphysical shift undergone by Buddhist thought during the period of the formation and fixation of the Abhidhamma. To make headway in comprehending the changing Abhidhamma doctrines they must be viewed in the light of this metaphysical shift.

What happened during this transitional period in the history of Theravadin thought is that the Abhidhammikas – in their attempt to elaborate on the Buddha's teaching (*Dhamma*), to construct it in theoretical terms and to provide an all-inclusive systematization of its set of truths and principles (*dhammas*) – inclined towards contemplating these principles as determined particulars, and in due course as primary elements (*dhammas*). They thus put more emphasis on the nature and status of the events constitutive of one's conscious experience as taught by the Buddha, rather than on how the consciousness process as a whole operates. As Rupert Gethin notes with reference to the transition from using the singular form *dhamma* to the plural *dhammas*,

[T]he relationship between *dhamma* and *dhammas* has been insufficiently examined by modern scholarship. This is in part the result of a tendency to view *dhammas* as the exclusive domain of the later Abhidhamma literature, both canonical and commentarial. The assumption is that the *dhammas* of the Abhidhamma constitute a scholastic elaboration somewhat removed in spirit and time from the 'original' *dhamma* of the Buddha.

Contemporary scholars have construed the major difference between the Buddha's teaching and the Abhidhamma in terms of a shift from *how* to *what*: from a concern with how one knows and how one experiences one's world, to asking what there is in the world. Gombrich has thus indicated that the consistency of the Buddha's interest in 'how' rather than in 'what' gains weight by his emphasis on physical and mental processes rather than on objects, as well as by his dismissal of ontological matters. Along the same line of thought, Sue Hamilton has suggested that the analysis of the human being into five *khandhas* is not an analysis of what the human being consists of, but of the processes or events by which one's experience is constituted and which one needs to understand. Ye t what are those phenomena – those physical and mental processes – that the Buddha discusses? They are all knowable phenomena as presented in consciousness; they are *dham-mas*. Hence, the shifting emphasis from 'how' to 'what' and the growing interest in ontology hinge, first and foremost, upon the concept of *dhamma*.

This means that at the kernel of what is perhaps the most striking doctrinal transition in the history of Theravadin thought and in the development of early Indian Buddhism in general, underlying the supposedly degenerative and scholastic character of the Abhidhamma, lies the tradition's changing outlook of the nature of a *dhamma*: of what it means to be a specific *dhamma*. This question is crucial to the objective of the present monograph and will be pursued throughout the following chapters.

An Outline of the Chapters

Chapter delineates the historical and doctrinal backdrop of the rise of the various Abhidharma schools: it surveys the contemporary intellectual milieu during the transitional period from the Nikaya mindset to the institutionalized tradition ancestral to the Theravada, advancing the prevalent scholarly accounts of the evolution of the Pali Abhidhamma and its literary genre. Assuming that at the heart of the doctrinal transition from the first teachings of the Buddha to the canonical Abhidhamma lies a shift in the tradition's construal of the concept of *dhamma*, Chapter explores the development of this concept and the formation of the *dhamma* theory. Examining the evolution of this theory along with two of its closely related doctrines – the doctrine of atomism and the doctrine of momen-tariness – this chapter shows that the major doctrinal shift in the history of early Buddhism is best understood in terms of a change in epistemological attitude and metaphysical foundation. Specifically, I find that the Abhidhamma theoreticians drew from the Buddha's epistemological position a metaphysical outlook that fostered a shift from analysing conscious experience in terms of processes to analysing it in terms of events, that is, from process to event metaphysics. The operative conceptual scheme implicit in the Buddha's teachings, which I identify with the concept of *dhamma* as a psycho-physical process, is thus replaced in the early Abhidhamma with the understanding of a *dhamma qua* an event as analytical primitive.

Chapter focuses on the Theravadin shifting apprehension of the term *sabhava*, a key concept in the evolution of Buddhist doctrinal thought, from its earliest occurrences in the para-canonical texts to its elaboration in the *Atthakatha* and the sub-commentaries. Drawing on the recognition that the doctrine of *sab-hava* cannot sensibly be isolated from the evolving *dhamma* theory and its underlying metaphysical shift, I show that the overall treatment of the concept of *sabhava* attests to the Theravadins' concern with matters of epistemology and language rather than of ontology, and that such an interest in ontology arose relatively late and was desultory rather than systematic.

Chapter 4 further investigates the Abhidhamma metaphysical vision. I identify the *dhamma* theory as centred on the individuation of one's conscious experience, and examine its application within the Abhidhamma event-based analysis of the consciousness process (*citta-vithi*). Discussing the Vaifesika and the early Grammarians' notions of definition and categorization as sources that are likely to have influenced the Abhidhamma *dhamma* theory, I clarify in what way the Theravadin conception of ontology is suffused with language and psychology. The chapter concludes with an appraisal of the Abhidhamma's growing interest in the individuation of *nibbana,* thus accounting for the post-canonical, fourfold *dhamma* typology.

Chapter 5 deals with another major aspect of the doctrinal transition undergone by early Buddhist thought, namely, the development of the Buddhist notion of causation. Having presented the doctrine of dependent co-arising (*paticcasamuppada*) as an account of causation that relies on the concept of *kamma,* I investigate the transition from this early doctrine to the Abhidhamma's complex theory of relations of causal conditioning (*paccaya*) as represented in its seventh book, the *Pa tthana,* showing that this theory is not about causation at all but rather forms an integral part of the overarching project of the individuation of the mental.

The book concludes with a reappraisal of the philosophical implications and tenability of the Abhidhamma's metaphysical vision, pointing to its weaknesses and to 'proto-Madhyamika elements' in the Buddha's teaching.

The translations from the Pali and Sanskrit are my own unless otherwise indicated.

2

The Further Teaching

THE ORIGIN OF THE ANCIENT BUDDHIST SCHOOLS AND THE ADVENT OF THE ABHIDHAMMA

The early history of Buddhism in India and of the school now referred to as Theravada is remarkably little known and the attempt to construct a consistent chronology of that history still engrosses the minds of contemporary scholars. There is, however, a generally accepted tradition that in the course of the second and third centuries after the Buddha's *mahaparinibbana* (hereafter BE) the Sakgha divided into a number of teacher's lineages (*acariyakula*), doctrines (*vada; acariyavada*) and fraternities (*nikaya*), and was subject to various doctrinal changes, refinements and shifts of emphasis that were part of the gradual systematization of Buddhism and its development from an oral teaching to an institutionalized tradition (*sasana*). To understand the processes in question it is necessary first to distinguish the formation of different sects and teachers' lineages around doctrinal issues from the notion of formal division in the Sakgha (*saðgha-bheda*).

It was but natural that in tandem with the Sakgha's spread across Northern India, and subsequently throughout the subcontinent, various groups of monks assembled around charismatic teachers and came to endorse divergent positions on certain points of the teaching. Ye t in addressing the complex problem of the origin of the ancient Indian Buddhist schools we must bear in mind that we are dealing with orthopraxy rather than orthodoxy: splitting the Sakgha is a technically precise matter and is always measured in terms of *vinaya* alone, so that holding a particular view of any doctrinal matter cannot be the grounds for a schism in or expulsion from the Sakgha. Noticeably, the fundamental acts of the Sakgha contrast in their plainness with the ritual elaboration involved in the public religious ceremonies of the lay Buddhist population. Two such communal acts are constitutive of the Sakgha and form the subject of the first two chapters of the *Khandhaka* portion of the *Vinaya-pitaka*: the first is the higher ordination (*upasampada,* as opposed to *pabbajja,* a novice's 'lower ordination'); the second, which the Buddha saw as the focal point of monastic life, is the fortnightly recital of the *patimokkha,* also known as the *uposatha* ceremony.

Since the quorum for holding a *patimokkha* ceremony is four, a Sakgha can split only when there are at least four votes on each side, and this occurs when a community of monks (and nuns) has a disagreement which causes two groups of more than three monks to hold separate *uposatha* ceremonies (and other ceremonies as well, but the *patimokkha* recital is both the most frequent and the most important). The disagreement is likely to be over a *vinaya* point, but whatever the source of the disagreement, the result is measured in terms of holding separate *patimokkha* ceremonies. It is a monk's or a nun's loyalty to a certain *patimokkha* code, then, that determines their Sakgha fellowship. When a body of monks or nuns who share the same *patimokkha* code develops as a separate entity by holding its own ceremony of higher ordination, it becomes a sect or fraternity (*nikaya*), and this is what incites the formation of different lineages within the Sakgha. Thus while the division into Sthaviras/Theriyas and Mahasakghikas, to which we shall refer in greater detail shortly, represents a formal splitting of the Sakgha into two fraternities, under each of these two groups there emerged numerous informal schools of thought and teachers' lineages.

Tradition has it that by the time the Mahayana doctrines arose, roughly in the first century BCE, there were eighteen sub-sects or schools of Sthaviras, the tradition ancestral to the Theravada, although different Buddhist sources preserve divergent lists of schools which add up to more than eighteen. The number eighteen is symbolic and has evidently become conventional in Buddhist historiography. In fact, as L.S. Cousins notes, this number is both too small and too large: on the one hand, the texts seem to struggle to identify eighteen different major schools, while, on the other hand, the likelihood is that the earliest Sakgha was only loosely organized and there must have been large numbers of independent local groupings of monks and monasteries. The 'eighteen schools' were indeed associated with distinct doctrinal views – often on moot Abhidhamma points – but the doctrinal opinion was unlikely to have originally caused their division. As long as distinct groups of monks adhered to essentially the same *vinaya* and recognized the validity of each other's ordination lineage, movement between the groups presented no problem and there was no ground for a formal split within the Sakgha. Moreover, not every school had its own distinctive textual tradition: in fact, the *vinaya* tradition suggests that there were roughly six distinct canonical traditions in addition to the Pali one. These are the Mahasakghika, the Vatsiputriya-Sammatiya, the Sarvastivada, the Kafyapiya, the Dharmaguptaka and the Mahifasaka.

An account of the first two Buddhist communal recitations or Councils (*saðgiti*) is found in all the surviving recensions of the *Vinaya-pitaka,* and according to all these versions the decisions taken at the second communal recitation, known as the Ve s ali Council (roughly 70–80 BE), were accepted by all parties. Later sources, however, suggest that at some point following the Vesali Council the primitive Sakgha formally divided into two parties, the Sthaviras and the Mahasakghikas, each of which thenceforth had its own ordination traditions. The traditional accounts of this event are much later, and hence are already the products of the sectarian division in question that have their own underlying ideologies. There are two inconsistent accounts of the emergence of this first division of the Sangha. The first, of Sarvastivadin origin, is based on the *Mahdvibhdsd* (third century CE) and on the *Samayabhedoparacanacakra* (T 49) - a Northern treatise attributed to a *Vasumitra (third or fourth century CE), extant in three Chinese and one Tibetan translation - as well as on many later sources that follow them. According to this line of thought, the division of the Sangha was provoked by a dispute over the 'Five Points' advanced by a monk named Mahadeva, concerning the behaviour of an *arahat* and whether he might be provided by others with material things or with mundane information due to his lack of knowledge and uncertainty, and whether he may make utterances and hear sounds while in a meditative attainment.

The second account, of Theravadin and Mahasanghika origin, attributes the division to a disagreement over certain questions of *vinaya*. The *Dipavamsa* (V 0ff.) (early fourth century CE) thus traces the origin of the Mahasanghikas as deriving from the defeated party at the Vesali Council, and is followed in this by the later Sinhalese chronicles. Yet, as Cousins remarks, the commentarial tradition of the Mahavihara was unlikely to have preserved an account of the origin of the 'eighteen schools', for the *Samantapdsddika* does not explain this issue while the commentary to the *Kathdvatthu* does, relating in this context to the *DipavamscCs* and *Mahavamsa's* reports. The source that attests to the Mahasanghika version of the first division of the Sangha is the *Sdriputrapariprcchd* (T 1465: 900b) - an eclectic text of a Magadhan origin extant in Chinese and dated roughly to the third century CE. Unlike the Ceylon tradition, this treatise sees the Mahasanghika not as the defeated party at Vesali, but as the conservative party that preserved the original *vinaya* unchanged against reformist efforts of the Sthaviras to create a reorganized and stricter version. Yet given the subjective perspective of this source the likelihood is that the Mahasanghikas were but the larger party resisting a reformist change in the discipline than the bearers of the 'original' *vinaya*.

The emerging picture as portrayed by recent scholarship is that the earliest division of the Sangha was primarily a matter of monastic discipline, though the Mahasanghikas cannot directly be traced through the defeated party at the Vesali Council. In view of the growing scholarly consensus that dates the Buddha's death at the end of the fifth century BCE, this fundamental division into Sthaviras and Mahasanghikas occurred some time around the beginning of the third century BCE. Throughout the subsequent two centuries or so doctrinal disputes arose among these two parties, resulting in the formation of additional sub-schools.

Again, the sources available to us of the history of these schools are quite late: aside from the references to the Buddhist Councils contained in the *vinaya* collections of various sects, these include certain inscriptions in KharosthI or Brahml from the Kusana period that indicate the presence of certain schools in various places, lists of masters, records of Chinese translators and the diaries of Chinese pilgrims, fragments of Sarvastivadin Abhidharma texts, and traditional works documenting the disputes among the schools, such as the later strata of the *Kathdvatthu,* the abovementioned treatise attributed to *Vasumitra, and Bhavya's *Nikdyabhedavibhangavydkhydna* (fourth century).

It is legitimate to assume, though, that the early Buddhist schools must have been for a long period fraternities based on minor *vinaya* differences only, and it may well be the case that at least some of these schools represent *de facto* divisions. Thus rather than portraying the Buddhist community in its early formative period as a homogeneous order within which an initial schism resulted in subsequent fragmentation, it might be better to adopt a model of a haphazardly scattered community in which natural variation in doctrine and in disciplinary codes was interpreted by the later tradition as the foundation of subsequent sects and schools of thought. We are not dealing here with schisms in the tradition, but with doctrinal dissensions; not with disparate denominations, but with informal intellectual branches that developed spontaneously due to the geographical extension of the community over the entire Indian subcontinent and subject to the particular problems each Sakgha confronted. In fact, differences in the *patimokkha* code may have arisen not so much from disagreements on *vinaya* matters as from the geographical isolation of different groupings of monks. Each monastic community tended to specialize in a specific branch of learning, had its own practical customs and relations with lay circles, and was influenced by the particular territories, economy, use of language and dialect, the types of clothing and food prevalent in its environment. Indeed the names of the 'eighteen schools' are indicative of their origins in characteristic teachings, geographical locations, or the legacy of particular teachers and founders: for instance, Sautrantikas, Haimavatas, or Vatsiputriyas respectively).

In conformity with the Sammatiya tradition cited by Bhavya and with the Sinhalese 'long chronology' which places Afoka's accession in 218 BE, all the 'eighteen schools' were already in existence by 200 BE, before Afoka came to the throne. Ye t according to both the 'short chronology' provided by Sanskrit works of Sarvastivadin origin and the treatise of *Vasumitra that places Afoka's accession in 100 BE (a suspiciously round figure which should properly be seen as ideal and symbolic), divisions among the Sthaviras do not begin until the third century BE, a century after Afoka came to the throne. Indeed *Vasumitra presents the early Sthavira schools as eighteen but, as Cousins explains in his study of the early schools ancestral to the Theravada, he intentionally exaggerates the degree of differences among the various schools and probably their number, thus pursuing his agenda of portraying Mainstream Buddhism as disputatious and dogmatic in contrast with the early Mahayana, which was put forward as a non-sectarian movement. It should also be noted that what has been presented as other divergent lists of schools based on additional sources, including the Pali version as found in the Sinhalese chronicles and in the *Kathavatthu-atthakatha,* are in fact variations derived from *Vasumitra's list. The only available textual source that is independent of *Vasumitra is contained in the **Tarkajvala.* Preserved in Tibetan, this treatise is attributed to *Bhavya or *Bha(va)viveka and dates to a period between the seventh and the tenth centuries, although the information it preserves is relatively early.

The Sinhalese Theravada tradition traces its lineage through the Vibhajjavadins. Inscriptional evidence from Nagarjunakojda and Amaravati *stupas* confirms that the Vibhajjavadins were part of the Theriya/Sthavira tradition, and links them to the Mahaviharavasin school at Anuradhapura as well as to the 'Tambapajjakas' – a name that is likely to have referred originally to monks living in the island of Taprobane and in the first centuries CE was adopted by their disciples, until it went out of use among the surviving non-Mahasakghika schools and was replaced by Theriya and Theravadin or by Mahaviharavasin. Cousins has shown that the evidence arising from a range of sources – the abovementioned inscriptions, various Pali texts (beginning with the *Cullavagga,* going through the *Dipavaµsa,* the *Visuddhimagga,* the Abhidhamma commentary, and up to later sources from the thirteenth century), and the doxographical material used in the **Tarkajvala* – combines to present a picture of several related Vibhajjavada branches, of which the primary four are the Dharmaguptakas, the Mahifasakas, the Kafyapiyas and the Tambapajjas, with the first three particularly strong in the North-West and the last predominating further south. Roughly in the first century CE, along with the demise of the other Vibhajjavadin schools in most parts of India, the Sinhalese Vibhajjavadin tradition was able to spread out in Southern India and parts of South-East Asia. It is the worldview of this Vibhajjavadin school that is preserved in the Pali canonical Abhidhamma.

The Sarvastivadins emerged as an independent school from within the Theriyas about the second or first century BCE, though this does not preclude the possibility that a certain group having Sarvastivadin tendencies had existed within the Theriyas from an earlier period. The traditional reason given for the recognition of the Sarvastivadins as a distinct sect is their 'All-exists' doctrine, meaning that the *dharmas* which constitute everything accessible to sentient experience exist in the three time periods. According to the Pali sources the Vibhajjavadins or 'Distinctionists' were the favoured party in a dispute over this Abhidhamma issue: they held that *dhammas* exist in the present, denied their existence in the future, while as regards the past made a distinction between *dhammas* that have issued their karmic fruit and hence no longer exist, and those past *dhammas* that have not yet issued their karmic fruit and can still be said to exist. The doctrinal dispute over this Abhidhamma matter is associated with a third communal recitation that took place at the Afokarama monastery (also known as Kukkutarama) in Pataliputra. This Council was presided by Moggaliputtatissa and lasted nine months, during which he composed the *Kathavatthu* that epitomizes the Vibhajjavadin worldview and refutes the positions of rival parties. The date of the Third Council is generally given as the year 236 BE, that is, eighteen years into Afoka's reign (or, according to the *Mahavaµsa,* seventeen), but in the *Atthasalini* Buddhaghosa prefers the year 218 BE, while recent scholarship agrees in dating Afoka's inauguration between 136 and 145 BE (277–268 BCE), a chronology that accordingly locates the third communal recitation between 154 and 165 BE (259–250 BCE). At any rate, the Theravadins cannot be directly equated with the Vibhajjavadins of this ancient dispute, for the traditional Theravadin position on the existence of *dhammas* in the three times as presented in the *Kathavatthu* is that present *dhammas* alone exist.

In fact, the reason for the dispute underlying the Third Council as given in the Pali sources seems to be far more closely related to a *vinaya* matter. Following Afoka's conversion to Buddhism, the lavish state patronage and the Sakgha's increasing revenue attracted non-Buddhists who were masquerading as Buddhist monks and teaching their own doctrines without being properly ordained or keeping to the rules of the *vinaya*. It was acknowledged that people who joined the monastic community simply to benefit from its security and the spiritual and material support it enjoyed corrupted the Sakgha, and the need to expel these people brought about a change in the early Sakgha's relationship to society. In his social-psychological exploration of the origins of early Buddhism, Torkel Brekke designates it 'a change from an outwardly minded conversionism to withdrawal and segregation – to introversionism'. This shifting attitude included four important aspects of early Buddhist monasticism: the gradual development of strict admission procedures, the emphasis on unity, the mental segregation by outward appearance and the physical segregation by separate dwellings. It is in relation to this social backdrop that the Theravadin account of the Third Council should be read.

According to this account discord prevailed among the inhabitants of the Afokarama roughly for seven years, and since the monks refused to co-operate with the non-Buddhists the *uposatha* ceremony was being celebrated by incomplete assemblies. After a violent, failed attempt to rectify this situation, the outsiders were identified and expelled from the monastery under Afoka's auspices. Subsequently, other monks (probably from affiliated monasteries belonging to the same *nikaya*) were summoned and declared that the Buddha was a Vibhajjavadin. Having confirmed this, Moggaliputtatissa organized the third communal recitation, during which he composed the *Kathavatthu*. In the Pali *Tika* the word *vibhajjavadin* signifies both an epithet for the Buddha and a name of the school whose members considered themselves to preserve the undistorted teaching of the founder. Cousins observes that the account of the third communal recitation gains its effectiveness from the double meaning of the word Vibhajjavadin and can only have been composed at a time when the word was already known as the name of that school. Indeed, as Richard Gombrich remarks, this account says nothing about Buddhist doctrine or Buddhist sect formation, as the false monks who merit expulsion were never Buddhist at all.

The story of the Third Council is peculiar to the Theravadin tradition and has been treated by scholars with scepticism because of various implausible features in it. Although Afoka's so-called Schism Edict buttresses the fact that some sort of dispute did occur at Pataliputra during his reign, it may be the case, as K.R. Norman suggests, that the account of a third communal recitation as given in the Pali sources conflates two different issues: the exposition of the *Kathavatthu* and a dispute over a *vinaya* matter. Certain *Vibhasa*-based sources from the sixth century CE, such as Paramartha's *Commentary on Vasumitra* (T 2300) and his pupil's *San lun hsüan* (T 1852), are also suggestive of a dispute at Pataliputra during Afoka's reign, but indicate that it was marked by the controversies provoked by the 'Five Points' of Mahadeva.

The inconsistencies clouding the emergence of the Sarvastivada as a distinct sect notwithstanding, archaeological and inscriptional remains show that by the time of the Kusaja empire (first half of the first century CE) the Sarvastivadins were well established in both Mathura and Kafmira. Various Sarvastivadin branches were developed, among which are the Vatsiputriyas-Sammatiyas and the Sautrantikas. That further divisions among these branches occurred over time is confirmed by the literary record of the debates of Sarvastivadin groups, but whether these various groups were independent sects in terms of the criterion of independent *vinaya* and ordination lineage or rather schools distinguished by doctrinal interpretation cannot be determined with certainty. Another notable branch is that of the Mulasarvastivadins: the historical and textual relationship between this school and the Sarvastivadins is by no means clear, but we do know that despite the affiliation between their Canons, these two groups transmitted different *Pratimoksas*, *Vinayas* and *Sutras*.

As for the Mahasakghikas, according to the Sammatiya tradition preserved by Bhavya the Mahasakghikas divided into two schools subsequent to the formation of the Puggalavada. The same two schools – the Kaukkutikas and the Ekavyavaharikas – are mentioned in the *Dipavaμsa* and in other Pali sources with reference to the first division of the Mahasakghikas. Several other North-Western sources count a third branch, the Lokottaravadins, while for *Vasumitra there were already eight Mahasakghika branches by the end of the second century BE.

The Abhidharma/Abhidhamma texts are by and large compositions contemporary with this formative period in the history of the early schools, providing the means by which one group could define itself and defend its position against the divergent interpretations and criticisms of other parties. Although much of the Abhidhamma mindset and something of its method go back to the earliest substratum of Buddhist thought alongside the *Nikayas,* the main body of its literature contains interpretations of the Sutta material that are specific to particular schools of thought, and philosophical elaborations of selectively emphasized doctrinal issues that continued to be refined by subsequent generations of monks who contributed to the consolidation of the schools.

According to Cousins, an analysis of the *Kathavatthu* evinces three primary phases in the development of Abhidhamma discussion. The first phase is the development of a literary genre consisting of constructed dilemmas, of which some contents proceed from older sources, albeit their formulation is indicative of Abhidhamma fashion. The *Puggalakatha* and the sections dealing with the Sarvastivada attest to the second and preponderant phase, which is marked by a three-way exchange between the Puggalavada, the Sarvastivada and the Vibhajjavada – the three schools for which we have textual evidence of a coherent doctrinal structure emerging from the early period (but of which the relationship to the Mahasakghikas is unclear). The third phase is the subsequent reshaping of Abhidhamma discussion in response to the growing contacts with the Mahasakghika schools. The Sammatiya tradition cited by Bhavya locates the first phase prior to the Mauryan period, while, approximately in line with Bhavya, the Pali sources suggest that the second phase corresponds to the reign of Afoka. This, however, cannot be reconciled with the 'short chronology' given by the Sarvastivadin sources.

The development of the Abhidhamma, though, was given impetus not only by monastic debates concerning the doctrine (*abhidhamma-katha*) between the ancestors of the Theravadins and their Buddhist rivals, but also by the intellectual challenges posed by the contemporary Brahmanical *darfanas*. It thus happened that the Abhidhamma texts became a medium by which Buddhist masters developed their positions through the stimulating debate with non-Buddhist opponents. These, with their evolving traditions of Vedic exegesis, logic and epistemology, impelled the

Abhidhammikas to adopt philosophical methods of analysis and discussion, to consolidate the Buddha's scattered teachings and to ground them in an ordered doctrinal framework.

ABHIDHAMMA LITERARY STYLE AND GENRE

The term *abhidhamma* is multivalent and amenable to various interpretations. Scholarly opinion has generally been divided between two alternative interpretations, both of which hinge upon the denotation of the prefix *abhi*. First, taking *abhi* in the sense of 'with regard to', *abhidhamma* is understood as a discipline whose subject matter is the *Dhamma* or Teaching. Second, using *abhi* in the sense of preponderance and distinction, *abhidhamma* has also been deemed a distinct and higher teaching, the further Teaching or its essence; that which goes beyond what is given in the Buddha's discourses, in a sense somewhat reminiscent of the term 'metaphysics'. One way by which the exegetical tradition describes the difference between the Sutta and Abhidhamma methods of instructing the teaching is in terms of a contrast between something that requires further exposition for clarity, because it is merely 'a way of putting things' (*pariyaya-desana*), and that which does not need any further explication, because it is couched in non-figurative, definitely put terms (*nippariyaya-desana*). Another similar commentarial differentiation is that the *suttas* explain the fundamental principles of Buddhist thought – namely, the five aggregates, the four noble truths, dependent co-arising, the sense spheres, the elements of cognition, etc. – only in part (*ekadesen' eva*), whereas the Abhidhamma expounds them in full, not restricting its elucidation to a single aspect (*nippadesena*), while applying the methods of Suttanta exposition, Abhidhamma exposition and catechism or interrogation (*pañhapucchaka*). Although the canonical Abhidhamma literature does not explicitly make such a distinction between the teaching in application subject to various circumstances versus the higher, ultimate teaching, it certainly contrasts Suttanta and Abhidhamma methods, as the structures of the *Vibhaðga* or the *Kathavatthu* emblematize.

The prevalent accounts of the historical origin and development of Abhidhamma literature proceed from two explanatory tendencies based on two distinctive characteristics of the genre. According to the first line of thought, there is a close relationship between the evolution of the Abhidhamma treatises and an established feature they manifest, namely, the arrangement of major parts of the material around lists of various types. In fact, such textual structuring dates to the beginning of Buddhist literature: the earliest Buddhist literature is an oral textual tradition and was built up around mnemonic lists. The *Nikayas* thus contain numerous classification lists, or, more literally, matrices *(matika/matrka)* of doctrinal topics, which offer summaries or condensed shorthand accounts of the Buddha's *Dhamma.* Among these lists we find the four noble truths, the four states of absorption in meditation *(jhana),* the five aggregates *(khandha),* the five hindrances *(nivarana),* the six sense faculties *(saayatana)* that along with their six corresponding object fields or sense data make up the twelve sense spheres (also called *ayatana),* the six higher types of knowledge *(abhinna),* the seven factors of awakening *(bojjhanga),* the noble eightfold path, the twelvefold chain of dependent co-arising *(paticcasamuppada)* or the eighteen elements of cognition *(dhatu,* namely, the twelve *ayatanas* plus their six corresponding types of cognitive awareness). There are also composite 'meta-lists' that appear to have evolved out of an analysis of extant lists and the categorization of the resultant items into further lists. Such are the analysis embodied in the *sattatimsa bodhipakkhiya dhamma,* that is, the post-canonical list of the thirty-seven *dhammas* that contribute to awakening, or the *khandhayatanadhatu* threefold scheme that embraces the five aggregates, the twelve sense spheres and the eighteen elements of cognition. The Nikaya lists are organized according to either topical or numerical criteria. Topically, the items enumerated are divided into different types based on some doctrinal principle. Lists of this kind abound in the *Samyutta-nikåya.* Numerically, the lists catalogue groups of identical number of items, or groups of items that sequentially increase in their number, commencing with one or two items and proceeding to higher numbers. This method is employed for example, in the *Sangiti* and *Dasuttara-suttas,* as well as in the *Anguttara-nikaya.*

The term *matika,* then, came to denote any ordered table of items summarizing the Buddha's teaching and sustaining further explication of fundamental doctrinal topics. This usage consolidated in the commentaries, where *matika* means 'a summary'. The term *matika,* however, originally had a narrower meaning and probably signified a set of kẹy words, similarly to *udana.* In the four primary *Nikayas* (most extensively in the *Anguttara* collection) and in the *Vinaya-pitaka* the term *matika* features as the first member of the compound *matika-dhara,* itself part of the stock description of the accomplished learned senior monk: 'one who has heard much, one to whom the tradition has been handed down, the bearer of the *dhamma,* of the discipline and of the *matika'*. This implies that monks who pursued the study of the Buddha's teaching and were involved in the doctrinal elaboration on key words from his sermons were called *matika-dhara.* The commentaries explicate *matika* in the compound *matika-dhara* as referring to the two *patimokkhas*, the bare lists of rules for fully ordained monks and nuns extracted from the *Vinaya'* s *Suttavibhaðga.* Ye t it seems that this interpretation is too restricted and that the sequence *dhamma vinaya matika* ought to correspond to the sequence of the three canonical collections, namely, *sutta vinaya abhidhamma* respectively. This surmise is supported by the extant Abhidhamma canonical works.

Towards the end of the Nikaya period, around the third century BCE, a new movement in Buddhist thought and literature emerged, to which the Abhidhamma treatises bear witness. As part of the natural development of the Buddhist *sasana,* the tradition ancestral to the Theravada underwent various doctrinal changes, and this natural course of development was enhanced by the debates that arose both with Brahmanical rivals and with other Buddhist circles. The Abhidhammikas were therefore required to clarify their doctrinal concepts and define them in clear-cut theoretical terms, to analyse each item of the Buddha's teachings and then synthetically construct its relations to all other items so as to reveal its proper place within the *Dhamma* as a whole. Moreover, the early tradition must have found the extant ordering of doctrinal topics lacking and supported a shift towards a more formal practice of analysing individual *dhammas*. This paved the way for numerous possibilities of *dhamma* classifications and categories, so that the process of drawing out *dhamma* lists became almost infinite – a practice that culminated in the tabulation of far more elaborate and complex *matikas*. Since *matikas* of one or other form underlie almost every Theravadin Abhidhamma work, it has been argued that *matika* must have been the early name equivalent to the *Abhidhamma-pitaka* and that the Abhidhamma texts evolved out of the Suttanta *matikas*.

The organization of the extant Abhidhamma texts supports this claim, for it derives from numerical and topical arrangement of the various *matikas* already found in the *suttas*. The *Abhidhamma-pitaka* comprises seven treatises: the *Dhammasaðgaji*, the *Vibhakga*, the *Dhatukatha*, the *Puggalapaññatti*, the *Kathavatthu*, the *Yamaka* and the *Pa tthana*. This division is given for the first time in the introduction to the *Milindapañha* and is described at length in the *Dhammasaðgaji* commentary. Questions regarding the structure, features and dating of these three canonical works are thus treated throughout the succeeding study. The central motif of the *Dhatukatha* is an investigation into the relations of various *dhammas*, or doctrinal concepts – a partial list of which includes the five aggregates, the twelve sense spheres, sense contact (*phassa*), the nine roots (*hetu*), feeling (*vedana*) and consciousness (*citta*) – to the eighteen *dhatus*. The classification schema of the *Puggalapaññatti* is based upon six *paññatti*, namely, concepts or designations, the sixth of which, *puggala* or person, is unique to this text that enumerates and classifies different types of person according to various guidelines (for instance, according to the way one strives for liberation, how one fulfils this wish, or the spiritual level one attains). The *Yamaka*, 'Pairs', derives its name from the method it applies in discussing various doctrinal concepts: it contrasts pairs of *dhamma* in numerous combinations and linkages, asking of each pair infinite questions and their inversions, for instance, whether when one *dhamma* arises and vanishes so does the other, then whether when the one does not arise the other also does not arise, or whether when the one is cognized so is the other, etc.

Unlike the six texts mentioned above, the *Kathavatthu* does not analyse *dhammas*, but rather aims at the refutation of non-Theravadin views, illustrating the second feature of Abhidhamma thought and its literary genre, which is discussed below. Excepting the *Kathavatthu*, the canonical Abhidhamma works rely on three sets of *matika*: the first two consist of the twenty-two triplets (*tika*) and one hundred couplets (*duka*) that set out the basic categories of the *dhamma* analysis, as documented at the beginning of the *Dhammasaðgaji*. This key list is referred to by scholars as the *abhidhamma-matika*. The third supplementary list is of forty-two Suttanta couplets, the majority of which feature in the *Saðgiti-sutta*. One must bear in mind, though, that the affinity between the Abhidhamma treatises and the early *suttas'* classification lists may also reflect the influence of Abhidhamma on the *suttas* themselves, for Abhidhamma-like activities may well have been extant before the completion of the *Sutta-pitaka*, and the final redaction of the latter overlaps with the composition of the Abhidhamma works. The two triplet-couplet *matika* sets also appear in three other Abhidhamma canonical works: the *Vibhaðga*, *Dhatukatha* and the *Pa tthana*. The *Puggalapaññatti* opens with an explicit *matika* arranged by numerical progression. The *Kathavatthu* and *Yamaka* do not have explicit *matika*, although the tradition describes their underlying discussion points and chapters as a *matika*.

I do not deny the relationship between the *matikas* and the evolution of the Abhidhamma, but find an oversimplification in equating the two, or in seeking to identify the more fundamental among the *matikas* and on that basis to establish a chronology of the texts. Based on a comparison of the *dhamma* analysis of works composed among the Northern Buddhist schools, such as Vasubandhu's *Abhidharmakofa* and Asakga's *Abhidharmasamuccaya*, Rupert Gethin has shown that such an attempt to settle the chronology of the texts amounts to a misunderstanding of 'the basic principle that determines the way in which the Abhidhamma develops out of the use of *matikas*'. This is because various *matikas* are fundamental to several texts and the Abhidhamma method consists in the interaction of those various *matikas*. Thus, on many occasions the categories of one list are analysed by the categories of another list, which suggests that the *matikas* represent but one aspect of the overarching growth of the Abhidhamma movement and its literature. As Cousins explains, this method would serve two different purposes: it would both sharpen one's comprehension and insight while at the same time securing more firmly the historical continuity of the tradition. In the meantime suffice it to mention Gethin's observation that the *matikas* are conducive to Buddhist meditation: the compilers of the *matikas* sought to distinguish physical and mental states and events in actual experience, and thus remind one of the richness and subtlety of experience, which, in turn, promotes awareness and provides a clue to the relationship between memory and awareness as expressed in the Buddhist conception of *sati/smrti.* With regard to the second element, the historical continuity of the tradition, here arises the Abhidhamma's self-awareness of the problems involved in the maintenance and continuity of its own oral tradition.

The frequent use of standard mnemonic registers of apparent synonyms to define particular mental or material occurrences requires a higher degree of formalization than the Sutta-based topical and numerical lists, and such a formalization can be successful only if the material is both well understood and contains no contradictory or incomplete elements. The Abhidhamma elaboration on the extant *matikas,* then, is a conscious attempt to fix the earliest Buddhist heritage and reflects a transition from an oral to a literary approach.

Another explanation of the origination of the Abhidhamma draws on a rather different feature of the Abhidhamma treatises, namely, their catechetical style. Scholars who favour this line of explanation ascribe the evolution of the Abhidhamma movement first and foremost to the influence of the contemporary intellectual milieu. The interaction between the Buddhist and the established Brahmanical schools, with their evolving traditions of exegesis, logic and episte-mology, must have been conducive not only to the development of the Abhidhamma but also to its growing bent for discursive hermeneutics through catechetical exposition. Moreover, the process of institutionalization undergone by Buddhist thought and the growth of the Sangha induced the rise of monastic debates and discussions concerning the doctrine among the Theravadins and their Buddhist rivals.

Such discussions are already represented by the *Maha/ Cuavedalla-suttas* and the division of the *Vibhanga-suttas* of the *Majjhima-nikaya,* which are characterized by a catechetical style and are formulated as an exchange of questions and answers. An elaborate catechetical style is the hallmark of the *Kathavatthu,* but a similar dialectical format also appears in several other Abhidhamma texts, such as the *Patisambhidamagga* and the *Vibhanga.* The structure of the last two is based on a series of statements from the *suttas (uddesa)* and their analytical exposition *(niddesa).*

The materials we have considered so far combine to present a picture of early Abhidhamma as a doctrinal movement and a distinct type of exegesis that gradually developed in tandem with particular theoretical as well as practical interests, resulting in an independent branch of inquiry and literary genre. What I wish to emphasize is that the two stylistic features of Abhidhamma literature - the abundant *matikas* and the catechetical format - are interconnected and that it would be inaccurate to relate the origins of the Abhidhamma solely and directly to either one of them. Rather, it is most likely that within the earliest Sangha there arose two approaches to discussing the *Dhamma:* the first intended to summarize and itemize the significant points of the teaching, the second to analyse and elaborate on the doctrines taught by means of the typical monastic disputations.

3

What the Buddha Taught and Abhidhamma Thought

THE DEVELOPMENT OF THE DHAMMA THEORY

The scholarly literature on the history of the term *dhamma* in Buddhist thought is fairly extensive and focuses on the ambiguity of the term caused by the wide range of meanings it covers. Among those meanings are included Buddhist teaching in general, any doctrine which forms part of that teaching, an element of experience, principle, phenomenon, nature, mental object, idea and others. A.K. Warder has shown that the Nikaya usage of the term *dhamma* (in both its singular and plural forms) is ambiguous and multivalent, and that its alleged ontological dimension is far from being clear. He indicates that

The four old *Nikayas* are not as clear about *dhamma* meaning an 'element' as is the Abhidhamma. They seem instead to offer discussions using the word a little more freely, apparently without defining it, out of which the precise concept of the Abhidhamma might have been extracted.

The prevailing scholarly notion of *dhammas* in their technical sense – as basic, irreducible and ultimately real elements constitutive of encountered phenomena – is strongly influenced by Theodore Stcherbatsky's pioneering study of *dharma*. Stcherbatsky concluded that this sense of element is a satisfactory equivalent for *dharma*. Ye t his study, Warder points out, is based on the position of the Vaibhaṡikas as documented by Vasubandhu's *Abhidharmakofa*, and hence Stcherbatsky's portrayal of what a *dharma* is should not be taken as valid for the Pali *Nikayas*. But is it valid for the Pali Abhidhamma? On this question I take sides with Rupert Gethin in his claim that it is not self-evident that the conception of a *dhamma* as a real, self-existing, irreducible element is fully attributable to the Pali canonical Abhidhamma. The present monograph shows that while the notion of a plurality of *dhammas* is clearly more developed in the post-canonical literature than in the *Nikayas,* the canonical Abhidhamma is not so clear about the 'precise concept' of *dhamma* as an element. In fact, the term retains its ambiguity and becomes ontologically laden only in the commentarial period. Despite the numerous extant studies of the term *dhamma* in Buddhist thought, the notion that this term conveys has remained indistinct. My hypothesis is that to make headway in understanding the notion of *dhamma* it must be viewed in the light of the broader doctrinal development of early Buddhism. We shall see that this development cannot sensibly be isolated from a fundamental metaphysical shift, while at the same time it is also subject to the Abhidhamma's soteriological concerns. To trace the development of the *dhamma* theory let us commence by reviewing the major modifications in the signification of the concept of *dhamma.*

On the Changing Meaning of Dhamma and Dhammas

To understand early Buddhist teaching one must see its genesis as conditioned by the religious and social milieu in which it arose, bearing in mind that the Buddha was propounding his ideas in a specific social context and that his central teachings originated in response to a particular spiritual environment. Buddhism, like all other major Indian religions, has elaborated its psychology, eschatology, epis-temology and metaphysics within the conceptual framework of Brahmanical thought and practice. This operated within the horizons set up by the fundamental categories of *samsara,* 'the round of rebirth', *karma,* 'action' and 'moral retribution', and *moksa,* 'liberation'. Early Brahmanical religion revolved around the sacrificial activity that came to be regarded as a constructive power essential to the cosmic scheme of things. The two Sanskrit terms that denote 'the scheme of things' are, in the *Vedas, rta,* and in later classical Sanskrit, *dharma* – the former, deriving from the root r, meaning 'that which is properly fitted together, ordered', the latter, deriving from the root *dhr,* meaning 'that which is (to be) upheld borne firmly, preserved'. *Rta* and *dharma* signify, albeit ambiguously, both the way the universe is ordered and the way it ought to be ordered thus blurring the distinction between fact and value. In due course the term *dharma* has become demonstrably beyond simple translation, conflating reality, the way things are, law, cosmic order, (caste) duty, righteousness, prescribed conduct, religious merit and truth in general all rolled into one. It is against this conceptual backdrop - of a closed universe constituted by sacrificial activity through which one creates oneself anew into the ritual world *(loka)* to perpetuate one's life and define one's identity - that the emergence of the Buddhist notion of *dhamma* ought to be situated.

In the *Tipitaka,* both the singular and plural forms *dhamma/ dhammas* ordinarily refer to the contents of the Buddha's talks, to the fundamental principles the Buddha taught. For instance, an exemplary *Samyutta* passage recounts the Buddha's description of what ascetics and Brahmins may or may not understand as follows:

Bhikkhus, as regards those ascetics and Brahmins who understand these things *(dhamme),* their origination, their cessation, the path leading to their cessation: what are those things they understand? They understand ageing-and-death, its origination, its cessation and the path leading to its cessation. They understand birth...becoming...clinging...craving... feeling .. . sense contact ... the six sense faculties. . .name-and-form . . . consciousness...and mental formations, their origination, their cessation and the path leading to their cessation.

This excerpt is succeeded by a passage that depicts a certain *bhikkhu* approaching the Buddha and asking him: 'Venerable sir, it is said "a speaker of the *Dhamma,* a speaker of the *Dhamma"* (*dhammakathiko*). How, now, is one a speaker of the *Dhamma*?' The Buddha replies as follows:

Bhikkhu, if one teaches the *dhamma* for the purpose of withdrawing from ageing-and-death, for its fading away and its cessation, one may be called a *bhikkhu* who is a speaker of the *Dhamma.* If one has entered the path for the purpose of withdrawing from ageing-and-death, for its fading away and its cessation, one may be called a *bhikkhu* who is practising in accordance with the *Dhamma.* [...] If one teaches the *Dhamma* for the purpose of withdrawing from birth...from becoming...from cling-ing...from craving...from mental formations...from ignorance, for their fading away and their cessation, one may be called a *bhikkhu* who is a speaker of the *Dhamma.*

That in this sense the singular and plural forms *dhamma/ dhammas* are interchangeable (like 'teaching' and 'teachings' in English) is illustrated by recurring passages that refer to the Buddha's ninefold teaching (*navaðgabuddha-sasana*), that is, the nine divisions of the Buddhist texts according to their form or style, although such passages must belong to a later period in which these distinct nine divisions were acknowledged. With reference to the principles taught by the Buddha, the word *dhamma* retains both the descriptive and normative senses it carries in Brahmanical thought. Thus, when the Buddha preached the *Dhamma,* he was at the same time describing his experience and prescribing a method to be followed.

Ye t the *dhamma* principles taught also signify experientially perceived physical and mental processes and states *qua* manifestations in one's consciousness: such are the twelve items that form the *paticcasamuppada* formula, and indeed numerous other phenomena the Buddha discusses, among which are delusion (*moha*), cognitive awareness in its six modalities (visual, auditory etc., including mental: *cakkhu-viññа~a, sotaviñña~a* etc., including *manoviñña~a*), one-pointedness of mind (*cittass' ekaggata*), bringing into being or development (*bhavana*), equanimity (*upekkha*), states of absorption in meditation (*jhana*), tranquillity (*passaddhi*), joy (*piti*) and many others. Since the *paticcasamuppada* doctrine explicates how sentient experience is, at bottom, a series of related processes arising and ceasing in a non-random order, and since the Buddha's teaching is in harmony with how things ultimately are, then knowledge of the *Dhamma* teaching is knowledge of the experiential world in terms of processes, which is but knowledge of *dhammas* in their various modes of operation. A stock phrase in the *Nikayas* describes the excellent, distinguished *Dhamma* teaching of Buddhas as encompassing *dukkha,* arising, cessation and the path, which is but a shorthand for the four noble truths. The *Nikayas* often explicate the first truth in terms of the five aggregates of grasping (*pañc' upadanakkhandha*), the second truth in terms of three kinds of craving (*kama-, bhava-* and *vibhava-ta~ha*), the third truth as the cessation of these types of craving, and the fourth truth in terms of the eight factors of the noble path. The

Dasuttara-sutta explains these categories as five *dhammas* to be fully known (*pariññeyya*), three *dhammas* to be abandoned (*pahatabba*), nine sorts of cessation referred to as nine *dhammas* to be realized (*sacchikatabba*), and eight *dhammas* to be fully developed (*bhavetabba*). This, Rupert Gethin observes, illustrates the Nikaya notion of the relation of *dhamma* and *dhammas:* to know the teaching is to know *dhammas* in their various aspects.

Knowledge of the teaching, and subsequently of how things really, truly are, is gained through meditative contemplation in which the practitioner strives towards the realization of the doctrinal points and topics taught by the Buddha. Within this meditative context a clearer distinction was drawn between *dhamma* and *dhammas*, whereby the meaning of the latter was gradually expanded and generalized. This tendency is demonstrated in the two standard texts on meditation, the *Satipatthana-* and *Mahasatipatthanasuttas:* here, in the context of the fourth foundation of awareness, namely, the contemplation of *dhammas* (*dhammanu-passana*), the plural form *dhammas* signifies the mental objects that appear to one's consciousness in the course of this meditation exercise. These, however, are explicated in terms of the Buddha's teachings: the texts state that a *bhikkhu* dwells watching *dhammas* with regard to the five hindrances (*nivara~a*), the five *khandhas* of grasping, the six internal (*ajjhatika*) and external (*bahira*) *ayatanas* (i.e. one's own physical and mental faculties in contrast to those of others), the seven factors of awakening (*bojjhaðga*) and the four noble truths. This implies that *dhammas* are both elements of the normative system to be applied and objects of experience in insight meditation; that what appears in consciousness to a practitioner while in meditative attainment follows the patterns laid down by the Buddha's teachings. Training himself along the Buddhist path, a monk moves from thinking about those teachings to thinking with them, as it were, for they are what makes up reality as taught by the Buddha. Steven Collins comments on this:

> The things, then, which a monk 'sees' in meditation clearly follow the patterns laid down by Buddhist doctrinal thinking. *Dhamma* are both elements of the normative system to be applied, and 'objects' of experience in insight meditation. For the Theravada tradition, the 'ultimate' psychological reality of these *dhamma* has never been a matter of question.

The meditative dimension ascribed to the meaning of the plural form *dhammas* led to the next step in the process of its generalization, whereby *dhammas* emerged as 'good psychological characteristics', or simply 'psychological characteristics' used for the sake of attaining meditative states. Such characteristics are listed under the seven sets known later on in the post-canonical literature by the collective title 'the thirty-seven factors contributing to awakening' (*satta-tiμsa bodhi-pakkhiya dhamma*), among which are included discrimination (*pavicaya*), concentration (*samadhi*), joy (*piti*), tranquillity (*passaddhi*) and others.

While this meaning of the plural *dhammas* is not peculiarly Buddhist, it was apparently subject to intended appropriation within early Buddhist conceptual framework and came to denote not only the objects that appear in one's consciousness while in meditative attainment, but also mental objects of the sixth sense faculty, namely, *manas*, alongside the objects of the five ordinary physical senses. *Manas* is one of the most ambiguous, multivalent terms in the Sutta literature: it may broadly be rendered as mind, suggesting that it undertakes processes that would be classified under one of the *arupakkhandhas* or the mental aggregates, while at the same time it is an *ayatana,* and hence is used as a generic term for the mind in its cognitive capacity as a mental sense that may be viewed as either an antecedent or a subsequent event with respect to the immediately following or immediately preceding phase in the cognitive process. Although when *manas* is translated as 'mind' *dhammas* tends to be rendered accordingly as 'thoughts' or 'ideas', note that *dhammas qua* the object of *manas* as the sixth sense faculty refer not only to thoughts, ideas or concepts, but to mentality in its broadest denotation: *dhammas* are the objects when one, for instance, remembers, anticipates or concentrates on something. There are six modes of cognitive awareness and five physical sense faculties; anything else is *dhamma.*

In the canonical Abhidhamma literature the term *manas* undergoes a process of systematization and is employed conjoined with various suffixes, having different technical meanings in different contexts and resulting in the distinctions between *manas, viññа~a, manodhatu, manayatana, manoviññа~a* and *manoviññа~adhatu.* These compounds already feature in the *Nikayas,* but the distinctions between their referents are marginalized by the Abhidhammikas. C.A.F. Rhys Davids observes that the Abhidhamma elaboration on the analysis of the scope of the mental as modelled on sense perception is set out in a fourfold formula taking into account the mental sense faculty, invisible and reacting; the mental object, also invisible and impinging; and the contact between the two. This analysis of sense perception includes (i) the fact of possible sensation, (ii) the actual impact of the appropriate object, (iii) the actual impact of the appropriate sense faculty and (iv) the resultant actual impression and possible results in the four *arupakkhandhas*. These four aspects, Rhys Davids explains, bring forward detailed time-reference ('has seen, sees, will or may see'), so that sense perception is emphatically stated as an experience in time. While *manayatana* is a generic term referring to the scope of the mental as a whole, and hence embracing the functions of *citta, manas* and *viñña~a* alike, the compound *manodhatu* (and also *manoviñña~adhatu*) is normally used to distinguish *manas* when it refers to the operation of the sixth, mental sense faculty as a distinct sphere of experience rather than to 'mind' in general.

In the *suttas, manodhdtu* is used in two different ways, both of which have been adopted by the canonical Abhidhamma and later on, by the commentarial tradition. On the one hand *manodhdtu* is understood as a unique 'quasi' sense; the basis of the ignorance-oriented cognitive process that prolongs one's experience in *samsdra.* This implies that whether one lives influenced by *samsaric* cognition or by liberating knowledge is determined by the cognitive faculties of which *manodhdtu* is in some way the sense, and hence the latter plays a unique role in the process of awakening that is not shared by the other sense faculties. On the other hand *manodhdtu* is also considered the sixth in a series of senses, and hence an 'ordinary' sense faculty of which the corresponding objects processed are mental and specific to its nature, just as, for instance, sound is specific to the ear. It does differ, though, from the five distinct sense faculties in that it plays the role of coordinator, synthesizing and unifying all the sense impressions brought in by the other five senses; it is the receiver of these incoming phenomenal data as raw material, prior to any specification as to visible objects, sound odour etc. In this respect *manodhdtu* is said to be the 'resort' *(patisarana)* for the five physical senses and to 'realize' their scope of activity Acting as their collator, *manodhdtu* renders these data comprehensible to the cognitive faculties. This implies, as has been stated by John Ross Carter and recently by Sue Hamilton, that *dhammas* as the objects of *manodhdtu* are a pluralistic representation of encountered phenomena; not merely mental objects, but all knowable sensory phenomena of whatever nature, that is, the *samsaric* world in its entirety as we experience it through the senses, *manodhdtu* accordingly signifying the receiver of these 'knowables'.

This broad rendering includes the narrower sense of *dhammas* as objects of *manas* when the latter signifies mental cognition *qua* an aspect of discriminative consciousness, or rather mental cognitive awareness *(manovinndna,* often translated literally as 'mind-consciousness'). As the sixth cognitive modality based on the faculty of *manas, manovinndna* refers to the distinctive awareness that is the cognitive basis of sense perception issuing from the contact between *manodhdtu* and its respective *dhamma* objects. In the *Nikdyas, vinndna* equally refers to this cognitive modality as well as to consciousness in its broad intentional denotation of 'consciousness of. The latter accompanies animated existence and is coterminous with one's *samsaric* experience as a whole; it preconditions not only the development of a new sentient body *(ndmarupa),* but also the emergence of mental formations *(sankhdra,* albeit it is simultaneously conditioned by *kammic* activities, viz., *anabhisankhdra).* The compound *manovinndna* specifies *vinndna* while functioning as the sixth modality of cognitive awareness, since it is a mental awareness that arises in conjunction with its appropriate mental objects. *Vinndna* as cognitive awareness occurs in six modes: visual, auditory, olfactory, gustatory, tactile and mental cognitive awareness, based on the concomitance of their respective sense faculties (the five physical sense organs plus *manas)* and their appropriate sense objects. A specific form of cognitive awareness arises when an appropriate sensory object enters the field of its respective sense faculty *(indriya),* impinging upon this unimpaired sense faculty, and there is sufficient attention on the part of the mind. The *Nikdyas* are at ease with the discordance between these two senses of *vinnana,* for at the metaphysical level they are both intertwined and mutually condition one another: *vinnana* as discriminative, cognitive awareness leads to future rebirths and hence to existence in *samsara,* the major medium of which is the continuous stream of consciousness, namely, *viññana,* which is, in turn, the very prerequisite for the occurrence of cognitive awareness itself. Both these aspects of *vinnana* are accommodated within the *paticcasamuppada* formula.

Now sentient beings experience the results of qualitatively different mental processes and states of mind in a variety of ways. Leaving aside the extreme cases of the highest, most subtle forms of consciousness possible, consciousness that is conditioned by actively skilful or unskilful mental occurrences is regarded as most commonly experienced in the process of sensory perception. In the *Abhidhamma-pitaka* emphasis is put on *manovinnana* in its denotation of mental cognitive awareness and it is deemed the central cognitive operation within the process of sensory perception. *Dhammas* as the cognitive objects of *manoviññana qua* mental cognitive awareness may now be better rendered as apperceptions in the sense of rapid mental events by means of which the mind unites and assimilates a particular perception, especially one newly presented to a larger set or mass of ideas already possessed thus comprehending and conceptualizing it. Insofar as these *dhammic* apperceptions interact with the five sensory modalities of cognitive awareness that arise in dependence upon their corresponding material phenomena, then they are fleeting 'flashes' of psycho-physical events.

A comprehensive theory of the consciousness process *(citta-vithi)* using such terms is set out in the Abhidhamma commentaries and manuals - mainly in Buddhaghosa's *Visuddhimagga* and *Atthasalini* as well as in Buddhadatta's and Anuruddha's works - but is based upon the description already found in the *Dhammasangani* and the *Patthana.* This theory portrays each moment of discriminative, cognitive awareness as involving not only the occurrence of sense perception itself, but also the derivation of a series of other related mental events. For instance, visual perception involves not only seeing itself, but such occurrences as adverting to the appropriate sense 'door', fixing of the visual object in the mind examination and recognition of its features and identification of its nature - and all of these are *dhammas.* For the time being suffice it to say that the canonical Abhidhamma portrays these *dhammic* apperceptions as diverse capacities or capabilities of psycho-physical events: short-lived minds or consciousness-types *(citta)* that interact with material phenomena, each of which arising and ceasing in sequential series while having its own function and capability. In accordance with this portrayal, *manoviññana* is necessarily temporal, processual and discriminative: it is not an act of cognition in the sense of an agent that acts upon its objects by cognizing them, but rather a discerning awareness of distinctions between the stimuli impinging upon the fields of the sense faculties that issues when the requisite conditions come together. This implies that the *dhammas* that condition such contextual distinctions and that co-arise with any given occurrence of cognitive awareness are themselves discrete and distinct psycho-physical events.

Two striking points emerge here: first, it now turns out that the above *dhammic* events as presented in consciousness, the product of our cognitive apparatus, are the constituents of sentient experience; the irreducible 'building blocks' that make up one's world, albeit they are not static mental contents and certainly not sub-stances. In this context Alexander Piatigorsky asserts that *dhamma* has never been meant to be explained or understood as the subject of any philosophical proposition, because it 'is' no thing, although it is an object of thought. The second point, as William Waldron observes, is that *manoviñña~a* appears not in conjunction with one, but with two sorts of cognitive object: with a previous moment of sensory cognitive awareness as an object and with its 'own' kind of object, namely, its appropriate *dhamma* that is a mental event. Waldron explains:

When a cognitive awareness of a sensory object occurs, it is often followed by an awareness *of* that awareness, that is, a reflexive awareness 'that such and such a sensory awareness (*viñña~a*) has occurred'. This is one of the 'objects' of mental cognitive awareness (*mano-viñña~a*). Mental cognitive awareness, however, also arises in conjunction with cognitive objects that occur independently of the sensory cognitive system, such as thinking, reflection, or ideas.

This means that at a meta-reflexive level *dhammas* are objects of discriminative, cognitive awareness inasmuch as they become objects of thinking and awareness *of* cognitive awareness itself. It is in this light that we may interpret a statement that recurs in the *Dhammasaðga~i* and reads: 'The five physical sense spheres comprise sense data (*rupa*) that are cognized by mental cognitive awareness (*manoviñña~a*), but all sense data [i.e. *manas* and *dhammas* inclusive] are cognized by the element of mental cognitive awareness [literally "mind-consciousness element"].' Piatigorsky accordingly claims that what stems from the Abhidhamma's approach to the scope of mind is a meta-psychology, by contrast to a reductionist psychology: meta-psychology investigates the conditions and states of our own thinking about mind, while reductionist psychology studies the substrata of mental processes. 'From the point of view of consciousness', Piatigorsky explains, 'it can be said that, when consciousness is conscious of one's mind, thought or consciousness directed to their objects, then it is "being conscious of " that may be named "a state of consciousness" or a *dharma*.' This, however, must not be seen as a definition of a *dhamma*, but rather as an indication to where within a descriptive system of interrelated, distinctive definitions it can be sought. From a meta-psychology that establishes the fact of thinking about *dhammas*, while dismissing the notion of a subject of consciousness or a person underlying the rise of thought, one cannot infer that a *dhamma* is an object, and this is to be understood 'in the sense that no psychology can be deduced from meta-psychology'.

I would say that no ontology can be deduced from this meta-psychology (yet). Does the post-canonical Abhidhamma also suspend ontological speculations, or may it be the case that at a certain stage its meta-psychology turned into a metaphysics conjoined with an ontology? And if so, what sort of ontology is it? The Abhidhamma exegetes distilled from the earlier *dhamma* analyses, especially those given in the *Cittuppddakanda* of the *Dhammasangani,* a comprehensive categorization of individual *dhamma* instances. They also supplemented the resultant *dhamma* theory with two major doctrines: the doctrine of momentariness and the doctrine of *sabhdva,* a laden concept that we may provisionally render as 'own-nature'. Underlying the succeeding two chapters are the questions of whether the post-canonical Abhidhamma assigns the doctrine of *sabhdva* an ontological dimension, what sort of metaphysics the developed *dhamma* theory embodies, and what role the doctrine of *sabhdva* plays in the formation of this metaphysics.

The early canonical position with regard to the *dhamma* analysis, then, aims at explaining the dynamics of sentient, cyclic experience in *samsdra.* This explanation appertains not only to human experience, for according to the basic principles of Buddhist cosmology, albeit these are merely scattered throughout the *Nikayas,* there is a hierarchy of several different realms of existence: the lower realms of hell beings *(niraya),* of animals *(tiracchdnayoni),* of hungry ghosts *(pettivisaya),* of human beings *(mantissa),* of various kinds of divine being collectively known as the lower gods *(deva),* and above the various heaven realms of divine beings known as Brahmas. Beings are continually reborn in these various realms in conformity with their actions. The Buddha taught that to understand this repetitive condition in *samsdra* is to see reality as it truly is - not a container of persons and 'things', but rather an assemblage of interlocking physical and mental processes that spring up and pass away subject to multifarious causes and conditions. In this respect it might be said that the Buddha had a distinctive, process epistemology: he taught that sentient experience is best understood in terms of dynamic processes that occur in a non-random order, and that to understand the causes and conditions of this dynamism is to gain insight into the way things truly are, which is equivalent to liberating knowledge.

In his talks the Buddha refers to several modes of analysis of sentient experience: in terms of physical and conceptual identity *(ndmarupa),* in terms of the five *khandhas,* in terms of the twelve sense spheres or *dyatanas* and in terms of the eighteen elements of cognition or *dhdtus.* The last three modes of analysis became the foundation for the later development of the *dhamma* analysis. In his comprehensive study of the development of the Theravadin doctrine of momentariness, Wan Doo Kim examines the *khandha, dyatana* and *dhdtu* lists along with their commentarial elaboration, referring to them as 'totality formulas', for each of the three represents a standpoint from which sentient experience is analysed in its entirety down to its final constituents. Kim indicates that the Abhidhamma employment of these lists testifies to its growing attempts to encapsulate everything that makes up lived experience in synthetic formulas. The present book evinces that along with this concern the Abhidhammikas were driven by another metaphysical goal, and that the latter is what distinguishes the *dhamma* theory from the *khandha, dyatana* and *dhdtu* totality formulas. The following section appraises these totality formulas inasmuch as they establish the foundations of the *dhamma* analysis.

Analysing Experience: the Khandha, Ayatana and Dhatu Formulas

The formula of the five *khandhas* is one of the fundamental doctrinal lists that constitute much of what Buddhism is about, retaining their importance within the Abhidhamma framework, wherein they still serve as categories of analysis. The five *khandhas* are: form *(nipa),* which here signifies the physical world as experienced by a sentient being, or rather body-endowed-with-consciousness *(saviññdna kayo);* feeling *(vedana);* conceptualization *(sannd);* volitional activities, or mental formations *(sankhdra);* and consciousness *(viññana)* in the broad sense of sheer sentience that continuously occurs throughout one's lifetime, and of one's awareness of oneself as having a series of perceptions and thoughts. The *khandhas* are normally portrayed by contemporary scholarship as the Buddhist alternative model of personal identity: a model that substitutes for an enduring self an assemblage of physical and mental processes. Nonetheless, the preferred Nikaya exposition of the *khandhas* is given in terms of the first noble truth: that is, the *khandhas* explain what *dukkha* is. As such they are named 'the five *khandhas* of grasping' *(pane updddnakkhandhd),* referring to the fact that prior to awakening one is fuelled by passions, cravings etc. What emerges from the texts, then, is a wider signification of the *khandhas* than merely the aggregates constituting the person. Sue Hamilton has provided a detailed study of the *khandhas.* Her conclusion is that associating of the five *khandhas* as a whole with *dukkha* indicates that experience is a combination of a straightforward cognitive process together with the psychological orientation that colours it in terms of unsatisfactoriness. Experience is thus both cognitive and affective, and cannot be separate from perception. As one's perception changes, so one's experience is different: we each have our own particular cognitions, perceptions and volitional activities in our own particular way and degree, and our own way of responding to and interpreting our experience *is* our very experience. In harmony with this line of thought, Gethin observes that the *khandhas* are presented as five aspects of the nature of conditioned existence from the point of view of the experiencing subject; five aspects of one's experience. Hence each *khandha* represents 'a complex class of phenomena that is continuously arising and falling away in response to processes of consciousness based on the six spheres of sense. They thus become the five *updddnakkhandhas,* encompassing both grasping and all that is grasped'.

The five *khandhas* are collectively said to be constructed or conditioned *(sankhata),* impermanent *(anicca)* and insubstantial or not self *(anatta)* In the *Nikdyas* the totality of each *khandha* is referred to by the stock formula: 'Whatever *riipa... vedana... sannd...sankhdras... vinñana* are past *(atita),* future *(andgata)* or present *(paccuppanna),* internal *(ajjhattam)* or external *(bahiddha),* gross *(odrika)* or subtle *(sukhuma),* inferior *(hind)* or superior *(panita),* far *(dure)* or near *(santike).'*

With regard to each of the *khandhas* one has to realize that 'this is not mine, I am not this, this is not my self'. The list of the five *khandhas* is largely taken for granted in the *Nikayas* and hence the series of their descriptive terms is left unexplained. This lacuna is filled by the *Vibhaðga,* the first of whose eighteen chapters deals with the *khandhas*. The *Vibhaðga'* exposition takes the above stock formula as characteristic of the Sutta account of the *khandhas*. We shall have more to say about the Sutta concept of time below, but in the *Vibhaðga* the terms 'past', 'present' and 'future' comply with their commonly accepted definition: the past is that which has come to an end, the future has not yet come into being and the present has not yet passed away. The pair internal/external is explained as relative to one's point of view, having as its point of reference any given person: one's own *khandhas* are internal, while those of other beings are external. The remaining pairs are also explained as relative, particularly when they are applied to the four mental *khandhas*: every instance of each *khandha* is said to be relative to another specific manifestation of that *khandha*. For instance, bad feeling may be gross, inferior and distant from both good and neither-good-nor-bad feelings, while good feeling may be subtle, superior and distant from both bad and neither-good-nor-bad feelings. The *Vibhaðga'* second section, the *abhidhamma-bhajaniya,* explicates how each of the five *khandhas* is divisible into various kinds and also applies the *abhidhamma-matika* to each of the four mental *khandhas*. This section thus provides hundreds of different sets of divisions for each of the five *khandhas* and a comprehensive analysis, by which any given conditioned *dhamma* can be categorized under one of the five *khandhas*. The *Vibhaðga* commentary further elaborates on the above canonical list of descriptive terms applied to each of the *khandhas*. It adds eleven pairs to the one triplet and four couplets of the list, thus forming sixteen aspects in terms of which the five *khand-has* are analysed. Six of these additional eleven pairs involve the temporal shape of the origination and cessation of the *khandhas,* their order of succession and limit of duration. This elaboration is pertinent to the Theravadin theory of momentariness, which I discuss below.

The two other totality formulas are the lists of twelve sense spheres, or *ayatanas*, and eighteen elements of cognition, or *dhatus*. These reflect sentient experience as encapsulated in the connections between the six sense faculties, their six corresponding sensory objects and six corresponding types, or modalities, of cognitive awareness. The first five sense faculties and their appropriate objects are the eye and visual form, the ear and sound, the nose and smell, the tongue and taste, and the body and tangibles respectively. The sixth sense faculty is *manas* and its corresponding mental objects are *dhammas*. The eighteen *dhatus* are formed by substituting the term *dhatu* for *ayatana* and by adding to these twelve sense spheres the six corresponding types of cognitive awareness, that is, visual cognitive awareness, auditory cognitive awareness, etc., up to mental cognitive awareness. This taxonomy is intended to facilitate direct insight into not-self by showing that in the final analysis personal identity is but a continuous sensory and cognitive process, of which any given element always refers to a distinct sphere of experience: a visual object is experientially distinct from an auditory object, from the faculty of sight, from cognitive awareness of sight; pleasant bodily feeling is distinct from unpleasant bodily feeling, from neutral bodily feeling, etc.

A straightforward passage stating that 'everything' (*sabba*) refers to all that is accessible to the twelve *ayatanas* is found in the *Sabba-sutta* of the *Saμyutta-nikaya:*

> What is 'everything', monks? It is the eye and visual forms, the ear and sounds, the nose and smells, the tongue and tastes, the body and tangibles, *manas* and *dhamma*. This, monks, is called 'everything'. Whoever should claim thus: 'having rejected this [version of] everything I shall define another', his words are unfounded. [...] Why is it so? Because, monks, there is nothing beyond this scope.

Another occurrence of the same idea, this time with an explicit reference to the term *ayatana,* is found in the *Niddesa* of the *Khuddaka-nikaya.* The *Cuaniddesa,* while commenting on the third *pada* of verse 1039 in the *Suttanipata,* introduces four alternative classifications describing how a monk should be skilled in all *dhammas,* the fourth of which claims that the twelve *ayatanas* alone represent the totality of all *dhammas.* This statement is repeated as part of the exegesis of *Suttanipata* verses (46, 181 and 187) in the *Mahaniddesa.*

The particular taxonomy of all-inclusiveness in terms of the twelve *ayatanas*, which is probably the earliest exegetical totality statement based on the *Sabba-sutta,* has been used by the Sarvastivadins to justify their ontological doctrine of the existence of *dharmas* in the three times. The *Sarva-sutra,* the *Saµyukta-agama* parallel of the *Sabba-sutta* (which, unlike its Pali counterpart, does explicitly mention the term *ayatana*), has become a main scriptural source for the Sarvastivada ontology. The Sarvastivadins identify the term 'everything' in the assertion 'everything exists' (*sarvam asti*) with this canonical passage, meaning that everything accessible to the twelve *ayatanas* exists. The Sarvastivada-Vaibhasika exegetical text, the *Mahavibhasa,* discusses in great detail the twelve *ayatanas,* explaining why of the three primary totality formulas the *ayatana* taxonomy alone is the most inclusive. The reason given is that the teaching of the twelve *ayatanas* is best suited to the highest degree of all-inclusiveness: the eighteen *dhatus*, despite their totality, are difficult to grasp, whereas the five *khandhas*, though easy to grasp, do not accommodate the unconditioned *dharmas* (these, according to the *Mahavibhasa,* include space (*akafa*), cessation resulting from consideration (*pratisaµkhyanirodha*) and cessation not resulting from consideration (*apratisaµkhyanirodha*)). The twelve *ayatanas,* however, encompass all *dharmas* whatsoever, conditioned and unconditioned alike, and hence embody the highest level of totality.

The Theravadin Abhidhamma rejects the Sarvastivadin conviction that 'everything exists' and accordingly does not pay much attention to the *ayatana* totality statement. In the *Abhidhamma-pitaka* there is no reference to the *Niddesa* declarations, although the *ayatanas* are conceded as one of the all-inclusive taxonomies. Nevertheless, the Abhidhamma does admit there is something unique about the inclusiveness of the *ayatanas* and the *dhatus*:

unlike the *khandha* formula, these taxonomies subsume *nibbana*. Wan Doo Kim notes on this that

> [A]lthough they attempted to present all the possible classifications of the *dhammas* within the confines of the *khandha* formula, in fact the early Abhidhammikas admitted that it could not accommodate the unconditioned, *nibbana* (i.e. *asaðkhatadhamma*). Therefore, they looked for another formula and discovered in the canonical texts the twelve *ayatanas* and eighteen *dhatus*.

Indeed the Abhidhammikas could place *nibbana* under the *dhamma* base in the twelve *ayatanas* and eighteen *dhatus*. Nevertheless, these two formulas, too, were found to be inadequate: the Abhidhammikas needed yet another mode of analysis, namely, the *dhamma* analysis, which turned into a whole theory. For what reason? I wish further to pursue this question.

What the Buddha and his immediate disciples would probably have understood by *dhamma,* then, was thought to reveal the nature of sentient experience in terms of *namarupa, khandha, ayatana* and *dhatu*. These standard modes of analysis represent a subjective and experiential treatment of mental and material phenomena from different standpoints, though none of them is definitive. That is, if each analysis is examined in relation to the others it is found amenable to further analysis. The *nama* component is thus analysed into the four mental *khandhas;* the five *khandhas* – as implied by that very term, which means 'a collection' or 'mass' of something – are further analysable into the eighteen *dhatus*, and the latter are but an elaboration on the twelve *ayatanas*.

Subsequent generations demanded further clarification of these modes of analysis and found them lacking. The *dhamma* theory was an outgrowth of their attempts to draw out the full implications of these types of analysis. The Abhidhammikas thus sought to make sense of meditative contemplation by drawing on yet another mode of analysis, which in their view was the most comprehensive and exhaustive, namely, the analysis of experience in terms of *dhammas*. In this context, the term *dhamma* refers to those items that result when the process of analysis is pursued to its ultimate limit, until it is not amenable to further analysis. In other words, *dhammas* are here the most basic, and in this sense 'atomic', physical and mental phenomena that make up one's experience, and in this sense one's world. This theoretical inquiry involves the categorization of all possible types of experiential occurrence, the scrutiny into their manifold conditional interrelations and the construction of these into an ordered, unified structure. By contrast to the prior listings of doctrinal concepts in the *suttas,* the Abhidhamma categorization of *dhammas* results in a comprehensive theory. In this specific context 'theory' denotes a systematic structure in which every single topic of the Buddha's teachings should find its proper place and be explained completely, both as it is in its exclusiveness and in relation to all other topics. The canonical Abhidhamma literature reflects the endeavour to provide such an all-encompassing theory. The fully fledged theory resultant from this enterprise of analysis and synthesis was finally settled in the commentaries and the later Abhidhamma manuals, and is referred to by modern scholars as 'the *dhamma* theory'. The *locus classicus* of the synthetic method is the *Patthana* that investigates the *dhammas'* manifold conditional relations, with which we shall deal in Chapter 5. The foundations of the analytic method are found in the *Dhammasangani.* Let us now consider this analytic aspect of the *dhamma* theory by looking at the Theravadin *dhamma* typology, the basic principles of which are shared by the Northern Abhidharma systems.

The Theravadin Dhamma Categorization

We have seen that within the Abhidhamma canonical framework *dhammas* are reckoned the physical and mental occurrences as presented in consciousness. These occurrences fall into various categories, the number of which is more or less finite: later Theravadin sources count eighty-two categories, whereas the Sarvastivada holds there to be seventy-five such categories. It should be noted that each category represents a possible type of occurrence and that the term *dhamma* denotes both any particular instance of a category of *dhammas* and the whole category. Thus, according to the Theravadin typology there are eighty-two possible types of occurrence in the encountered world not eighty-two occurrences. Eighty-one categories are conditioned *(sankhata),* which means that the many and various *dhamma* combinations they embrace constitute the conditioned cyclic experience in *samsdra* from the lowest realms of hell to the highest heavens of the *devas* and *brahmas.* The eighty-second *dhamma* category is unconditioned *(asankhata)* and has one single member, namely, *nibbdna.*

The eighty-one conditioned *dhammas* fall into three broad categories: consciousness *(citta),* associated mentality *(cetasika)* and materiality, or physical phenomena *(rupa).* The five *khandhas* of the Suttanta method fit within these three categories: the *rupakkhandha* is included within the *rupa* category that will be divided into twenty-eight types of material phenomena; the *viññanakkhandha* is subsumed by *citta* that here refers to different types of consciousness distinguished among other things, by their concomitants; while the remaining three *arupakkhandhas* are all accommodated within the *cetasika* category as mental states that arise along with consciousness performing diverse functions, with the *vedandkkhandha* and the *sanndkkhandha* each counted as one *cetasika,* the *sankhdrakkhandha* finely subdivided into fifty distinct *cetasikas.*

Consciousness, *citta,* encompasses a single *dhamma* category and in conformity with the early Buddhist intentional model of consciousness, has the sense of being aware of something. We can never experience bare consciousness in its own moment of occurrence as a single isolated *dhamma,* for consciousness always directs itself to some object; it cannot eventuate as a *dhamma* in isolation from other *dhammas*. Rather, it always occurs associated *(sampayutta)* with other mental states that enable the mind to be aware of perceived objects. There are fifty-two such *dhammas* that form the category of associated mentality. According to the post-canonical Abhidhamma the minimum number of associated mental states required for any thought process is seven: sense contact (*phassa*), feeling (*vedana*), recognition or conceptualization (*sañña*), volition (*cetana*), one-pointedness (*ekaggata*), life-faculty (*jivitindriya*) and attention (*manasikara*). These mental occurrences are common to all types of consciousness (*sabbacittasadhara~a*) and perform the essential and most basic cognitive functions without which the thought process would be impossible. Together with bare consciousness, this means that any conscious process requires a minimum of eight *dhammas*. The number of *cetasikas* will vary from the minimum seven in the simplest form of sense consciousness up to a maximum of thirty-six in a developed skilful consciousness. They will also vary qualitatively according to the type of consciousness in question.

The third category, materiality, groups twenty-eight types of *dhamma*. Any given physical occurrence is analysable into these *rupa-dhammas*, apart from which no other matter is recognized; the elusive metaphorical entity that we call 'matter' is but our own mental construction. For the sake of explanation, each *rupa-dhamma* is postulated as if it were a discrete entity, but in actual fact it always occurs inseparably associated with a set of other *rupa-dhammas*. A significant distinction is drawn between primary and secondary *rupa-dhammas*. The category of primary material *dhammas* includes the four great elements (*mahabhuta*), namely, earth, water, fire and wind (*pathavi-, apo-, tejo-, vayo-dhatu*) or, according to the Abhidhamma elaborate and more abstract explanation, the elements of solidity, fluidity, heat and mobility. The category of secondary material *dham-mas*, called *upada-rupa*, subsumes those material elements that are always coexistent with and necessarily dependent on the *mahabhutas*. Twenty-four such items are enumerated: the first five physical sense faculties and the first four corresponding sense objects (excluding tangibles); three faculties (femininity, masculinity, material faculty of life); two modes of self-expression (bodily and vocal); three characteristics of matter (lightness, plasticity and pliability); four phases of matter (integration, continuity, decay and impermanence); the space element, nutriment and the heart basis. Although the Abhidhamma framework shows more uniformity in the application of the term *rupa* than do the *Nikayas* (note that *rupa* in the sense of subjective phenomena is given up), the diversity of the *dhammas* grouped under the *rupa* category suggests that even in the Abhidhamma the term *rupa* was used with some degree of fluidity. The constituents of the *rupa* category are not as uniform as might be expected: some represent certain elements of matter and others certain facts (phases, modes, limitation) connected with matter.

The fourfold categorization of *dhammas* into *citta, cetasika, rupa* and *nibbana* is already anticipated by the *Dhammasaðga~i*, though only implicitly: it is not given straightforwardly, but it may be gleaned from the text's method and structure. The first two categories become manifest if we take into account the fact that the *dham-mas* investigated by the *Dhammasaðga~i* always prove to be factors of *citta* in its broadest sense of a series of particular mental occurrences. Indeed, Book I is entirely devoted to the uprising of *citta* (*cittuppada*) and aims at a comprehensive mapping of one's consciousness. That *citta* is regarded as inseparable from its associated mental states is shown by the couplets enumerated in the *mdtika* of the *Dhammasangani,* known as the *abhidhamma-mdtika,* and especially by the couplets of the *mahantara-duka,* among which we find *'dhammas* that are associated with/dissociated from *citta' (cittasampayuttdf-vippayuttd), 'dhammas* that are conjoined with/ detached from *citta' (cittasamsatthdAvisamsatthd)* and *'dhammas* that arise/do not arise simultaneously with *citta' (no citta-/ cittasahabhuno).* The *Dhammasangani,* though, also deals with the category of *rupa:* in fact, Book II is devoted to an inquiry into *rupa,* while Book III broaches the idea that the entire domain of *dhammas* is divided with respect to *rupa,* for the *dhammas* are shown to be either *rupino* or *arupino.* The former group incorporates the four great physical elements and all material form that is derived from them, whereas the latter refers to whatever is included under the four mental *khandhas* and to the unconditioned element. The fourfold *dhamma* categorization can thus be drawn from the *Dhammasangani,* and in this sense it is also present in the other Abhidhamma treatises which are familiar with the *Dhammasangani* and presuppose its ideas. It is explicitly stated for the first time, though, in the *Abhidhammdvatdra* - a post-canonical Abhidhamma manual ascribed to Buddhadatta (*c.*430 CE).

The fourfold *dhamma* typology became fundamental to and representative of Abhidhamma thought. One is, then, bound to wonder again: Why did the Abhidhamma theoreticians need this particular fourfold typology if the extant *dyatana* and *dhdtu* totality formulas could account for human experience in its entirety, *nibbdna* inclusive? What role did the intellectual milieu at that time play in the development of the *dhamma* categorization? This book argues and demonstrates that the Abhidhammikas sought to establish a metaphysical theory of mental events, and that for this purpose the extant totality formulas were found to be wanting. Motivated not only by a concern with the dynamics of sentient experience in its entirety, but also by a specific interest in accounting for what an awakened mind is as opposed to skilful consciousness experienced by an ordinary being *(puthujjana),* the Abhidhamma theoreticians attempted to set out criteria for determining what any given *dhamma* that may possibly occur in one's consciousness is. It is this metaphysical undertaking that distinguishes the *dhamma* analysis from the extant totality formulas. My argument, as primarily unfolded in Chapter 4, is that philosophically the

Abhidhammikas grappled with the problem of individua-tion and that, attempting to reconcile the tension between the systematic-doctrinal and the experiential-practical dimensions of their tradition within the specific context of Buddhist soteriology, they offered a method of individuating the *dhammas* as a means for individuating the scope of the mental.

This section has dealt with the major transformations in early Buddhist conception of *dhamma.* We have shown that in the Sutta literature *dhamma* was used as a generic term related to the Buddha's teachings and enabling one to refer to any subject matter in the broadest sense, similarly to 'thing'. In the canonical Abhidhamma the concept of *dhamma* underwent a gradual process of concretization and gradually acquired a narrower, more technical meaning. Here a clearer distinction was drawn between *dhamma* and *dhammas,* and the notion of the plurality of *dhammas* became the basis of an intricate theory of consciousness, or rather a metaphysics of mind. The *dhamma* theory was accompanied by closely related doctrines that together shaped the development of Buddhist systematic thought. The following section examines these doctrines.

ON DHAMMAS, ATOMS, SUBSTANCES AND THE DOCTRINE OF MOMENTARINESS

The Intellectual Backdrop: the Vaiçesika View of Atoms and Substances

The further systematization of *dhammas* was given impetus by their construal as psycho-physical events *qua* analytical primitives and, in the post-canonical period particularly, by their portrayal as momentary, atomic occurrences subsumed into a comprehensive categorial theory. This theory is not intended to provide an inventory of external existents, but rather distinguish the physical and mental events that may possibly occur in one's consciousness while making progress on the path to awakening. Ye t in their systematization of the *dhamma* theory, the Abhidhammikas must have been influenced by the contemporary Indian philosophical schools and their disputes over the notion of being and its extension. Within the Brahmanical arena, the Nyaya, the Vaifesika and the Purvamimaµsa take a leading role in the competition against the Buddhist anti-substantialist, process-oriented position. It is the Vaifesika, though, that sets up the most inclusive categorial system in classical Indian metaphysical discourse, and indeed there are conspicuous interrelations between the Abhidhamma's shift in understanding the concept of *dhamma* and Vaifesika doctrinal thought.

Although the full-fledged expression of the Vaifesika's ideas as found in the

a i fesika-sutra and in its ensuing textual tradition is posterior at least to the early strata of the canonical Abhidhamma, the idea of categorization and the conceptual roots of the Vaifesika go back to as early as the ancient Grammarians' (Vaiyyakaraja) analyses of language into its various components. The tradition of grammatical thought as documented in the *Mahabhasya* (second century BCE?) provides significant counterparts for Vaifesika metaphysics and abounds with analogues of the Vaifesika categorial theory. Modern scholarship has broached arguments in favour of both the thesis that the Vaifesika theory borrows from the *Mahabhasya* and was fixed roughly a century later (because it is more elaborate), and the opposite assumption that Patañjali's grammatical categories presuppose the

a i fesika categories. The extant sources, however, do not enable us conclusively to determine their dating, or the direction of intellectual transference between the Va i fesika, the Grammarians and the canonical Abhidhamma, and hence it would be more appropriate to substitute 'doctrinal exchange' for 'one-sided influence'. At any rate, we may safely assume that the Vaifesika and the Abhidhamma schools emerged in an intellectual atmosphere that was at least mediated by, if not originated from, ancient linguistic and grammatical circles. This intellectual milieu, on the one hand, fostered doctrinal interrelations between the above schools and, on the other hand, supported metaphysics and the reification of entities and qualities.

Much of the Abhidhamma doctrinal thought is essentially built upon the analysis of consciousness, and its paradigm for the way consciousness operates is consciousness experienced in the process of sensory perception. The Vaifesika and the Buddhist theories of sense perception show remarkable resemblance, although in the Vaifesika system the concepts of substance and of soul play a major role. Like the Abhidhamma theory of perception, the Vaifesika theory deals with the qualities of the elements that construct the objects of the different sense organs. Underlying this theory is the assumption that things are perceived with their qualities because the sense organs come into contact (*saµyoga*) with them. One perceives a certain colour, for instance, when there is a contact between the eye and the substance in which the colour inheres. The Vaifesika position, however, is that substances themselves are perceived, although their perception is necessarily bound up with the perception of their qualities. *Manas,* which is a substance on the Vaifesika list of categories, denotes a sixth, internal organ, intrinsically unconscious and in itself incapable of any cognitive activity. The internal organ receives sensory data from the five physical sense organs and passes them on to the soul or the knowing subject (*atman*). It passes only one sensory datum at a time so that the soul will not be swamped with too many data at once – which explains the fact that knowing does not occur all in an instant. Perception thus follows through contact with the objects and is assisted by the internal organ.

Interrelations are also found between the Vaifesika atomistic theory and the Abhidhamma explication of material reality in terms of atoms, although this affinity may have been mediated by the Sarvastivada. The Vaifesika deals with the analysis of nature into its ultimate constituents, incorporating the elaborate list of these constituents in a categorial scheme. Postponing the detailed discussion of the philosophical significance of a categorial theory to Chapter 4, in the present context suffice it to say that, ontologically, categories provide a means to analyse reality according to the distinct types of entity that supposedly constitute it. Categories represent the modes of being of all things in the encountered world, and hence are aspects of reality, differently from the items that they enumerate, which are parts of reality. A metaphysical system will arrange its categories in a certain hierarchy: the members of the preponderant category or categories are regarded as what really exists, while the members of the remaining, secondary categories are seen as either dependent upon the former or as illusory.

The first three categories on the Vaifesika list are substance (*dravya*); attribute, or 'quality instances'; and motion, or 'action-moments'. There are nine types of substance: earth, water, fire, air, ether, time, space, self and mind. Substance is defined as that which possesses attribute and motion, and as the inherent cause of all objects. It is the locus, the supportive substratum and the constitutive cause of all things. Substances are divided into permanent (*nitya*) and impermanent (*anitya*): all nine classes of substance are essentially irreducible, indestructible elements that occur in their permanent form as eternal, indivisible atoms (*parama~u*). The four primary substances (earth, water, fire and air) also occur as impermanent, destructible compounds of atoms that form the concrete, empirical objects and phenomena we encounter in everyday experience. In both their modes of existence substances are real substrates of real attributes having *astitva*, 'isness'.

The Vaifesika conceives of atoms, then, as infinitely small, eternal and uncaused material substances. According to this mechanistic philosophy of nature, everything in the encountered world is made up of and reducible to these imperishable atoms that conglomerate and separate, but themselves remain unchangeable. The origination and disappearance of all existents depend on the connection and the separation of atoms respectively. The latter also possess definite, permanent qualities (excepting the earth atoms, the qualities of which could change under the influence of heat), so that whatever apparent change in empirical phenomena results from the mixture of different atoms. Through the connection of parts (*avayava*) of which a thing is composed there ascends a new entity: a uniform whole (*avayavi*) different from its parts but that inheres in these parts. The new material compound emerges from the substance of its atomic elements, although its qualities, such an extension, may differ from those of its elements.

The Vaifesika pluralistic realism and atomistic theory, then, are grounded in what may be called a substance-attribute ontology. Such an ontology was dominant in classical Western philosophy for a long period, albeit it founded itself upon a supporting substance metaphysics that does not neatly match ancient India's conceptual framework, first and foremost in the significance this metaphysics ascribes to the postulate of transcendence. The charges of doctrinal divergence, scholasticism and 'ontologization' levelled against the Abhidhamma notwithstanding, it is yet unclear to what extent these charges are justified, let alone in the case of the canonical Abhidhamma. Moreover, even if the later Abhidhammikas did develop what may provisionally be called 'ontology', given that their adhered event metaphysics had been rooted in process thought, then the resultant ontology may well be of an order different from substance-attribute ontology. To come to grips with these issues, we must first clarify what the Abhidhamma metaphysics is *not*, namely, substance metaphysics.

Substance Metaphysics: An Overview

From the time of Aristotle onwards, Western metaphysics has been dominated by the ontology of substance. The concept of substance has mainly been used in philosophical attempts to account for an ordinary, commonsense conceptual scheme that presupposes the existence of individual entities – substantial continuants such as persons, trees, animals, events, times and places. Even though philosophical scepticism, post-modernist movements and empirical science have operated in the direction of eradicating this widespread scheme, it is not clear that the idea of the existence of substances has been completely dispensed with (consider, for example, science's reference to 'particles'). This idea is deeply rooted in the language we operate, of which the basic subject–predicate structure expresses a two-category ontological scheme: there are objects or 'things', namely, particulars that exist at unique place-times, and these objects have various attributes, that is, characteristics and modes of action. Our subject terms typically refer to particular objects, our predicate terms to their attributes and properties. Although the concept of substance is multivalent and has noticeably changed throughout the history of philosophy, it has retained the basic metaphysical sense of 'that which is': a concrete particular, and the only true particular, in which properties inhere.

Different metaphysical systems propose alternative schemes for the structure of reality. Each such scheme typically exhibits a hierarchy of levels of ontologi-cal categories. The topmost category is that of Being or Entity, which instantiates everything that exists. Then some schemes take at a lower level the categories of the Concrete and the Abstract. It is assumed that this division is exhaustive and exclusive: every entity is necessarily either concrete or abstract. A concrete entity, while 'monopolizing' its location, as it were, is the totality of the being to be found where its features are. Abstract entities, by contrast, do not exist in space and time, and it is often held that they lack causal powers and hence that they are incapable of entering into causal relationships with other entities. At the next level the Abstract is divided into various types such as Property (e.g. redness, squareness), Relation (e.g. identity), Proposition (e.g. 'Human beings are mortal') and Number. The Concrete, on the other hand, includes a different set of categories, the most important of which are Substance, Event (e.g. the eruption of Mt Vesuvius), Time (e.g. instants and durations), Place (points or regions of space), Limit (e.g. corners, surfaces) and Privation (e.g. holes or the absence of something). Finally, the category Substance is divided into Matter that includes all sensible objects, and Mind. Thus, the most fundamental feature of substance to be found in all its different accounts throughout the history of philosophy is that it is a concrete, particular entity; a specific, definite object rather than any other.

The concept of substance has occupied a central position in philosophical attempts to organize and categorize entities into various types. At the opening of *Metaphysics* VII Aristotle situates his inquiry into the nature of substance in relation to the traditional perplexity over the nature of being. What is the nature of being *qua* being, which is universal and necessary to all things? Aristotle maintains that this nature is located only in the primary or first instance, that is, in substance. Aristotle mentions various ways in which being is spoken of, though he focuses on the distinction between essential and accidental being. Substance, as the fundamental kind of being, denotes the subject of accidental change and is contrasted with its accidents: with things such as properties, qualities or attributes of substance, affections of substance, processes towards it and things that are productive of and relative to substance. This asymmetry rests on the assumption that the world contains two sorts of entity – substance and non-substance – that stand in a relation of one-way ontological dependence.

Substance is assigned an ontological priority: whereas all non-substances exist in substances that are their subjects (substrata), substances do not exist in subjects; they are separate and independent of non-substances. In this sense, substances may be reckoned as the ontological foundations of what there is; there is nothing more basic than them. But there are two additional aspects to the priority of substance. The first is a logico-grammatical priority: building on the logical notion of a subject, by 'sensible substances' Aristotle intended fundamental objects of predication, things that are neither predicated (said of) a subject nor in a subject. Contrarily, what needs to have a subject included in its definition is not a subject in the primary sense, and hence cannot be a substance.

On Aristotle's view, we can predicate various attributes of sensible substances, but we cannot predicate substances of anything else, and in this sense their being is independent. For instance, we may say of the sky that it is blue, but we cannot say of any other subject that it is sky. This primacy of substance is, then, characterized by a priority in definition: the definition of any non-substantial being will include the definition of a substance, but not vice versa. The second aspect, and the third priority assigned to substance, is epistemological. Here it is stated that the definition of a substance is crucial for knowing what a thing is. We presume we know each entity fully, Aristotle says, when we know what its nature is, for example, what a man is, rather than when we know its accidental features, such as its quality, its quantity or its place.

The elements of Aristotle's metaphysical scheme laid the conceptual infrastructure of his scholastic heirs' worldview. Those medieval thinkers kept elaborating on the Aristotelian project of articulating the structure of substance, supplementing and refining Aristotle's account in accordance with their metaphysical and theological concerns. The scholastics' concern with the Aristotelian metaphysics of substance was prompted by their interest in the notion of individual substance, and especially in the problem of individuation, which we may provisionally render as the question of what makes an individual substance this very particular rather than any other individual. What the medieval thinkers emphasize is that an individual substance is defined and distinguished from all other substances by its position in a hierarchy of levels of generality among categories. First, it is distinguished by the generic distinction holding among genera, next by the specific distinction holding among species, and finally, within a species, by the numerical distinction among the various particulars (e.g. 'animal' '! 'human being' '! 'Socrates').

The dawn of modern philosophy brought changes into the traditional articulation of the structure of substance. Nonetheless, the fundamentals of a substance-attribute ontology persisted in subsequent philosophy and retained Aristotle's authority long after the notion of substance came to be understood differently. René Descartes (1596–1650), the founder of modern philosophy, applies the term substance

> [T]o every thing in which whatever we perceive immediately resides, as in a subject, or to every thing by means of which whatever we perceive exists. By 'whatever we perceive' is meant any property, quality or attribute of which we have a real idea.

Now Descartes' idea of substance significantly differs from the Aristotelian-scholastic tradition's in that substance is no longer assigned an epistemological primacy. 'We cannot initially become aware of a substance', Descartes says, 'merely through its being an existing thing, since this alone does not of itself have any effect on us'. Rather, from the fact that we perceive certain attributes, which must inhere in something in order to have existence, we name the thing in which they inhere 'substance' and conclude that it must also exist. The ontological primacy, though, is retained: whatever is real can exist independently of any other object, and that which can thus exist is a substance.

Empiricists from John Locke (1632–1704) onwards turned the traditional epistemological and ontological hierarchy between substance and attribute completely on its head. They rejected the ontological priority of substance and instead argued that qualities alone are observed, and hence that qualities alone can be said to exist. In the words of Locke, substance is something the idea of which 'we neither have, nor can have by sensation or reflection'. It is something we accustom ourselves to suppose to be the support of certain qualities that are capable of producing simple ideas in us, as these are conveyed to us by the senses. Substance is the supposed, though unknown, substratum of those qualities we find existing, which we imagine cannot subsist without something to uphold them. On Locke's view 'substance' signifies 'the bearer of properties' and is approximated to what is indicated by the term 'object' – a sense which is remarkably different from 'the most basic kind of being'. Qualities or properties, though, are general and can apply to an infinitely large number of individual instances.

To pin down a particular by progressively specifying a complete set of its properties thus by no means assures that any group of properties, which is the set of all these properties, has that thing as its unique instance. Qualitatively identical things may be numerically distinct. This implies that the unique individuality of a thing is something over and above its attributes and possible appearances. Thus, although this Lockean line of thought strongly criticizes the concept of substance, once it has admitted the idea of an individuator it is compelled to accept the idea of a unifying substratum.

To sum up, Western metaphysics has been dominated by the ontological model of substance, which has a marked bias in favour of 'objects'. The mainstays of substance metaphysics are that the world contains individual entities that endure through time and in which properties inhere (leaving aside whether those entities are material or immaterial and the exact nature of their inherent properties). What is perhaps the main derivative of the concept of substance is the view that reality is such that there is something 'out there' which is abiding, enduring and unalterable, despite the diversity and change we witness. Substance is that immutable core, what underlies an object and enables it to remain the same despite the novelty of its fea-tures. The concept of substance is therefore tied in with realism, according to which we are, by and large, capable of acquiring knowledge of the world and of comprehending it, because our categories, beliefs and statements fit with the features of a mind-independent reality. The Vaifesika pluralistic realism and atomistic theory are on a par with these assumptions. The point is that although the Theravadin Abhidhamma analysis of matter is likely to have been informed by the Vaisesika ontology it is grounded in a disparate metaphysical approach.

The Buddhist Notion of Atomic Dharmas

Within Buddhist circles the idea of material atoms is explicitly stated for the first time in the *Abhidharmahrdaya* of Dharmasri (*c.* second century CE). It is given a detailed formulation in the *Mahdvibhdsd* and later on plays an integral part in the works of Vasubandhu and Sanghabhadra (fifth century CE). The Sarvastivada-Vaibhasika position, as documented by Vasubandhu in the

Abhidharmakosabhdsya, distinguishes between two layers of material entities: the unitary atom *(dravya-paramdnu)* and the collective atom *(sanghdta-paramdnu).* The unitary atom is the smallest unit of matter: it consists of the four primary elements *(mahdbhuta,* i.e. earth, fire, water and wind), albeit it is partless and without dimensions; it never springs or passes away in isolation, but is combined with other unitary atoms. A collection of atoms that emanate and discontinue simultaneously with each other is called a collective atom, the smallest of which consists of a minimum of eight elements: the four primary elements and four secondary elements. The latter are four of the five types of sense object (form, odour, taste and touch; sound is not regarded as necessary for the occurrence of material objects) - what Nelson Goodman has coined *qualia,* meaning those sensible things such as shades of colour, smells and tastes.

The *Nikdyas* allude to the distinction between the *mahdbhutas* as primary material elements *(rupa-dhamma)* and the secondary, derived material elements *(upddd-rupa),* but no attempt is made to explain how and why the latter are secondary to the former. The *Dhammasangani* does not go much beyond the *Nikdyas* in this respect. Preliminary information is found in the *Patthdna,* wherein it is said that the four *mahdbhutas* stand in relation to the *upddd-rupas* as causal conditions *(paccaya)* by way of simultaneity *(sahajdta),* support *(nissaya),* presence *(atthi)* and non-disappearance *(avigata).* The *upddd-dhammas* thus emanate simultaneously with the *rupa-dhammas,* but they are elements that describe how material phenomena are perceived through our senses, and hence they are secondary to the latter. The *mahdbhutas* are assigned a primary position in the sense that they are recognized as the ultimate, irreducible data of matter. Although all four primary elements are present in every instance of matter, there is no quantitative difference *(pamdna)* between them: they enter into the composition of material things in equal proportion. The diversity of material objects is not due to a difference in the quantity of their components, but in their capability *(sdmatthiya).* That is, in a given material phenomenon one element is more intense than the others. For instance, if in a given material aggregate the earth element is characterized by a comparatively high degree of intensity or capability, then that material aggregate is also called 'earth' or 'earth-preponderant' *(adhika).*

Note that this is not an account of matter as constitutive of external, mind-independent reality, and indeed ontologically it might be said that the schema of material reality as made up of the atoms of the four elements does not specify the status of material phenomena other than that they arise from the elements. The above Abhidhamma analysis depicts material phenomena as they appear to the different types of cognitive awareness, revealing that every instance of matter in all its possible states other than sound has eight components: four elements and four types of sensible phenomena (form, odour, taste and touch). Sound alone has nine components: the former eight plus sound.

Nevertheless, the analysis of matter into atomic components undermines this phenomenological dimension. Georges Dreyfus observes that the latter is more distinctly retained in the Sautrantika divergent version of the atomistic theory. For the Vaibhasika the five types of sensible phenomena – and hence the four secondary elements – are included in the list of the seventy-five *dharmas* under the *ayatanas*. Therefore they are as real as the four primary elements, despite being composed of, and thus dependent on, the former. But this is contradictory, for if they are merely mental constructs made of unitary atoms how can they be real?

The Sautrantika view, as represented by Vasubandhu in his commentary to his own *Abhidharmakofa*, deals with this problem by distinguishing between two different senses of 'real' (*dravya*): ontological and phenomenological. Although from a phenomenological standpoint the sense spheres constitute one's experiential world and may be taken as real, ontologically speaking they are not so. Vasubandhu thus refutes the Vaibhasika interpretation that large material objects are made up of eight elements. For him, only the four primary elements are real in the full sense of the term; they constitute all material objects that are mere conceptual constructs. Accordingly, the sense spheres are excluded from the list of real phenomena (*dravya*). According to this Sautrantika explanation, infinitesimal atoms and moments of consciousness alone are real. Everything else, such as shapes or shades of colour, is taken as real only inasmuch as it has the efficacy to produce appropriate effects (visual cognitions, in the present example) and is taken as an object of conventional practice. Our perception of sense objects is not due to their reality, but is the result of the causal efficacy of their constituent atoms. Whatever disputes may have existed between the Sarvastivada-Vaibhasika and the Sautrantika on these ontological and phenomenological issues, they all agreed on the view that material reality (*rupa-dharma*) can be reduced to discrete momentary atoms, namely, the four primary elements. These momentary atoms, through their spatial arrangement and by their concatenation with prior and posterior atoms of the same type, create the illusion of persisting things as they appear in our everyday experience. Atomic reality is thus understood first and foremost as change, though not in the sense of a thing *x* transforming into *y*. That is, change itself is the very nature of atomic reality rather than its being made of enduring substances the qualities of which undergo change. Atoms that appear to endure are, in fact, a series of momentary events that ascend and fall in rapid succession and in accordance with causal relations. Unlike the atoms of the Vaifesika, the atoms of the Sarvastivada-Vaibhasika and the Sautrantika are not permanent: they come into being and cease from one moment to the next, going through a process of birth, continuance, decay and destruction. Yet the material compounds that consist of these atoms are real, if only in the minimal, phenomenological sense.

For our present purpose it is important to note that the Theravadins did not incorporate the Northern Buddhist atomistic theory as such into their system. As Karunadasa indicates, the Theravadin canonical texts do not mention the idea of a unitary atom or the term *parama~u*. Rather, the post-canonical texts employ the term *kalapa* (literally 'package'), which corresponds to the collective atom of the Sarvastivada-Vaibhasika, that is, the smallest material unit that contains the eight elements. The idea first appears in the commentaries to the *Dhammasaðga~i* and the *Vibhaðga,* as well as in the *Visuddhimagga,* using both the singular form and the plural form *kalapa*. Yet only in the period of the sub-commentaries and the medieval manuals did *kalapa* become the standard term for the collective atom.

Moreover, the four *mahabhutas* – although postulated as if they were discrete entities – do not exist independently. Rather, they always occur simultaneously (*sahajata*) with each other: the rise or cessation of one always synchronizes with those of the other three. Their relation is therefore described in the *Patthana* and in the Abhidhamma commentaries as conditioned by mutuality and simultaneity (*aññamañña-, sahajata-paccaya*). Fundamental to these two types of causal conditioning is the principle that the occurrence of one element must simultaneously be accompanied by whatever is related to that element. Each of the primary elements thus becomes at one and the same time the condition as well as what is conditioned in relation to the others. Each element assists the remaining three by performing its peculiar function: the earth element is a condition for the other three primaries by acting as their foundation; the water element acts as their cohesion; the fire element acts as their maintenance; the air element acts as their distension.

Even if this analysis of matter eventually ends in 'atomism', the notion of the material *dhammas'* simultaneity is not abandoned: the so-called atom is a collection of *rupa-dhammas*, each of which is inseparable from the others. Their interconnection is explained with reference to relations of causal conditioning rather than to inherence of some sort, such as that between substances and their intrinsic attributes or qualities. No distinction between substance and attributes is introduced here: instead, a distinction is made between primary and secondary elements. The Buddhist atomistic theory, regardless of its different interpretation by each Abhidharma school, thus stands in contrast to Vaifesika atomism. The Va i fesika theory exhibits the substance-attribute ontological model, whereas for the Buddhists sensibilia are not the attributes or qualities of the *mahabhutas*; they are a set of secondary elements dependent on the latter. The *Atthasalini* declares: 'Who has said that visual forms etc., are qualities of heat, and so on? For it is not permissible to say of indivisible phenomena "this is a quality of that."' Although the *mahabhutas* are deemed the ultimate and primary elements of matter, they are not to be understood as substances. Each element is always found to be conditioned by, related to and co-arisen with the others – and this stands in utter contradiction with the definition of substance as that which exists independently of any other thing, ontologically, epistemologically and linguistically. All four primary elements are present in each *rupa-kalapa*, the smallest unit of matter, but they are not permanent, independent entities: they are subject to the laws of causal conditioning, liable to destruction and have no underlying, enduring essence. In short, they are characterized by the three marks of *anicca, dukkha* and *anatta*.

The early Theravadin Abhidhamma, then, did not simply adhere to the theory of atomic *dhammas* and there is no allusion to the unitary atom in the Theravadin canonical texts. Only in the post-canonical literature does the idea of a collective atom (*kalapa*) appear, and even the mature theory of *rupa-kalapas*, the Theravadin form of atomism, is incommensurate with a substance metaphysics. Nonetheless, the idea of atomizing the encountered world did leave its mark upon the Theravadin mindset. This is evinced in the Theravadin reconciliation of the *dhamma* typologies with the doctrine of momentariness espoused by the Northern Abhidharma schools. The next section reviews the salient principles of this doctrine and its metaphysical implications.

The Doctrine of Momentariness

The doctrine of momentariness does not appear as a topic in its own right in the earliest stratum of Buddhist teaching. It was initially developed within the framework of the Abhidharma traditions and thereafter became an integral part of their doctrinal systems. The theory appears to have originated from the early Buddhist analysis of impermanence (*anicca*) in terms of the constant rise and fall of all mental and physical phenomena. This analysis, however, was subsequently elaborated by the Buddhist schools into a schematic and radical theory that departed from the ancient view of impermanence as found in the *suttas*, where it is presented as an empirically oriented teaching about the nature of sentient experience. The Buddhist doctrine of momentariness atomizes phenomena temporally by dissecting them into a succession of discrete, momentary (*ksa~ika/kha~ika*) events that pass out of existence as soon as they have originated. As one event is exhausted, it conditions a new event of its kind that proceeds immediately afterwards. The result is an uninterrupted, flowing continuum (*santana*) of causally connected momentary events. These succeed each other so fast that we conceive of the phenomena they constitute as temporally extended.

There is no surviving textual material that documents how the original Buddhist postulate of impermanence came to be conceived in terms of momen-tariness. Pioneering research on the

Buddhist doctrine of momentariness began in the 1930s, but produced a picture of the final form this doctrine assumed in the Sautrantika and Yogacara schools. Alexander von Rospatt's comprehensive study of the early history of the doctrine of momentariness fills this gap, although it focuses on the Sarvastivada-Vaibhasika and Yogacara texts. Wan Doo Kim has recently provided an erudite reconstruction of the early formation of this doctrine in the Theravada tradition. The following presentation of the development of the Theravadin doctrine of momentariness is informed by these two studies, and especially by Kim's work and its conclusions.

Most scholars agree that the Buddhist doctrine of momentariness cannot be traced back to the early canonical sources, that is, the *Nikayas* and their equivalents in other Buddhist traditions. Accordingly, it has been argued that the Theravadins did not develop the doctrine of momentariness in the early stage of their history, that it was adopted from other Buddhist circles following the division into divergent doctrinal movements, and is thus a post-canonical development which dates back only to the first century CE and possibly even later, being introduced by Buddhaghosa in the fifth century CE. In contradistinction to this position, Kim shows that the doctrine of momentariness is embedded in the Old Sinhalese commentaries and has its roots in the Theravadin canonical sources.

The doctrine of momentariness probably originated in conjunction with the teaching of impermanence and the three characteristics of conditioned phenomena *(tisankhatalakkhana,* namely, *anicca, dukkha* and *anatta).* The characteristic of impermanence lies at the root of Buddhist thought and is emphatically insisted upon in the canonical texts. This conviction is expressed by the renowned formula *sabbe sankhara anicca.* It is part of the basic position of the Buddha's teaching that all empirical phenomena - physical and mental alike - are impermanent, in a constant process of conditioned construction, and are closely linked being dependently originated. The Sutta elaboration on these three interlocking ideas results in the statement that conditioned phenomena *(sankhdrd/sankhatad-hamma)* are of the nature of origination *(uppdda)* and dissolution *(vaya).* They are sometimes also depicted as having the nature of 'change of what endures' *(thitassa annathatta),* as the Buddha says: Origination of the body, feeling, conceptualization, karmic volition and consciousness is evident, [its] dissolution is evident, [its] change of what endures is evident. Origination of these phenomena *(dhammdnam)* is evident, [their] dissolution is evident, [their] change of what endures is evident.

Kim suggests that this is the stock phrasing that paved the way for further schematization of the idea of impermanence, and from which a redactor or reciter of the Canon eventually derived the prototype *tisankhatalakkhana* formula of the *Anguttara-nikdya,* later known as the *Trilaksana-sutra:*

There are, monks, these three conditioned characteristic marks of that which is conditioned. What three? Origination is evident, dissolution is evident and change of what endures is evident. These, monks, are the three conditioned characteristic marks of that which is conditioned.

Interestingly, the couplet of origination and dissolution, or rather cessation, also appears in the *Yamaka.* Each chapter of this canonical Abhidhamma treatise is divided into three sections: Distribution of Designations *(pannatti-vdra),* Process *(pavatti-vdra)* and Comprehension *(parinnd-vdra).* The rationale of the second section is especially significant for the concerns of this study, as it complies with the earliest Buddhist process metaphysics, that is, the assumption that the encountered phenomena constituting one's experience are best represented and understood in terms of processes rather than substantial 'things'. The Process section in each of the *Yamaka* chapters examines various doctrinal concepts in terms of origination *(uppdda-vdra),* cessation *(nirodha-vdra)* and origination-cessation *(uppddanirodha-vdra).* As Kim notes, this is probably the first occurrence of the term *khana* in the sense of the subdivision of a moment into origination and destruction moments *(uppadakkhana, bhangakkhana).* This is also a milestone in the development of a radical theory of momentariness which replaced the early teaching of impermanence.

The full-fledged threefold scheme of subdivision of a moment, adding an endurance moment *(thitikkhana),* first appears in the Pali commentaries. Relying on the recurring canonical doctrine of the three marks of conditioned phenomena, the commentators taught that each moment *(khana)* of every single phenomenon is subdivided into three different instants of origination *(uppadakkhana),* endurance *(thitikkhana)* and dissolution *(bhangakkhana).* The *Samyutta* commentary declares:

Hence the Ancients said:

'Arising was called birth and dissolution referred to passing away. Change referred to ageing and endurance to maintenance.'

Thus each *khandha* has three characteristic marks called arising, ageing and dissolution, of which it is said in the passage (A I 152): 'These are, monks, the three conditioned characteristic marks of the conditioned *[khandha].'*

On the basis of a stanza handed down by the Ancients, the commentator identifies *uppdda* withyarf (birth), *vaya* with *bhanga* (dissolution), *thiti* with *anupdland* (maintenance) and *annathatta* with *jard* (ageing). Then, referring to the *Anguttara* formula of the *tisankhatalakkhana,* he reduces these four categories to three, namely, *uppdda, jard* and *bhanga.* The *Anguttara* commentary refers to three categories only, glossing *uppdda with jdti, vaya* with *bheda* (destruction) and *thitassa aññathatta* with *jard.* It then explicitly refers to time, applying the concept of a moment to each phase of the *tisankhatalakkhana:* origination is said to appear at the origination moments, ageing at the subsistence *(thana)* moments and dissolution at the destruction moments.

In the Abhidharma tradition of the Sarvastivada-Vaibhasika the term 'moment' *(ksana)* is used in a highly technical sense as the smallest, definite unit of time that cannot be subdivided the length of which came to be equated with the duration of mental entities as the briefest conceivable events. This usage presupposes an atomistic conception of time in the sense that time is not reckoned indefinitely divisible - indeed *ksana* is often discussed in juxtaposition to the concepts of material atoms and syllables, which are likewise comprehended as indivisible. The Sarvastivadins took the stance that the four *samskrtalaksanas* exist separately as real entities within each moment. This induced a host of problems, the primary of which is that such a definition of *ksana* is difficult to reconcile with the conception of the moment as the shortest unit of time.

The Theravadins, though, did not share this conception of the moment and instead used *khana* as the expression for a short while, the dimension of which is not fixed but may be determined by the context. For example, *cittakkhana* refers to the instant taken by one mental event. In this basic sense as denoting a very brief stretch of time, the term *khana* does not entail an atomistic conception of a definite and ultimate, smallest unit of time, but leaves open the possibility that time is infinitely divisible. In the canonical texts *khana* covers a wider range of meaning than merely 'moment' and often denotes 'opportunity' or 'auspicious moment'. In the context of the *tisankhatalakkhana, khana* acquires the specific sense of the threefold subdivision of a moment and is prefixed by the words *uppada, thiti* and *bhanga.* Here the three moments of origination, endurance and dissolution do not correspond to three different entities. Rather, they represent three phases *(avattha)* of a single momentary phenomenon and are defined as one single consciousness-moment *(ekacittakkhana):* a *dhamma* occurs in the first sub-moment, endures in the second sub-moment and perishes in the third one. In this way, the Theravadins avoided the predicament of the Sarvastivada-Vaibhasikas, who had to face the difficulties of how to compress the four *samskrtalaksanas* -conceived of as four different realities, as really existent entities - into one single indivisible moment, and of how to account for their ontological status.

Despite their different interpretations of the concept of momentariness, the early Buddhist schools all derived this concept from the analysis of imperma-nence in terms of the dynamics of whatever mental and physical phenomena eventuate. The equation of *ksana/khana* with the duration of these transient phenomena as extremely short occurrences - even the shortest conceivable - led to the direct determination of the moment in terms of these occurrences. This, along with the schematization and subdivision of the moment into the phases of origination, endurance and dissolution, resulted in the mature theory of momentariness. In the framework of the Sarvastivadins, the Darstantikas and the Sautrantikas, the theory is applied to material and mental phenomena alike. These schools portray consciousness as a succession of discrete moments of awareness, that is, single instants of thought, the occurrence and passing away of which transpire extremely rapidly in accordance with a sequence of particular sense objects. Thus, the ratio of change between material and mental phenomena in a given moment is one to one, so that they occur in perfect synchronicity. As opposed to those schools, the Theravadins claim in the *Khanikakatha* of the *Kathdvatthu* -the earliest evidence of the theory of momentariness - that only mental phenomena are momentary, whereas material phenomena endure for a stretch of time. The Theravadin commentarial tradition subsequently elaborated on this proposition and produced the unique theory that a material phenomenon lasts for sixteen or seventeen thought moments.

So far we have located the Theravadin doctrine of momentariness within the broader intellectual milieu of early Buddhist doctrinal thought. We have seen that this doctrine testifies to a transition from an empirically oriented postulate of impermanence to an all-encompassing schematization of experience-in-time construed in terms of moments: from *anicca* to *khanikavdda.* This transition led the Theravadin masters into conceptual reification and hypostatization: although the doctrine of momentariness entails that all conditioned phenomena are intrinsically momentary and subject to constant origination and destruction, each such constitutive moment came to be hypostatized through its analysis into discrete phases corresponding to the characteristics of the conditioned. What is perhaps the most striking embodiment of this doctrinal move is the endurance moment, *thitikkhana,* and its respective conditioned characteristic of *thitassa, annathatta.*

The endurance moment posed a host of problems for the Buddhist schools and was interpreted in various ways. The Theravadins explain *annathatta* as ageing *(jara)* and in accordance with the distinction they draw between the duration of a moment of thought and one of matter, they are particularly concerned with the incongruity of the idea of ageing when it applies to immaterial phenomena. Hence, they claim that the marks of such phenomena as feeling, conceptualization etc. should be understood either in terms of an existence moment *(atthikkhana)* or in terms of recurrence *(santati):*

But some declare: 'The ageing-moment cannot be made known in the case of immaterial phenomena. [...] Those [three characteristic marks] are obtained with reference to the moment of existence.' [...] They further say: 'Or alternatively, "endurance" is a state to be understood in terms of recurrence.' It is difficult to determine from this *Samyutta* commentary passage what exactly is meant by *atthikkhana.* To judge by the sub-commentary, the term refers to the fact that a mental phenomenon changes so rapidly that there is no separate endurance moment, because the very brief moment of its existence is denoted by the origination moment itself. Later sub-commentators, notably Sumangala, reject the concept *of atthikkhana* and interpret the phrase *thitassa annathatta* as *pubbdparavisesa,* namely, the difference between the preceding and the succeeding phase that constitutes a series of *dhammas.* This position is on a par with the second alternative in the above citation, wherein *thiti* is understood in terms of continuity. Most Theravadin commentators, however, do not endorse this position. The *Samyutta* commentary thus states that *thitikkhana* is a state in the occurrence of a *dhamma* distinct from the stages of its arising and dissolution, during which the *dhamma* endures 'in the face of its own dissolution' *(bhangabhimukhavattha).*

Another difficulty regarding *thitikkhana* and its identification with ageing is that ageing implies a qualitative change or modification in a given *dhamma* during the moment of its endurance, and change, in its turn, implies numerical difference, that is, the loss of identity and the substitution of the old by the new. The problem is how to reconcile this change with the Buddhist avoidance of the metaphysical notion of substance and its position that, beyond their properties, the *dhammas* have no underlying substrate which could account for their identity at the time of their origination and dissolution. In this context, both Buddhaghosa and Buddhadatta observe that ageing is manifested as the loss of the newness (*navabhavapagama*) of a *dhamma,* and not as the loss of its intrinsic nature (*sab-havanapagama*). Now the idea that the *dhammas* retain their intrinsic nature seems to be at odds with the very teaching of impermanence and with the fundamental rejection of an underlying substrate serving as the common thread upholding the moments of those *dhammas* together. The succeeding chapter takes up the development of the concept of *sabhava,* its alleged ontological bearing and its position within the wider context of Buddhist epistemology and metaphysics. What I wish to emphasize here is that there appears to be a disparity between the early Buddhist teaching of impermanence and the later Abhidhamma analysis of each and every phenomenon at the microscopic level into its constitutive moments and their discrete phases. A tendency towards reification and hypostati-zation of the *dhammas* is attested by the conceptual shift from *anicca* to *thiti* and by the introduction of such ideas as *sabhava* and *atthikkha~a*.

The development of the theory of momentariness, then, along with its closely related atomistic theory, is part of the gradual systematization of Buddhist thought and ought to be seen in the broader context of the developing *dhamma* theory. As Gombrich has indicated, this doctrinal shift in the history of Buddhist thought is marked by two factors: the first is what he calls scholastic literalism, namely, a form of exegesis which reads more meaning into words at the cost of disregarding what those words were originally intended to describe. The second factor is debate, that is, the fact that monks were arguing about various doctrinal topics among themselves as well as against rival Buddhist and non-Buddhist circles. The two factors are interrelated: literalism may provide ample matter for debate and induce the preservation and assimilation of more than one side of an argument, whereas debates can often degenerate into excessive schematization and reification of terms. Accordingly, Gombrich suggests that the problem of *thitassa aññathatta* could be an instance of this doctrinal shift within early Buddhist schools:

> It would be possible to see the passage in the *Trilaksa~a-sutra* in a different light, as consonant with the simple twofold description of all conditioned phenomena as just arising and passing away. This could be done by interpreting *thitassa aññathatta* as simply synonymous with *uppada* plus *vaya* – another way of expressing the same thing. True, the passage exactly as we have it seems to suggest three perfectly parallel clauses, and since *vaya* is clearly different from *uppada*, parallelism suggests that *thitassa aññathatta* is different again. However, since the text (in any case not a perfect recording of the Buddha) may have undergone some slight rephrasing, this is not an overwhelming argument. Moreover, if a true tri-partition were intended, one would expect the chronological sequence: *uppada, thitassa aññathatta, vaya*. On our interpretation of the text's original meaning, *thitassa* should not be translated 'of what endures' but 'of what there is'.

The theory of momentariness and the dissection of each phenomenal moment at the micro-level, then, are subject to the *dhamma* theory and its broader vision of analysing experience into its ultimately basic elements. Such a project would be susceptible to the danger of reifying these elements and assigning them an ontological status. This, Gombrich has argued, is precisely what happened in the Abhidhamma. As already indicated, the Abhidhammikas attempted to construct a systematic theory that would account for meditative experience. In this specific context of meditation the plural form *dhammas* refers to mental objects; the contents as they appear in the practitioner's consciousness and that through mediative contemplation are revealed to reflect the Buddha's teachings in propo-sitional form. The latter, by virtue of their status as propositions, do not have to be conceived ontologically, as 'things' existing 'out there'. Nevertheless, generalizing from this specific context of meditation, Gombrich explains, the Abhidhammikas began to treat these *dhamma* lists that the Buddha had referred to 'as an inventory of what the Buddha had taught to *exist*, as the building blocks of the universe [...] There were many more abstract than concrete *dhamma*, and some were still the names of processes, like anger, but the list was a closed one'. The result is that the Buddha's empirical approach and original concern with the processes that make up one's cycle of lives are replaced with scholastic doctrines, schematic analyses and ontological apprehensions remote from one's conscious, lived world.

In contradistinction to this expository position, L.S. Cousins comments on the Abhidhamma *dhamma* theory that 'the aim of this Abhidhamma analysis is not really theoretical; it is related to insight meditation (*vipassana*) and offers a worldview based upon processes in order to facilitate insight into change (*anicca*) and no-self (*anatta*) so as to undermine mental rigidity'. Rupert Gethin similarly claims that in taking the traditional *matikas* and exploring their application,

> [T]he early *abhidhammikas* were not contributing to the ossification of Buddhist teaching, but were rather developing something that was at the heart of early Buddhism. The concerns of the early Abhidhamma were precisely the same concerns as those of the Nikayas. The concerns of the early Abhidhamma are practical rather than purely theoretical or scholastic; they arise directly out of the concerns of the Nikayas themselves: what is

going on in the mind when one tries to train it and wake it up? Thus the Abhidhamma enterprise continues a way of conceptualizing and exploring the processes of meditation and spiritual development that is clearly evidenced from the beginnings of Buddhism.

I suggest that to comprehend the nature of the canonical Abhidhamma and its place in the history of early Buddhist thought we need to reframe our conception of what ontology is, and seriously look into the possibility of grasping the doctrinal shift in the history of Theravada Buddhism not in ontological terms, but rather in epistemological terms. Indeed the next section shows that the Buddhist doctrine of momentariness, albeit subject to a gradual process of concretization and reification, attests to certain epistemological, rather than ontological, constraints that are common to both early Buddhist teaching and the canonical Abhidhamma.

BUDDHIST THOUGHT IN THE MIRROR OF PROCESS METAPHYSICS

Time and its Experience

The doctrine of momentariness is an elaboration on and an extremely radical formulation of the teaching of impermanence, although it does not challenge our ordinary perception of occurrences as such, but only the interpretation of these occurrences at the micro-level of their constitutive moments. Yet is this doctrine an analysis of time at all? To answer this question one should bear in mind that the doctrine of momentariness and the analysis of each and every *dhamma-constitutive* moment into its sub-moments originated in conjunction with the *tisankhata-lakkhana,* or in the Sarvastivada framework, the four *samskrtalaksanas.* In the case of the Sarvastivada, the soteriological and epistemological significance of the canonical formula regarding the impermanence of all conditioned phenomena is combined with deliberations on the ontological status of past and future *dharmas.* The Sarvastivada theory of momentariness thus has to be viewed against the backdrop of its notion of *sarvam asti,* which recognizes the existence of past, present and future *dharmas* (not the existence of the three times). The Theravadins rejected this notion and admitted only the existence of momentary present *dhammas.*

Much has been written regarding the Buddhist debate over the existence of past and future *dharmas* – a complex topic that exceeds the scope of the present study. What I wish to emphasize here is that whatever disputes may have existed between the early Sarvastivada and Theravadin Abhidhamma on this issue, no distinction is drawn between a *dharma* and its temporal determination, and both traditions agree that it is the operation of the characteristics of whatever is conditioned that accounts for a *dharma/dhamma* being past, present, future or present only. We have seen above that the equation of the *ksana/khana* with the duration of transient, momentary occurrences led to the direct determination of the moment in terms of the characterization of these occurrences. As Alexander von Rospatt points out:

> Thus, the Sarvastivada definition of the moment as the time taken by the four characteristics to discharge their function implies that momentary entities are exposed to the causal efficacy of each of the four characteristics. In fact, these specifications of the moment no longer convey a concrete idea about its duration at all, but only serve to characterize the momentary entity.

On another occasion Rospatt indicates that the object of the Buddhist doctrine of momentariness is not the nature of time, but existence within time. Rather than atomizing time into moments, this doctrine atomizes phenomena temporally by dissecting them into a succession of discrete momentary entities.

Let us now replace the ontological emphasis of this claim with an epistemologi-cal focus. While the ontologist asks how time as a transcendental category contains and determines occurrences, the epistemologist searches for features in experience that make us conceive of occurrences the way we do. This epistemological reading of the doctrine of momentariness accords better with the earliest Buddhist process-geared outlook and demonstrates Gethin's abovementioned contention that the concerns of the Abhidhamma ensue from the concerns of the *Nikayas*. Such a shift of emphasis from ontology to epistemology evinces that the object of the Buddhist doctrine of momentariness is not so much existence within time, nor the passage of time as such, but rather, in a somewhat Bergsonian sense, experience within time or, more correctly, the way we experience events in time. This doctrine does not analyse time in line with classical

Newtonian physics as a transcendental category, seeing time as a matrix of order imposed on natural events form without, or as a static container that sets the stage on which such events must play themselves out. Rather, time is itself but an inherent aspect of the manifold patterns of causal conditioning by which physical and mental events interrelate; it is an event-constituted, inherent feature of the structural operation of psycho-physical events.

This means that the doctrine of momentariness deals not with temporality as such, but with the construction of temporal experience; it analyses *dhammas* as they transpire through time: as psycho-physical events that appear in consciousness and, in fact, construct time. The Suttanta exposition interprets the three times as referring to past, present and future lives, while the Abhidhamma method explicates them as referring to the three subdivisions of the moment undergone by any conditioned *dhamma*. As Steven Collins remarks, this distinction is made by the commentaries on two canonical texts that list the three times. Collins then observes:

> 'But,' the commentary continues, 'this division into past (present and future), is (a division) of *dhamma*-s, not of time; in relation to *dhamma*-s which are divided into past, etc., time does not exist in ultimate truth, and therefore here "past", etc., are only spoken of by conventional usage'.

Within the Abhidhamma framework, then, the sequence of the three times is secondary, generated in and by the process of conditioned and conditioning *dhammas*. We have already seen that the Buddha's modes of analysis of sentient experience in terms of *namarupa*, the *khandha*, the *ayatana* and the *dhatu* formulas represent an empirical treatment of mental and physical dynamic processes from various standpoints. The Buddha talks about greed, hatred, delusion, ignorance, grasping, craving, sense perception, becoming, ageing, concentration, non-attachment, dispassion, equanimity, tranquillity, trust, gladness, super-knowledges and liberation-by-insight – to name but a few of the phenomena with which he is concerned. Even though all these may well function as meaningful linguistic referents and be referred to as 'things' in the broadest and non-technical sense of that word, they are not 'objects existing out there'; they are not substances, but rather processes and states that belong to the category of occurrence. This same anti-substantialist thread also runs through Abhidhamma doctrinal thought. Taking the *Dhammasaðga~i* and the *Vibhaðga* as representative of early Abhidhamma thought and of its analysis of human experience into *dhammas,* one may say that the *dhamma* theory is meant to individuate one's conscious experience according to one's position on the noble path, thus distinguishing the ordinary mind from the awakened mind. The *dhammas* investigated by the Abhidhamma, too, are subsumed under the category of occurrence: they always prove to be factors of *citta,* in its broadest sense of a series of particular mental occurrences.

There is, however, a striking difference between the Nikaya and the Abhidhamma views of these occurrences that makes up one's experience: whereas the *suttas* depict them as ongoing processes, the Abhidhamma portrays them as evanescent events. This is evidenced in the tradition's espousal of the doctrine of momentariness and the shift from *anicca* to *kha~avada*: from seeing phenomena as undergoing a repetitive process of emergence and cessation to regarding them as momentary. Cousins thus observes that the Abhidhamma sets out a description of mental processes and their interaction with the physical and the transcendent (*lokuttara*) by giving detailed accounts of specific events. These were seen as short-lived minds (*cittas*) related to specific sense objects and accompanied by a number of structures composed of basic mental elements (*dhammas*). These minds are viewed as constantly changing in level, object and content in a sequential stream.

On another occasion Cousins indicates that the earlier Abhidhamma works 'seek to describe specific events or occasions using the categories which the suttas rather employ to refer to sequences or processes', and that it is this shift from a sequential, process orientation to a momentary or event orientated approach which accounts for the most characteristic difference between the two currents of thought. But what is the nature of processes and events, and how is the difference between them to be explained?

Towards a Distinction between Processes and Events

Over the last century processes and events have attracted attention among philosophical circles – mainly those concerned with the philosophy of mind – largely because of the demise of the metaphysics of substance and its subsequent recognition that there is no such 'thing', strictly speaking, as the mind. Beliefs, desires, feelings, thoughts etc. were no longer conceived of as modifications of a substance such as the soul or mind, but rather as dynamic entities that construct the mind. According to this alternative picture the mind is a collection of mental events, processes and states, about whose nature and connection with physical reality questions can then be raised. Events have attracted most of the scholarly attention and various theories have been offered in order to account for the nature of these enti-ties. What is significant for our concern is the fact that events and processes belong to the category of occurrences: they happen – as distinct from objects, which rather endure, and from states, which rather obtain. This means that events and processes, differently from objects, bear direct relation to time and necessarily involve change. Objects' relation to time is indirect: they do not occur, begin or culminate; they are located in space, which allows one to say that they are *in* the world in a very straightforward sense, but they do not take place at a certain time.

Numerous linguists and philosophers have attempted to articulate criteria for the categorization of occurrences into events, processes and states, given their relation to time. The typologies offered are not flawless: they are over-neat and by no means exhaustive. I wish to highlight only those features which are most pertinent to distinguishing processes from events in the context of Buddhist thought. First, any attempt to explain the differences between these entities would have to draw on a richer conception of their temporal character than the one based simply on temporal duration. Although we tend to think of events as relatively short-lived whereas processes are regarded as rather more permanent and long-lasting, these are contingent facts rather than necessary truths essential to the categories of event and process, and hence there can be long events (e.g. wars which last for years) as well as short-lived processes (e.g. drawing breath). It is not the amount of time they occupy, but rather the way they occupy time which marks the distinction between events and processes. As Helen Steward indicates, it is the *way* in which that item fills the relevant period of time – whether it *persists through* the time, or *occurs during* the time, or *obtains throughout* the time, etc. Continuants, for example, persist *through* time and exist, as wholes, at every moment of their existence, whereas events occur *at* times or *during* periods of time and are unlike continuants in having temporal parts.

Steward renders these differences in the relation of events and processes to time as their 'temporal shape'.

The temporal shape of events reveals them to be properties of *moments* of time, whereas processes are found to be properties of *periods* of time. The most pertinent questions to be asked about mental and physical processes are of the 'how' type: how such happenings are distributed in time, how they unfold, how they come about and how they can be ended. By contrast, once events have been analysed into their sub-phases, they are ordinarily found to be instantaneous. For this reason it does not make sense to ask how they transpire throughout time. Occurrences of an event, such as the ascent of a certain *citta*, can be counted and so it is more appropriate to ask how often a given event occurs. Not so with processes, of which correct measure is not frequency but rather duration. This is demonstrated by the temporally sensitive adjectives applicable to processes. As Steward notes, a process, such as craving, dispassion or auditory perception, can be persistent, continuous, ongoing, incessant, perpetual, unremitting, sporadic, intermittent, irregular, steady. None of these adjectives can be comfortably applied to an event. Processes, says Steward, are things which, as it were, go on throughout periods of time – and so we can sensibly ask how they went on through that time – whether they went on constantly, or intermittently etc. But events simply happen – there is a 'when' and a 'how long' to be asked, but it does not make sense to ask a certain kind of 'how' question, the kind which asks for the distribution of the happening in time.

Bear in mind that by contrast to universals – such as qualities and properties, numbers, species and propositions – and along with material objects and people, events are regarded as concrete particulars, that is, occurrences of which nature and individuality can be determined. Hence a rather more suitable set of questions about an event is of the 'what' group: what its temporal parts are, what makes it up, what its starting and culmination points are, and above all, what it means to be this particular event. The notion of events as particulars would, in turn, urge one to establish the principles of their categorization into types and the criteria for individuating the innumerable tokens of each type by virtue of their causal origins.

The present section has shown that the preliminary construction of the transition from the Nikaya to the Abhidhamma worldview in terms of a shift from asking 'how' to 'what' is rooted in a fertile theoretical ground. Accordingly, early Buddhism is an attempt to provide a coherent picture of human experience in terms of a whole conceived as a process. The Abhidhamma is concerned with this very objective, but at the same time seeks to retain the uniqueness of the irreducible events which go into the making of the process. Although processes and events equally belong to the category of occurrence, they should not be understood as composing two exclusive ontological subcategories. Most of the attempts to provide criteria for the identity of processes and events rely on grammatical principles, and these fail to establish the status of processes and events as ontologically distinct entities. Rather, it would seem that the distinction between process and event results from the different viewpoints of occurrences that we have at our disposal and is merely a by-product of our language. In other words, the distinction is epistemological, not ontological.

In her paper 'On the Metaphysical Distinction between Processes and Events', Kathleen Gill shows the difficulties in the transition from grammatical distinctions to an ontological categorization of processes and events. First she indicates that speakers' choices when describing occurrences are guided by pragmatic interests. For instance, a certain occurrence may be depicted as having varying degrees of dynamics, in its part, excluding any reference to an end-point, or in its totality – all in order to emphasize its different aspects and achieve different effects. 'Our choices are not arbitrary,' Gill notes, 'they are based on conventions which reflect our world and our experience of it, e.g. causation and perceptual salience. But they do not simply mirror an ontological sub-categorization of occurrences'.

It would be preferable, then, to interpret the question of how events and processes differ in epistemological rather than ontological terms. This is not to dismiss the importance of grammatical distinctions for ontology, nor the repercussions that the bipartition in question has for the problem of what there is. Attesting to the relation between grammar and ontology is the long-lasting conviction in classical philosophy that language mirrors reality, and that there must be some sort of correspondence between what is said and what there is, between grammar and reality. My claim, however, is that the major emphasis in the sub-categorization of processes and events is put on the problem of individuation, rather than on ontology: on the question of what it means to *be something or other* according to what we say about being, rather than on the questions of being *per se* or of what there is – and epistemology supplies a perfect lodging for the question of individuation. As Gill notes, we would gain a better grasp of the distinction between processes and events if we realized that the relevant philosophical issue involved in it is an examination of those principles and guidelines that we use in separating off our experience and in dividing phenomena into distinct occurrences.

Viewed from this standpoint, the Abhidhamma's move away from the earliest Buddhist teachings is not as remote in spirit as it has been assumed to be. Different as they may be in their metaphysical foundation and, by the time of the commen-tarial tradition, in their divergent concern with epistemology vs. ontology, both the Nikaya and the Abhidhamma lines of thought agree in what they are *not*, namely, substance metaphysics. They are both subsumed under the category of process philosophy. To clarify these claims a preliminary discussion of the nature of process philosophy is due.

Process Philosophy: Basic Themes

We have already seen that Western metaphysics has been dominated by a substance-attribute ontology, which has a marked bias in favour of 'objects'. Plato's view of reason and his doctrine of the realm of Forms illustrate the predominance of the notion of substance, but it is in Aristotle's writings that substance metaphysics reached its highest perfection, and has thereafter dominated much of traditional philosophy from the ancient Stoics, through the scholastics of the Middle Ages and up to the distinguished authors of modern philosophy. Notwithstanding this dominance and its decisive ramifications for much of Western history of ideas, from as early as the period of the pre-Socratics there has been present another standpoint that goes against the current of much of Western metaphysics. This variant line of thought, designated by modern scholarship as 'process metaphysics' or 'process philosophy', focuses on the ontological category of occurrences – mainly events and processes – rather than on that of material objects, and is concerned with the notion of becoming rather than of being. Nicholas Rescher has provided a detailed account of process metaphysics and its principles in his two books called *Process Metaphysics: An Introduction to Process Philosophy* and *Process Philosophy: A Survey of Basic Issues*. The following presentation of the central ideas of process metaphysics largely draws on these two sources.

Process metaphysics has deliberately chosen to reverse the primacy of substance: it insists on seeing processes as basic in the order of being, or at least in the order of understanding. Underlying process metaphysics is the supposition that encountered phenomena are best represented and understood in terms of occurrences – processes and events – rather than in terms of 'things', and with reference to modes of change rather than to fixed stabilities. The guiding idea is that processes are basic and things derivative, for it takes some mental process to construct 'things' from the indistinct mass of sense experience, and because change is the pervasive and predominant feature of the real. The result is that *how* eventualities transpire is seen as no less significant than *what* sorts of thing there are. Traditional metaphysics, drawing on the substance-attribute ontological model, sees processes as the manifestations of the changing properties that inhere in enduring substances. By contrast, process philosophy holds that things are simply what they do and are manifestations of processes: to *be* a substance (thing-unit) is to *function* as a thing-unit in various situations, and to *have* a property is to *exhibit* this property in various contexts – a reversal of perspective that is buttressed by the fact that processes are pervasive both in nature and in human life. The internal variations in process thought stem from different positions with regard to what type of process is taken as paramount and paradigmatic: some renowned processists, like Alfred North Whitehead (1861–1947), see physical processes as central and other sorts of process as modelled on them. Those who espouse the approach of Henri Bergson (1859–1941), though, deem biological processes fundamental and conceive of the world in essentially organismic terms. Still others, especially William James (1842–1910) and his followers, base their ideas of process on a psychological model that takes human thought as a paradigmatic process. These differences in style and emphasis notwithstanding, the teachings of the major processists are all variations on a common theme.

Process philosophy begins with the ancient Greeks, of whom Heraclitus (*c*.540 BCE) is recognized as the founder of the process approach. His book *On Nature* depicts the encountered world in terms of opposed forces interlocked in mutual rivalry and constant conflict, and contends that the ultimate 'stuff' of which the world is made is not some material substance, but rather the workings of a natural process, namely, fire. The constant variations of fire are the source of all change, which is so pervasive that 'one cannot step twice into the same river'. The river is not a 'thing', but a sort of activity or a changing process and, like a river, 'everything flows'. Heraclitus's doctrine stood in sharp contrast to Parmenides's static system with its claim of the ultimate unreality of change, as well as to the atomism of Leucippus, Democritus and Epicurus, who set up the paradigm of substance ontology in classical antiquity, having portrayed nature as composed of enduring material atoms whose sole commerce with processes is the alteration of their position in space and time.

Much of traditional Western philosophy since the ancient Stoics has stressed the stabilities and fixities characteristic of the world as based on a lawful order. The new propounder of the process approach in modern philosophy is Gottfried Wilhelm Leibniz (1646–1717). Leibniz maintained that everything that figures in our experience consists of monads – centres of force, as it were, or bundles of minute processes and activities, each of which is an integrated whole of non-random change that dominates it as a single, unified, long-term process. The idea of a bundle was also developed by Locke, and indeed process philosophy owes much to his critique of substance. In accord with his empiricist worldview, Locke insisted that we have no experiential contact with substances as such: rather, we can come to grips with their causal impetus alone, and hence it is in their powers that the nature of so-called substances resides, that is, in the effects they produce in us. This position marks a turning point in the history of philosophy, which here begins to see substances as bundles of powers possessing a functional unity, instead of bearers of powers individuated by a qualitative nature of some sort. David Hume (1711–76) later used the idea of a bundle in relation to his notion of personal identity: given that observational confrontation with a personal core substance or a self is doomed to failure – for all we can get hold of observationally about ourselves are the body and its activities and sensations – the human being, on Hume's view, is but a bundle of different perceptions that succeed each other extremely rapidly and are in a perpetual flux. From a processual standpoint, the person is simply a structured system of processes and activity, so that the unity of person is a unity of experience; the coalescence of one's diverse micro-experience into one unified macro-process.

Leaping over to the nineteenth century, Bergson is another prominent proces-sist who regards processes and temporality as pivotal features of the world and as central to human life and consciousness. The process approach also plays a major role in the work of the American pragmatists – Charles Peirce (1839–1914), William James and John Dewey (1859–1952) specifically. In recent years, though, 'process philosophy' has become a code word for the doctrines of Whitehead, especially as given in his book *Process and Reality* (1929), and for those of his followers, who have developed a holistic view of science, in which a leading principle is that nature is a process.

In his late philosophical writing, Whitehead developed a metaphysical system called 'philosophy of organism' that seeks to obtain an account of human experience by putting its various elements into a consistent relation to one another. Inspired by the paradigm of biological systems, this schema favours the idea of macro-processes that organize micro-processes into systematic wholes. Hence the idea of a system is prominent to it, and it renders witnessed reality as organically integrated systems of coordinated processes, assigning primacy to the categories of occurrence and relatedness. The latter, by contrast to Aristotle's category of relation, implies that all phenomena are *inter*connected. The traditional notions of being and substance are thus regarded here as subordinate to and derivative from the notion of interrelations among actualities. On Whiteheads view the empirical world and whatever things there are in any sense of existence are derived by abstraction from actual occurrences in their process of becoming. Actual occurrences are the microcosmic elements and the ultimately real constituents of the world, although they are not substances, but temporal foci of dynamic, evanescent physical and mental processes that perish as soon as they become determinate and definite. To borrow Rescher's rendering, on this account a processual occurrence is made into the item it is 'not through its continuing ("essential") properties, as with a classically conceived substance, but by its history, by the temporal structure of its descriptive unfolding across time'. It might thus be said that the identity of a process is constituted through a sequential pattern of action, and that temporality is the definitive characterizing feature of the processual nature of the real. This ties in with the fact that in the natural philosophy of process the idea of time is correlative with a transient present of ever-changing creativity. Process philosophy abandons the Newtonian hypostatization of time as a container within which natural processes transpire – a view that goes back to the Greek Atomists and plays into the hands of substance ontology. Rather, it sees time as itself an inherent aspect of natural, physical processes and as conditioned by the interrelationships of such processes.

It should be noted that a number of scholarly studies have already suggested that Buddhism belongs to the category of process philosophy. With reference to the Pali tradition these studies centre on the rough analogy between the doctrine of dependent co-arising and the principle of impermanence *vis-à-vis* the notion of a process. Excepting this analogy, however, they leave much to be desired as regards the relationship between the Theravada's idea of a process and its construal of the concept of *dhamma*, thus overlooking the Abhidhamma's shift from a process-based to an event-based approach in analysing conscious experience. David Dilworth has drawn a comparison between Whitehead's process metaphysics and the Abhidharma so-called realism, but his interpretation is ontologi-cally oriented, whereas, as this book illustrates, when addressing the Pali Abhidhamma a distinction should be made between the epistemological concerns of the canonical Abhidhamma and the ontological orientation of the post-canonical tradition. Western process thought is a reaction to a major current in the history of philosophy that is rooted in presuppositions and concepts which may not be attributable to early Indian Buddhism. The reason I broach process philosophy as part of the present monograph is that as a general line of thought it expounds an anti-substantialist metaphysical attitude conducive to understanding what the Buddha's successors extracted from his first, implicit teachings, and what they later on developed in accordance with their specific doctrinal and practical concerns.

In sum, what is characteristically definitive of process philosophizing, as Rescher indicates, is an insistence on seeing processes as constituting an essential aspect of everything that exists – a commitment to the fundamentally processual nature of the real. A process philosopher holds that what exists in nature is not just originated and sustained by processes, but is in fact ongoingly and inexorably *characterized* by them. On such a view, process is both pervasive in nature and fundamental for its understanding.

This implies that process philosophy has two closely interrelated dimensions: the one conceptual, or epistemological, the second ontological. The former draws on the idea that our experience is best represented in terms of processes rather than in terms of things, and that any attempt to explain the idea of a 'thing' necessarily has recourse to the notion of process. The suggestion is that substance concepts are reducible to process talk; that it would be more instructive to analyse the items we categorize as 'things' in terms of instantiations of process-complexes. The ontological dimension of process philosophy, by contrast, centres on the idea that processes are the ultimate units of which the world consists and are ontolog-ically more fundamental than 'things'. It holds that the above conceptual state of affairs obtains because all phenomena are reducible to processes. Process philosophy, then, is more a general line of thought and a venture in metaphysics than a thoroughly worked-out system. It can be oriented phenomenologically (seeing processes as fundamental to human experience and cognition), or biologically (seeing processes as fundamental to organic existence), or physicalistically (seeing processes as fundamental to nature and to physical existence).

This book argues and demonstrates that the doctrinal transition from the first teachings of the Buddha to the canonical and post-canonical Abhidhamma is best understood in terms of a change in epistemological attitude and metaphysical foundation. More specifically, what the present study shows is that from the Buddha's processual and epistemologically geared approach to sentient experience, which is one of the earliest embodiments of process philosophy in the history of ideas, the subsequent Buddhist tradition teases out an underlying metaphysics. The canonical Abhidhamma transforms this process metaphysics into an event metaphysics, albeit its approach to the analysis of sentient experience is still epistemological, whereas the post-canonical Abhdihamma takes an even further doctrinal step in shifting the emphasis of this event metaphysics from epistemology to ontology. What the Abhidhamma gradually establishes, however, is a metaphysical theory of mental events, that is, a metaphysics of mind rather than a comprehensive ontology. While my argument is demonstrated in the succeeding three chapters, the following section concludes the present chapter with a construction of the transition from the Nikaya mindset to the Abhidhamma framework in terms of process philosophy.

The Abhidhamma Path from Process to Event Metaphysics

Tying in together the motifs of this chapter – the Buddhist tradition's changing conception of *dhamma,* the doctrines of atomism and of momentariness, the principles of process philosophy and the philosophical distinction between process and event – we are now in a position to recognize that the Nikaya and the canonical Abhidhamma part from one another in their metaphysical foundation: from the implicit, process-based epistemology, or conceptual scheme, operative in the Buddha's teaching the Abhidhammikas distil an underlying metaphysics in which the idea of a psycho-physical process is replaced by the notion of a *dhamma qua* a mental event as analytical primitive. Ye t in the canonical Abhidhamma the focus of this event metaphysics is still epistemological. Only in the commentarial period does this event metaphysics yield an ontological model, though the question remains as to what sort of ontology this is.

Indeed, the shift from the Nikaya mindset to that of the canonical Abhidhamma is metaphysical, for in their notion of a comprehensive picture of the world – and thus in their metaphysical vision – these two traditions draw on two divergent foundations.

Whereas the *Nikayas* describe sentient experience in terms of empirically discernible physical and mental processes, the Abhidhamma texts dissect these processes into their constitutive stages, shifting the focus to the micro-scale of each and every moment undergone by each particular psycho-physical event. Such a shift, however, is not necessarily destined to distort the 'original' teaching. Processes and events are not incommensurable categories: after all, one single occurrence can equally be described as a process or as an event, and the fact that we separate off our experience into distinct occurrences does not necessarily reflect what exists 'out there'. In fact, a major part of the early Buddhist teachings may be expressible in momentary terms, for to a large extent the Buddha's teachings, to which the *dhammas* of the old *matikas* refer, expressed stages in transient meditative attainment. Indeed both the Nikaya and the canonical Abhidhamma lines of thought are accommodated within the category of anti-substantialist philosophy, and in both cases their analysis of sentient experience is epistemological rather than ontological, that is, concerns the conditions of the psycho-physical occurrences that arise in consciousness – and in this sense form one's 'world' – not with what exists *per se* in a mind-independent world.

To endorse an event metaphysics need not necessarily imply that a momentary event must be seen as a philosophical point-instant. This view may characterize the Sarvastivada-Vaibhasika construal of the *dhammas*, but is not directly attributable to the Theravadin Abhidhamma, particularly in its canonical period. In fact, the Pali Abhidhamma does not take much interest in ontology, if 'ontology' means a preoccupation with the classical substance-attribute model and the question of being. If any notion of ontology is to be found in the Abhidhamma framework, then it is one of which demarcation from psychology is far less clear than what is customarily conveyed by its standard meaning; indeed, a notion similar to the sense of ontology prevalent in philosophical discourse nowadays. In this context Paul Williams observes that:

> What is involved in seeing dhammas as events, in seeing all as based perhaps on an event-ontology, rather than a substance-ontology, seems to be relatively unexplored in the Pali Abhidhamma or indeed in the Theravada thought which follows it. To that extent, one could argue, the everyday practicalities of insight

meditation remain paramount. An interest in specific questions of the ontological nature of dharmas is found not so much among Theravadins, but among Sarvastivadins and their rivals.

This means that the canonical Abhidhamma event metaphysics and its ensuing *dhamma* analyses are systematized in the post-canonical literature and result in a metaphysics of mind that may have an ontological dimension, although it is not a comprehensive ontology as such.

Underlying the doctrinal shift from the first teachings of the Buddha to the Abhidhamma are not two different ontologies, but rather two different viewpoints into human experience and its relation to the environment. Since events and processes are not two ontologically exclusive categories, then an elemental experience dissolves into manifold processes, which in turn divide into their constituting sequential events, each of which is a living unit of elemental experience that can be further analysed into its sub-phases according to the way it transpires in time and thus constructs time, rather than is contained in time. In Western thought, with its marked bias in favour of substantial objects, it is customarily accepted that what holds for discrete events also holds for discrete objects, which are then explained in terms of substances and essences. But substance metaphysics is not the only conceptual scheme at one's disposal. Both early Buddhist teaching and the canonical Abhidhamma originate from a common source that may be referred to as process philosophy: a general line of thought that hinges on the notions of becoming and change, construing sentient experience as a dynamic flow of physical and mental occurrences, rather than in terms of persons and objects. Still, the two traditions differ in their orientations, emphases and concerns: the *Nikayas'* predominant concern is with one's experience throughout one's present birth and rounds of rebirth. From this perspective the crucial question is how exactly this recurring process of becoming and dissolution is triggered and how it may be brought to a halt. The Abhidhamma, albeit it is concerned with the same process, shifts the focus to the micro-scale of its inside constituents, zooming in, as it were, on the evanescent, onetime particular events of which it consists. Like the earliest Buddhist teaching, the Abhidhamma also accounts for conscious experience, but from a different perspective, along a different timescale and urged by a different motive, namely, to account for the nature of this experience. The Abhidhammikas thus had to individuate every possible occurrence in one's consciousness, and for this purpose an analysis into events is more appropriate than into processes. Events and processes alike are dynamic happenings that involve change and are directly related to time. Processes, though, are properties of stretches of time, while events are properties of moments, and hence they suit better as the unit of analysis when consciousness is investigated at the micro-level of its constituents. The Abhidhamma is indeed led from construing the consciousness process as a flow of brief events (the duration of which is unspecified) to its portrayal as a complex sequence of momentary particulars.

This undertaking, as we shall see in the course of the next three chapters, is not necessarily ontological, at least not in the canonical Abhidhamma. Yet the Abhidhamma appears to have been liable to the risks of reification and doctrinal excrescences, to such an extent that its process-based worldview has been criticized as a scholastic development that resulted in but another version of substance ontology. Can this development be traced to its exact phases and grounded in the Abhidhamma treatises? What are the implications of this development for the Abhidhamma soteriology? One of my objectives in this study is to reconsider the position of soteriology within the Abhidhamma framework, and examine how the Abhidhamma contends with the controversial question, prevalent during the centuries after the Buddha's death, of what Buddhism is all about. This concept is bound up with the advent of the *dhamma* theory and its ancillary doctrines of momentariness and atomism. *Sabhava* is also inextricably related to the alleged Abhidhamma ontology. It is therefore necessary to locate this concept as part of the broader doctrinal transition from the early Buddhist teaching to the canonical Abhidhamma and up to the commentarial tradition.

4

Sabhåva and Buddhist Doctrinal Thought

The preceding chapter has shown that the Buddha clearly had a distinct epistemology, from which the canonical Abhidhamma distilled a well articulated metaphysics. We have identified this conceptual framework as process metaphysics and observed that its basic units analysing experience, the *dhammas,* fall into the category of occurrences rather than of substance. This has revealed that the primary difference between the Nikaya worldview and the canonical Abhidhamma is epis-temological, not ontological: the *Nikayas* construe the occurrences that make up conscious experience as mental and physical processes, whereas the Abhidhamma sees them as short-lived, psycho-physical events. Throughout the Abhidhamma's formative period Buddhist thought was subject to a gradual process of institution-alization, schematization and conceptual assimilation, part of which were a growing tendency to reify those *dhammic* events and an increasing interest in establishing their true nature. Fundamental to this doctrinal development is the concept of *sabhava*. This concept plays a major role in the systematization of Abhidhamma thought, is closely related to the consolidation of the *dhamma* theory and is regarded as that which gave an impetus to the Abhidhamma's growing concern with ontology.

The present chapter traces the evolution of the concept of *sabhava* in Pali literature and appraises its implications for the alleged Abhidhamma ontology. Various renderings of *sabhava* are found in the extant scholarly literature, the paramount of which are 'particular nature', 'own-nature', 'self-existence' and 'individual essence'. We shall examine the different senses of *sabhava* and their philosophical significance in the para-canonical texts and in the commentaries, with an emphasis on the distinction between *sabhava qua* nature as opposed to essence. The starting point of this investigation is the assumption that the concept of *sabhava* ought to be understood in the wider context of the *dhamma* theory and its underlying process philosophy. We shall see that *sabhava* occupies a primary position in a conceptual scheme that seeks to explain the workings of the mind rather than reflect the structure of an external reality. My claim is that if Buddhist thought eventually teased out an ontology from the concept of *sabhava* and the *dhamma* theory – a possibility that calls for a reassessment of what is meant by 'ontology' – then this state of affairs may apply to the post-canonical period, but should not be read into the early Abhidhamma, the primary interest of which in the notion of *sabhava* is epistemological rather than ontological.

To judge from the *suttas*, the term *sabhava* was never employed by the Buddha and it is rare in the Pali Canon in general. Only in the post-canonical period does it become a standard concept, when it is extensively used in the commentarial descriptions of the *dhammas* and in the sub-commentarial exegesis. Ñajamoli notes that there is merely a single occurrence of the term *sabhava* in the *Tipitaka*, namely, in the *Pa tisambhidamagga*. Ye t the term does feature on various occasions in four other canonical or para-canonical texts: the *Pe takopadesa*, the *Nettippakaraja*, the *Milindapañha* and the *Buddhavaµsa*. These texts, of which the *Pa tisambhidamagga* and the *Buddhavaµsa* are included in the *Khuddaka-nikaya*, are customarily thought of as later additions to the Canon. Ye t they may be dated back to a relatively early period, or may at least contain parts that predate the latest works of the *Abhidhamma-pitaka* and that are certainly older than the main Pali commentaries. Any attempt to trace the doctrinal transition from the *suttas*, through the canonical Abhidhamma and up to the *Atthakatha* must therefore examine these para-canonical texts.

THE CONCEPT OF *SABHÅVA* IN THE PARA-CANONICAL TEXTS

The Patisambhidamagga

Although included in the *Khuddaka-nikaya*, the *Pa tisambhidamagga* is clearly a work of the Abhidhamma. Erich

Frauwallner explains the absence of this treatise from the *Abhidhamma-pitaka* as due to its being the latest of the Abhidhamma works, and dates it to a time when the compilation of the Canon had essentially been completed. A conceptual mapping of the *Pa tisambhidamagga,* though, suggests that at least parts of the text are earlier than the main body of the *Abhidhamma-pitaka.* If so, then this early textual layer belongs to and may shed light on the formative period of the Abhidhamma and its doctrinal move away from the Nikaya thought-world. To settle this hypothesis we should briefly deal with the *Pa tisambhidamagga*'s method.

Translated as *The Path of Discrimination,* the *Pa tisambhidamagga*'s purpose is to expound the actual way by which one comes to discriminate and comprehend the Buddha's teachings. This type of discrimination (*patisambhida*) has four aspects. The first aspect is the discrimination of *dhammas,* wherein *dhammas* in this context refer to the principles or elements constituting human experience, such as the sense faculties, knowledge or recognition, but also to such items as the four noble truths, the five 'spiritual' faculties (*indriya*) and five powers (*bala*), the seven factors of awakening or the eight factors of the path. These are taken in the sense of objects of thought, and testify to what Gombrich has identified as a shift from thinking *about* the Buddha's teachings to thinking *with* them, thus seeing the world through Buddhist spectacles, as it were. The second aspect is the discrimination of the *dhammas' attha. Attha* here signifies the *dhammas'* operation or function, for the enumerated *atthas* are those of establishment *(upatthdnattho),* of investigating *(pavicayattho),* of calm *(upasamattho),* of non-distraction *(avikkhepattho)* and others, all with reference to their corresponding *dhammas.* The discrimination of *attha,* then, concerns what the *dhammas* do and how they act - an aspect fit for the processual construal of the *dhammas* as dynamic occurrences. The third aspect is the discrimination of the language *(nirutti)* expressing the *dhammas* and their *atthas,* and the fourth is the discrimination of perspicuity or penetration *(patibhdna).* The latter is 'meta-knowledge', namely, the apprehension of instances of the first three types of discrimination, which are regarded as its supporting object *(drammana)* and its domain *(gocara).* Discrimination of penetration, then, is the knowledge of the differences between the various types of *dhamma,* their functions and the language in which they are articulated.

It is worth noting that the same four types of discrimination are also discussed at the *Vibhanga* 293-305 (chapter XV). The *Vibhanga,* however, portrays the discriminations of *dhamma/s* and *attha* differently from the *Patisambhiddmagga.* On the one hand *dhammas* are the physical and mental events constituting human experience, whereby their discrimination is the knowledge of the causal conditions *(hetu)* through which these *dhammas* have been originated and the discrimination of *attha* is the knowledge of the conditioned occurrences, namely, the eventuating *dhammas.* On the other hand *dhammas* here are also the Buddha's statements and doctrines, and so *attha* refers to the corresponding meaning of whatever *dhamma* has been spoken. The different views of the two discriminations taken by the *Vibhanga* and the *Patisambhiddmagga* may suggest that these two texts developed their positions independently of each other.

The *Patisambhiddmagga* presents a practice based on the coupling of calm *(samatha)* and insight *(vipassand),* which is made possible when the practitioner gains such fourfold discrimination of the nature of reality as taught by the Buddha. Its move away from the *suttas* is evinced by the attempt to provide a more systematic and all-embracing account of this path than previously supplied by the Buddha's scattered descriptions on various occasions. To this end the *Patisambhiddmagga* distinguishes and discusses the prior doctrinal concepts in their manifold aspects. Commenting on this method Frauwallner opines that the *Patisambhiddmagga* differs from the older Abhidhamma works in that 'several "excrescences" of the "method" which are so unpleasantly obtrusive in the old Abhidharma are missing here'. Following this statement Frauwallner says:

> The systematic approach as such is purely superficial [...] In addition, the attempts at treating larger complexes of problems systematically, signs of which we have seen in the *Dhammasangani* in particular, were not continued here. There is nothing that goes beyond the pedantic treatment of the individual doctrinal concepts.

The *Patisambhidamagga'* alleged systematization falls short even compared to the *Dhammasangani,* which is the first and probably the oldest work in the *Abhidhamma-pitaka.* Frauwallner is, indeed right in his criticism of the *Patisambhidamagga*'s systematization and in claiming that it is found to be wanting compared to the *Dhammasangani.* But the reason for the undeveloped systematic structure of the *Patisambhidamagga* may be that major parts of it overlap with, or perhaps even predate, the *Abhidhamma-pitaka.* If the *Patisambhidamagga* is markedly earlier than Frauwallner assumes it to be, then it may be the first Pali text to use the term *sabhdva.* The dating of this work is therefore worth further consideration.

The *Patisambhidamagga* is not of one piece and is probably not all of the same date. Like the other canonical Abhidhamma works, it is likely to have grown by expansion of its *matikas* and it presupposes much of the *Sutta-pitaka:* in fact, its first part is based on the *Dasuttara-sutta* of the *Digha-nikdya.* The *Patisambhidamagga* presupposes the *Dhammasangani,* for it is acquainted with the latter's analysis by 'planes' or 'spheres' *(avacara)* and with its first triplet (I83-5), and occasionally quotes descriptions or definitions from it. Alternatively, the two texts may have originated from a common source. The *Dhammasangani* is a remarkable example of the increasing emphasis on the formalization and elaboration of the practice of listing *dhammas:* the text enumerates and describes the *dhammas* by applying to them the triplet-couplet *abhidhamma-mdtikd,* as well as anticipates the fourfold *dhamma* categorization into *rupa, citta, cetasika* and *nibbdna,* although it does not employ it explicitly. On the other hand the *Dhammasangani* does not yet embody the full-fledged *dhamma* theory, as this is found in the commentaries, and its method is open-ended. It does not enumerate all possible *dhammas,* but rather ends the lists by mentioning 'these or whatever others may occur on that occasion', while these 'others' are not specified. Yet even compared to this somewhat loose method the *Patisambhidamagga* manifests a lesser degree of systematization in its *dhamma* categorization. Although it employs several *dhamma* definitions and categorizations that also feature in the *Dhammasangani,* on the whole the work does not seem to be aware of the *Dhammasangan's* elaborate triplet-couplet *mdtikd.*

Moreover, to judge from the *Patisambhidamagga*'s method of explaining the *dhammas,* the work is likely to antedate the Atthakatha period. In the commentaries the method of *dhamma* exegesis is based on a fourfold scheme specifying the defining characteristic *(lakkhana),* the mode of manifestation *(paccu-patthdna),* the immediate cause *(padatthdna)* and the quality *(rasa* in a special, technical sense) that are peculiar to each *dhamma.* Concentration *(samddhi),* for example, which is equated with one-pointedness of mind is assigned the defining characteristic of non-scattering or non-distraction, the quality of combining co-arisen *dhammas,* the manifestation of calm or knowledge and being the immediate cause of happiness. Thus, each *dhamma* is defined by means of a particular characteristic peculiar to itself, in addition to the *tisankhatalakkhana* shared by all conditioned phenomena, namely, *anicca, dukkha* and *anattd.* The idea of *lakkhana* as a defining characteristic of a set of *dhammas,* and later on as the own-mark *(salakkhana)* of any given *dhamma,* is closely related to the concept of *sabhdva* and to the development of the *dhamma* theory and will have played a major role in the tradition's changing view of the plurality of *dhammas.* We shall refer in greater detail to the idea of *lakkhana* below.

In the *Patisambhiddmagga,* though, the method of explaining the *dhammas* consists in stating their *atthas,* following the second of the four discriminations. The *lakkhanas* of the *dhammas* are, indeed brought forward yet they do not refer to the actuality of these *dhammas* as entities of any sort, nor to particular, distinguishing features peculiar to each and every *dhamma.* Rather, they signify the impermanence, unsatisfactoriness and insubstantiality of the *dhammas* in their totality, as well as their origination, cessation and ongoing change, which they all have in common. For instance, the term *lakkhana* is repeatedly employed throughout Chapter 6 of Treatise I in the first division of the text, which deals with the knowledge of the rise and fall *(udaya-bbaya-hdna)* of *dhammas.* There it is stated of each of the five *khandhas,* which are qualified as presently arisen *(paccuppanna)* and as born *(jdta),* that the defining characteristic *(lakkhana)* of its origination is rise whereas the defining characteristic of its change is dissolution. Further on, in Treatise XII of the second division, which concerns the four noble truths, we also find an extensive use of the term *lakkhana.* It is there said that the four truths have two *lakkhanas:* the conditioned *(sahkhata)* and the unconditioned *(asahkhata).* The conditioned are, in their turn, qualified by the marks of rise *(uppada),* fall *(vaya)* and change of what is present *(thitassa ahhathatta).* In the case of the unconditioned it is said that no such marks are discerned.

Lakkhanas as the characteristics of *dhammas* are but concepts referring to the common features of the conditioned *dhammas* in their totality rather than to the individuality or actual existence of any given *dhamma.* The idea *of lakkhana* thus falls short of being either an epistemological determinant ascertaining the discernibility of a *dhamma's* particular nature or an ontological determinant attesting to a *dhamma's* existential status. What does point to a doctrinal novelty is the occurrence of the characteristic of *thitassa ahhathatta* that is intimately connected to the Theravadins' espousal of the doctrine of momentariness, and which illustrates the commentaries' growing tendency to reify and hypostatize the *dhammas.* The very idea of assigning each *dhamma* an endurance phase is at odds with the Buddha's teaching, let alone when the commentators load on this phase the idea of an existence moment *(atthikkhana)* - although they describe each phenomenon dissected within their system as a wave that follows patterns of recurrence rather than of continuity, having phases of origination and of dissolution. The *Patisambhiddmagga's* use of the characteristic of *thitassa ahhathatta* thus showcases what are perhaps the earliest traces of the later relationship between the Theravadin endorsement of the mature theory of momentariness, on the one hand and the commentarial inclination towards ontological interpretation of *sabhdva* and *dhamma,* on the other hand. This new tendency notwithstanding, within the framework of the *Patisambhidamagga thitassa annathatta* is a *lakkhana,* that is, a characteristic mark of whatever is conditioned, just like the other two marks of origination and cessation. None of these three characteristics is associated with time or with the idea of momentariness. This part of the text, then, belongs to a layer composed before the establishment of the theory of momentariness.

Assuming that a chronology of Buddhist doctrinal development may be deduced from conceptual systematization, elaborate categorizations and contemplation of the *dhammas* as definite constituents that exist as real entities by virtue of their particular characteristics and unique functions, then not only is the *Patisambhidamagga's* method of explaining the *dhammas* earlier than that espoused in the *Atthakatha,* but it also predates the one found in the final, extant version of the *Dhammasangani.* In the light of these findings, Warder has suggested that 'a substantial part of the *Patisambhidamagga* may have been elaborated in the same period of the composition of the *Dhammasangani,* parallel to it and using some of its contents in an earlier form'. Moreover, as already indicated the *Patisambhidamagga*'s position on the discriminations of *dhamma* and *attha* is different from the *Vibhanga's,* and was probably constructed independently of it. The *Patisambhidamagga* thus represents a doctrinal progression parallel to the *Dhammasangani* and the *Vibhanga,* relying on a source common to these two texts, albeit taking a divergent course of development. In this connection, Warder suggests that the *Patisambhidamagga* goes back to as early as the third century BCE, adducing in support of this possibility the text's position on the nature of insight *(abhisamaya).* The text bespeaks the Theravadin idea that the penetration of the four noble truths in the path moments occurs as a sudden flash of intuition, or a single breakthrough to knowledge *(ekabhisamaya),* rather than as separate intuitions of each truth. The idea of a spontaneous insight emerged in relation to the Sarvastivadin view of the spiritual path and is propounded for the first time in the *Kathavatthu.* This strengthens the impression that the *Patisambhidamagga* was composed during the period of the great doctrinal divisions as a summation setting out the doctrines accepted by the Theravada, perhaps as a positive counterpart to the *Kathavatthu*. Cousins also notes that the *Patisambhidamagga* is certainly a work of the period of the first doctrinal division related to the Second Council of Vesali that took place roughly in 70-80 BE. On the basis of all these pieces of evidence the suggestion that the *Patisambhidamagga* dates to the period of the Abhidhamma's formation and of the doctrinal divisions among the ancient Buddhist schools is more convincing than the claim that this text is the latest of the Abhidhamma works.

Nevertheless, this suggestion primarily applies to the first division of the *Patisambhidamagga,* but some parts of the second division are probably later than the earliest compositions of the *Abhidhamma-pitaka,* for they introduce several concepts that are not to be found in the latter. The last major stage of the *Patisambhidamagga*'s composition is likely to have taken place in the early or mid-second century BCE, with only minor later additions. The *Patisambhidamagga* is a transitional text residing somewhere in between the *suttas* and the *Atthakatha.*

It introduces new concepts and ideas that depart from the Nikaya outlook, while at the same time its method of explaining these concepts and ideas is not yet as consolidated as that of the commentaries, and the ideas themselves are not fully worked out, or indeed are still latent. One such concept that belongs to the textual layer posterior to the *Dhammasangani* is *sabhdva.*

The term *sabhdva* is introduced in the Suññakatha of the *Patisambhiddmagga,* Treatise XX at the end of the *Patisambhiddmagga's* second division, which discusses the qualifier 'empty' *(sunnam).* The treatise opens with a quotation of a Samyutta passage describing an occasion on which Ånanda, referring to the alleged claim 'The world is empty' *(sunno loko ti),* asks the Buddha to explain in what way it is so. In reply, the Buddha affirms the validity of that claim on the grounds that the world 'is empty of self or of what belongs to self'. He then expounds what exactly it is that is empty of self or of what belongs to self, enumerating the six sense faculties *(sadyatana)* along with their appropriate sense objects, that is, the twelve *dyatanas,* adding their six corresponding modalities of cognitive awareness, thus referring to the eighteen *dhdtus.* Included in the above list is also whatever feeling originates from the contact between the sense faculties and their appropriate objects, whether pleasant, or painful or neither.

At this stage the Buddha lists various types of the state of being empty, one of which is empty in terms of change *(viparindma-sunnam).* His reply to the question 'What is empty in terms of change?' is:

Born materiality is empty of *sabhdva (sabhdvena suññam);* disappeared materiality is both changed and empty. Born feeling is empty of *sabhdva;* disappeared feeling is both changed and empty...Born conceptualization...Born volitions...Born consciousness...Born becoming is empty of *sabhdva;* disappeared becoming is both changed and empty. This is 'empty in terms of change'.

Obviously the entire meaning of this excerpt depends on how the phrase *sabhdvena sunnam* is interpreted. Taking into account the context, namely, expounding the predication of the world by the term 'empty', and which *dhammas* are listed in the above *mdtikd,* this extract means that the totality of human experience is devoid of an enduring substance or of anything which belongs to such a substance, because this totality is dependent on many and various conditions, and is of the nature of being subject to a continuous process of origination and dissolution. Bear in mind that the twelve *dyatanas* and eighteen *dhdtus* (along with the five *khandhas)* are totality formulas, methods of classifying the totality of *dhammas* that make up all conditioned phenomena. Hence the passage deals with the totality of *dhammas* and with classes of them as they work together, not with each and every single *dhamma* separately. Inasmuch as the issue at stake is the *dhammas* in their totality and their being subject to constant change, it is close in spirit to the teaching of impermanence as expressed in the *Nikdyas.* There it is frequently repeated that impermanent, conditioned phenomena are of the nature of origination and decay, whereby the word employed to denote this nature is *dhamma.*

In this context, then, the term *sabhava* appears to be interchangeable with *dhamma* in its sense of 'nature'. This sense may be taken as roughly corresponding to the nontechnical, broad meaning of *pakati.* In the Pali texts *pakati,* the equivalent of the Sanskrit *prakrti,* is not a technical philosophical term and unlike in the Sarnkhya-Yoga, it has a limited metaphysical bearing. *Pakati* denotes the regularity with which things normally occur in nature: the normal custom or innate predispositions of persons, the order of occurrences in the environment and that which is common to all or shared by all. For instance, *pakati* is employed with reference to the innate character - virtuous or bad - of people, to the inborn capacities of sense perception or the natural strength of the body; when a habit has become so natural that one performs it automatically and effortlessly, or when it is raining during the rainy season. In this respect the Pali usage of *pakati* is similar to the meaning of the term *dham-matd,* namely, the regular orderliness of the encountered world. The word *dhammatd* is used in the *suttas* to denote events which are natural, normal and regular, such as the flowing of water, the blowing of wind or the behaviour of a monk endowed with right view. These events should not be understood as occurring because of *dhammatd;* rather their happening is itself *dhammatd.* In the commentaries, this sense of *dhammatd,* which has no metaphysical or ontological bearing, is equated with *sabhava qua* 'nature' and with *niydma* in the sense of the 'order of things'.

The *Patisambhiddmagga* endorses a broad notion of *sabhava* as the nature that the *dhammas* essentially share, but it is by no means clear that this nature necessarily defines what a *dhamma* is, or that a *dhamma* exists by virtue of this nature which it possesses. Nor is the relation between *lakkhana, sabhava* and *dhamma* spelled out. Nowhere is it stated that a *dhamma* is defined determined or exists by its *sabhava;* or that it is marked by a set of *lakkhanas* or by any single, unique *lakkhana;* or that a *dhammas sabhava* is to be identified in any way with its set of *lakkhanas;* or yet again that the latter is possessed by or constitutes those *sabhava* and *dhamma.* The text presents the Buddha as saying that things have no *sabhava,* in a way that parallels his saying that they have no *attd.* This suggests that the *Patisambhiddmagga's* author is simply showing that this basic point applies equally when one uses the Brahmanical term *svabhdva.* As *dtman,* too, was a Brahmanical term, history is more or less repeating itself.

That this notion of *sabhava* represents a shifting point between the Sutta and the Atthakatha periods, and does not yet carry the technical sense attached to it in the commentaries, is shown by comparing the *Patisambhiddmagga* with its exegesis in Mahanama's Commentary, the *Saddhammappakdsini* (sixth century CE). In this work Mahanama seeks to present the text as a systematic exposition of the way to *arahantship.* In doing so, he draws heavily on the *Visuddhimagga* and his exegesis is often laden with metaphysical implications that exceed the laconic, aphoristic account of the original text. Mahanama initially analyses the compound *sabhava* as *sayam bhdvo,* or *sako bhdvo,* that is, 'essence by itself or 'essence of itself', explaining this to mean 'arising by itself *(sayam eva uppddo)* or 'own-arising' *(attano yeva uppddo).* Given this interpretation, to translate *bhdvo* as 'nature' is inappropriate, for the commentator points to the narrower and more technical sense of essence. Mahanama then turns to an explication of the coupling *sabhdvena sunnam.* First, he states that essence, *bhdva,* is but a figurative designation for *dhamma,* and since each single *dhamma* does not have any other *dhamma* called 'essence', it is empty of essence other than itself. This, in fact, reveals a different analysis of *sabhdva,* as 'the essence that it has of itself *(sakassa bhdvo).* It thus follows that every single *dhamma* has a single 'essence-hood'*(ekassabhdvatd).*

In ordinary language the term 'essence' is often employed synonymously with 'nature', but there is a significant difference between the two. Essence is bound up with the notion of necessity, for it singles out what necessarily determines a particular individual as that very item, thus assuming the role of an item's individuator. Essence has the status of a particular: it is not a property had by a certain object (whether a substance, process or event), but the latter's definition, and hence it cannot be predicated of other members within the domain of that object. In this sense essence is detached from ontology altogether: it does not account for the existence of its possessing item - a *dhamma* in our case - but determines what this item is in distinction from any other item of that kind. *What* something is and *that* it is are two distinct issues and the latter is not necessarily implied by the former. Unlike an essence, a nature does not individuate its associated particular and may be common to many different particulars within a certain domain; its metaphysical status is that of a universal. Essence, though, may also have an ontological significance: a renowned line of thought in the history of metaphysics holds that essence is meant to account for its associated particular's existence as an individual. Accordingly, an essence is what constitutes its possessing individual as the very particular it is: it does not merely define the individuality of this particular within its domain, but is the cause of this particular's being an actual, unified individual. This causal role, too, is not shared by a particular nature: the latter is the sum total of the concurrent attributes a particular possesses; it is neither what determines the individuality of this particular nor is it the cause of its existence as such. The essence alone is the cause of there being an actual individual.

Mahanama oscillates between an epistemological and ontological interpretations of *sabhdva* as essence: his initial explanation of *sabhdva* as *sayam/sako bhdvo* draws on the epistemological sense of essence as an individuator of a *dhamma.* His analysis *of sabhdva* as *sakassa bhdvo/ekassabhdvatd,* though, relies on the ontological aspect of essence as the cause of a *dhamma's* being. The meaning suggested here is that a *dhamma* is independent of other *dhammas* for its existence; it bears its own reality all by itself. The *sabhdva* is the cause of the *dhammas* actual existence and its evidence. The commentator begins by analysing *sabhdva* as *sva+bhdva,* 'own-nature', but eventually divides the compound into *sat+bhdva,* 'real essence'. The latter has ontological repercussions for the *dhammas'* ęxistential status that the former explanation lacks.

This exegesis over-interprets the concise indications of the original text and may induce the impression that Mahanama was here trying to accommodate the text to the intellectual milieu of his own epoch. Interestingly, he next offers an alternative elucidation of *sabhavena sunnam* – and a preferred one, as implied by the particle *athavd* that normally introduces the preferred explanation in a commentary - namely, 'empty through having emptiness as its individual essence'. This interpretation is more in harmony with the *Patisambhidamagga*'s spirit. Yet even here Mahanama discloses the influence of his contemporary intellectual milieu: first, he refers to 'every single *dhamma'(ekassa dhammassa),* thus attesting to the view that the emptiness of essence is a distinguishing mark unique to every single *dhamma.* The *Patisambhidamagga,* as already noted is concerned with the totality of *dhammas* and the universal nature they all share. Second Mahanama rejects the argument that the latter rendering of *sabhavena suññam* means that the *dhammas* are completely empty, having no reality at all, by claiming that *dhammas* exist as real actualities, though only momentarily The commentator refers to *dhammas* as *sat,* real existents, whereas the *Patisambhidamagga* neither ascribes to the *dhammas* any ontological status nor mentions the doctrine of momentariness.

In summary, the *Patisambhidamagga* sheds light on the origination of the concept of *sabhava,* for it contains one of the rare canonical occurrences of the term *sabhava* in Pali literature; indeed it may be the first one. The text exemplifies the conceptual shift from the *Nikayas* to the Abhidhamma, anticipating the later Theravadin description of the *dhammas* according to their own-nature, quality and defining characteristic *(sabhava-rasa-lakkhana).* This conceptual framework, though, gained currency only at a later stage in the history of Theravadin doctrinal thought, so that in the *Patisambhidamagga* the above concepts are indistinct and not yet endowed with their later technical meanings as found in other para-canonical texts and in the *Atthakatha.*

Let us turn to two other para-canonical texts in which this doctrinal elaboration is carried out, namely, the *Petakopadesa* and the *Nettippakarana.* These texts represent a watershed in the development of the concept of *sabhava* and of the *dhamma* analysis as a whole.

The Petakopadesa and the Nettippakarana

The *Petakopadesa* and the *Nettippakarana* are hermeneutical manuals primarily concerned with methodology rather than with Buddhist doctrine as such; they deal with all aspects of interpretation of the Buddha's teaching and set forth a method of correct reformulation, explanation and expounding of the *Dhamma.* The Burmese Buddhists classify both works as canonical, forming part of the *Khuddaka-nikaya,* but other Theravadin traditions consider them to be non-canonical. Yet they are traditionally ascribed to the Thera Mahakaccayana, who is identified in the Theravada tradition as the Buddha's disciple, albeit this attribution is more explicit in the case of the *Petakopadesa.*3 Although this traditional dating is by far too early, the *Petakopadesa* and the *Nettippakarana* are considerably prior to the main Pali commentaries: they were probably composed in North India around the first century BCE and, because they are both known to Buddhaghosa, were reintroduced to Ceylon well before the fifth century CE, though not necessarily at the same time. Therefore they are invaluable documents for the study of the history of Pali exegesis and of the shift from the Nikaya worldview to the Abhidhamma framework.

Conceptually supporting a relatively early dating of the *Petakopadesa* is the text's discussion of the idea of *ekabhisamaya,* a simultaneous flash of knowledge of the four noble truths. Like the *Patisambhiddmagga,* the *Petakopadesa* also espouses the view that the penetration of the four noble truths occurs as a sudden flash of intuition - an idea expounded for the first time in the *Kathdvatthu,* the earliest portion of which is likely to date from the third century BCE or very soon thereafter, which suggests that if parts of the two texts originated around the same period then the *Petakopadesa* is rooted in a fairly old tradition. Ñanamoli indicates that the words *Tipitaka* or *Pitakattaya* are found in Pali only in the main commentaries, but the word *petakin,* 'one who knows the *Pitakas*', appears in an inscription at Sañci dated from the first or the second century BCE, and hence the work could be as early as that date. Oskar von Hinüber points to additional philological evidence in support of this date, indicating that the *Petakopadesa* bridges the gap between Southern (Burmese) and Northern Buddhist texts like the *Mahdvastu* and the *Uddnavarga.* On this basis he concludes that the *Petakopadesa* was most probably composed in India roughly in the first century BCE.

Stefano Zacchetti has recently discussed the dating of the *Petakopadesa* as part of his exploration of the *Yin chi ru jing* (T 603, hereafter YCRZ), an early Chinese text corresponding to Chapter 6 of the *Petakopadesa,* translated by An Shigao, the earliest translator of Buddhist scriptures into Chinese (active since 148 CE, during the Later Han Dynasty). Based on his examination of this Chinese parallel, Zacchetti argues that the extant *Petakopadesa* is the result of a long formative process and that it presupposes the prior existence of its sixth chapter. The latter represents a particularly ancient layer of Buddhist exegesis and had probably been an independent text by the time it was introduced into China around the second half of the second century CE. This old *mdtrikd-based* work translated by An Shigao as the YCRZ, Zacchetti conjectures, had been one of the sources of the *Petakopadesa's* method, and only at a later stage was it inserted into the latter text as one of its chapters. This means that the extant *Petakopadesa* should be dated somewhat later than has been assumed in the past by Ñanamoli.

Buddhological scholarship has repeatedly discussed the relation of the *Petakopadesa* and *Nettippakarana* deriving from the resemblance in their contents, but their relative chronology remains, on the whole, obscure, despite the extant significant sources for studying the tradition from which they ensue. Ñanamoli, who challenges E. Hardy's position on this matter, argues that the *Petakopadesa* predates the *Nettippakarana,* for the latter is far better organized, thus making the exegetical method more comprehensive and applicable to a wider range of texts (a superiority that may explain why of the two texts only the *Nettippakarana* has a commentary). More recently however Hinüber has adduced an important point in favour of the view that the *Nettippakarana* is the older of the two works: the same *arya* verses occur in both texts, but while these are well arranged at the beginning of the *Nettippakarana,* in the *Petakopadesa* they are dispersed all over and are badly preserved which shows that the *Petakopadesa* took over those verses and rearranged them, and hence that it is the younger text. Yet Hinüber qualifies this conclusion by suggesting that the two texts may not depend on each other, but rather deal separately with the same material derived from a common source used for the same purpose. In this context he draws attention to Lamotte's mention of Kumarajiva's fifth-century translation of the *Upadesa* (T 1509), which refers to Mahakatyayana as the compiler of a *Pi-lê* corresponding to 'Petaka' that had been used in South India. Kumarajiva's quotations from this **Petaka* in Pali literature, however, cannot be traced to the extant *Petakopadesa,* and hence, Hinüber opines, there could even be a third text similar to the *Nettippakarana* and the *Petakopadesa.*

Supporting this possibility is Zacchetti's investigation of the **Petaka* passages of a Chinese text called *Da zhidu lun* (T 1509, hereafter DZDL), in which he exposes traces of such a 'third text'. Zacchetti shows that the *Nettippakarana* makes use of material that is not found in the *Petakopadesa* but is in part paralleled by the **Petaka* quoted in the DZDL. This points to a third text in addition to the *Nettippakarana* and *Petakopadesa,* thus corroborating the hypothesis that all these works independently adopted some material from a possibly fairly old common tradition in which it was not yet systematically organized and that the *Nettippakarana* ought not to be considered as a direct revision of the *Petakopadesa;* rather, the history of this textual tradition must have been more complex. Nevertheless, removed as they may be in their place or time of composition, both the *Nettippakarana* and the *Petakopadesa* set forth virtually the same method and may be considered in tandem regarding their application of the term *sabhdva.* For a brief outline of this hermeneutical method I shall refer to the *Petakopadesa.*

The *Petakopadesa* provides two exegetical principles for ascertaining the Buddha's statements: one with reference to their phrasing *(vyañjana),* the other with reference to their meaning *(attha).* The analysis of these two aspects of the *Dhamma* by means of five meaning guidelines *(naya)* and sixteen phrasing categories *(hara,* or in Ñanamoli's rendering 'modes of conveying a communication') reveals its unity and inner structure. This method introduced new concepts that played a significant role in the subsequent development of Theravadin doctrinal thought and its *dhamma* exegesis. One of these concepts we have already encountered namely, *lakkhana,* is intimately related to the concept of *sabhdva.*

The term *lakkhana* features in the fifth of the sixteen categories of investigation, namely conveying the characteristics of an utterance *(lakkhano haw).* This mode of investigation is intended to clarify whether a word or a phrase states the unique feature of a set of *dhammas.* The text says: 'when one *dhamma* is mentioned, all those *dhammas* which have the same characteristic are mentioned by that. This is the category called "characteristic".' Here emerges the notion of a general characteristic common to a set of *dhammas* and distinguishing them from other such sets, namely, a class-inclusion concept that determines a *dhamma* type, cataloguing all those *dhammas* that possess the same characteristic mark as a set that belongs to the same class. Given the purpose of the *Pe takopadesa,* it is more likely that *dhammas* here refer to the statements comprising the Buddha's teachings rather than to 'thoughts' or 'ideas' (as Ñajamoli renders them). The fifth category of 'conveying characteristics' is thus intended to scrutinize the phrasing of the Buddha's utterances by pointing out their shared characteristics. What is asserted by utterances are propositions, and propositions are logico-linguistic entities that do not themselves have an ontological status. Hence a *dhamma* in this sense of phrasing need not be apprehended ontologically and does not signify an actual substance, either 'out there' or in some 'inner' reality. By the same token, the characteristic mark of a *dhamma* is not an instance of an existing universal, but rather a class-definition statement.

The term *sabhava* first appears in the *Pe takopadesa* within the framework of the fifteenth category of phrasing investigation, that is, 'conveying requisites' (*parikkharo h aro*). This category is expounded as the search for the cause (*hetu*) and condition (*paccaya*) of a *dhamma.* The *Nettippakara~a* further explains that a *dhamma* generating some other *dhamma* is its requisite and that there are two sorts of generating *dhammas*: a cause and a condition. That is, the topic under discussion is dependent co-origination, wherein an attempt is made to distinguish between the cause and the condition of a *dhamma.* Two notable issues unfold in this context: the first is that the distinction between *hetu* and *paccaya* as cause and condition respectively attests to a watershed in the development of Buddhist doctrinal thought. A widespread view in modern scholarship is that this distinction is already present in the earliest strata of the Canon, but, in fact, no such distinction is to be found in the *Nikayas,* where *hetu* and *paccaya* are regarded as synonymous and are used interchangeably along with a series of other terms – like *kara~a* and *nidana,* to name but two – all of which denote causal relatedness. Only in the Abhidhamma literature do *hetu* and *paccaya* become distinct and signify 'cause' and 'condition' respectively – a distinction later taken up by the commentaries. The *Pe takopadesa* and the *Nettippakara~a* are the only canonical or semi-canonical texts upholding this demarcation outside of the *Abhidhamma-pitaka.*

The second notable issue concerns the term *parikkhara* in the title of the category of investigation under discussion. *Parikkhara* is an early Vinaya term denoting the set of four necessities of a wandering *bhikkhu.* The employment of this term in the present context may point to the tradition's growing concern with doctrinal thought: a term that was originally applied to the practical, daily life of monks now signifies a category of philosophical investigation. von Hinüber indeed observes the possible connection between the *Nettippakara~a* and the *Parivara* (Vin V) – a *Vinaya* handbook providing a systematic survey of monastic laws and legal matters. Whereas the *Parivara* summarizes the *Vinaya* for practical purposes, the *Nettippakarana* – and, by the same reasoning, the *Petakopadesa* well - may be reckoned as Suttanta handbooks applying pragmatic Vinaya terms to metaphysics.

The investigation into the distinction between a *dhamma's* cause and condition under the category of conveying requisites begins thus:

> What is the difference between cause and condition? The cause is the own-nature *(sabhdva),* whereas the condition is the other-nature *(parab-havd).* Although the other-nature's condition is a cause, too, the condition of any other-nature whatsoever, excepting the own-nature's cause, is not called 'cause'; it is called 'condition'.

That is, the own-nature is the necessary condition of the occurrence of a specific *dhamma* series under certain circumstances, whereas the other-nature is the contributory condition of the eventuation of this circumstantial setting, and this condition is another *dhamma.* The own-nature is further explained as internal *(ajjhattiko)* to a stream of *dhammas,* as unshared or not held in common *(asadharano)* by them, and is likened to a producer *(nibbattako)* and to a resident *(nevdsiko).* By contrast, the other-nature is said to be external *(bdhiro)* to a stream of consciousness, held in common *(sddhdrano)* by its constitutive *dhammas,* and is likened to a receiver *(patiggahako)* and to a visitor *(dgantuko)* respectively In the *Dhammasangani* the terms *ajjhattiko* and *bdhiro* form one couplet of the *abhidhamma-mdtikd,* based on which internal *dhammas* are explicated as the six sense faculties *(cakkhdyatanam* etc., up to *mandyatanam),* external *dhammas* as the six corresponding object fields *(rupdyatanam* etc., up to *dhammdyatanam).* In accordance with this sense of *bdhiro, sabhdva-as-cause* characterizes a set of *dhammas* constituting a certain series consciousness, as opposed to *jara*M*ava*-as-condition that marks some other set of *dhammas* external to that series.

Hetu is identified as a cause in the sense of a *dhamma*'s own-nature: that which operates within the *dhamma*'s series and determines what it is to be that specific *dhamma. Paccaya,* by contrast, is regarded as a condition in the sense of other-nature: what operates in conditioning the series of another *dhamma.* Despite its contribution to the occurrence of that series, the condition is not what makes any given *dhamma* of that series what it is as this particular event, and so it may well be a contributory condition of other *dhammas.* This distinction between *hetu* and *paccaya* was further elaborated into a demarcation between *hetu* in the sense of 'horizontal causation' coordinating the *dhammas* of a certain consciousness series, and 'vertical causation' precipitating the activation of a common effect by that series. This elaboration marks a turning point in the history of Buddhist thought and is coupled with the increasing doctrinal sys-tematization characteristic of the Abhidhamma. Chapter 5 deals with the distinction between *hetu* and *paccaya,* grappling with the question of whether the idea of horizontal causation harmonizes with what is ordinarily intended by 'causation'. What I wish to emphasize in the present context is the *Pe takopadesa*'s acknowledgment of the idea that the *dhammas* possess particular natures intrinsic to them. The ambiguity encompassing the *Patisambhidamagga*'s treatment of *sabhava* (which gave its commentator much trouble) fades away here. Instead of the mere, vague sense of 'nature', *sabhava* is now assigned a narrower, more technical sense of own-nature *qua* an indi-viduator. This may eventually have led the later tradition into drawing conclusions with regard to the ontological status of the *dhammas*, stating that *sabhava* is the cause of its *dhamma*'s actual presence as an independently existing reality. This signification, however, is not yet worked out in the *Pe takopadesa*, and what is insisted upon is *sabhava* as an individuator rather than as an ontologi-cal determinant of primary existence: *sabhava* is what determines the individuality of a *dhamma* as this particular instant rather than that, and what makes it discernible as such. *Sabhava* therefore serves as a guideline we use for marking off our experience and separating it into its constitutive momentary events. Moreover, the *sabhava*-possessing *dhammas* are not point-instant, continuously existing entities, but the Buddha's teachings to be applied and the contents of ones experience as they appear to one's mind. Let us now look more closely into the *Nettippakara~a*'s employment of the terms *sabhava* and *dhamma*.

The *Nettippakara~a* contains a parallel discussion of the distinction between cause and effect under the same category of conveying requisites. It repeats the idea that the cause, as opposed to the condition, is not held in common by the *dhammas*. This is expounded by the following simile: 'While earth and water are common to the occurrence of every sprout, the seed is unique to a particular sprout. For earth and water are each a condition of a sprout, but own-nature (*sab-hava*) is its cause.' The seed is the sprout's own-nature and the cause of its occurrence. One may argue that insofar as *sabhava* is interpreted as the cause of a *dhamma*'s actual production or existence, then explicit metaphysics indeed creeps into this framework. As we shall see in Chapter 5, though, it is not self-evident that the early Buddhist concept of causation has the sense of production, for it concerns physical and mental processes whose eventuation follows patterns that are causally conditioned, not substances whose production is causally determined. Moreover, the above statement is ambiguous and oscillates between two senses of *sabhava*: one is indeed ontological, but the other is epistemological. Ontologically, the passage introduces the notion of a seed as a particular entity and the cause of the existence of another such entity, namely, the sprout. Epistemologically, the passage implies the idea of a seed-nature as a principle that determines and distinguishes the sprout-natured phenomenon conditioned upon it. Åcariya Dhammapala's commentary to the *Nettippakara~a* (sixth century CE) testifies to this ambiguity: 'The same existing own-nature, the seed, is the cause. But is it not a fact that the seed is not like the sprout, etc.? There is no (saying) that it is not; for there is no arising of that kind (of sprout) from any other kind (of seed).'

A second occurrence of the term *sabhava* in the *Petakopadesa* further supports the epistemological interpretation of *sabhava* as a particular nature. Here, explicating the idea of one's being afflicted tormented or disturbed *(samkilesa), sabhava* features in a section dealing with the five hindrances *(nivarana),* where it is stated that 'there are four hindrances that are afflictions by own-nature *(sabhava),* but sloth-and-torpor *(thina-middha)* are afflictions by being subordinate to the hindrances'. This claim is then explained with reference to the four corruptions *(dsava):* the four hindrances, we are told are corruptions by their own-nature, that is, due to their possessing the nature of *asavas,* but afflictions such as sloth-and-torpor are corruptions because they pertain to *citta* that is subject to the *asavas*. Here, too, the text does not interpret the *dhammas* ontologically, as 'things'. No certain conclusion can be drawn from the above employment of the term *sabhava* as regards the meaning of *dhamma* in the dimension of existence *(bhava).* The *dhammas* to which the term *sabhava* is applied are the five hindrances, that is, states of mind and mental events. Nothing is explicitly stated regarding their status as real existents: they are not said to possess a peculiar characteristic marking them as irreducible realities, neither as a class nor as individuals, and *sabhava* in this context does not determine the existence of these *dhammas.* What the text does mention is their own-nature as an intrinsic essence, and this, as we have seen above, does not necessarily have to be reckoned in ontological terms. *Sabhava* is first and foremost what demarcates, distinguishes, determines and defines the individuality of its *dhamma,* thus rendering it as knowable and nameable.

Both the *Petakopadesa* and the *Nettippakarana* establish the epistemological significance of *sabhava* as a category determining what a *dhamma* is, but its identification with *hetu* in the sense of cause introduces the metaphysical dimension of *sabhava* as the cause of a *dhamma's* individuality; that which in the internal constitution of a *dhamma* makes it the individual it is. Although the metaphysical sense of *sabhava* as the principle of a *dhamma's* individuality may lead one to construe both *sabhava* and *dhamma* as existing entities, at this stage their ontological status is not yet discussed. Even the *Nettippakarana* commentary is hesitant on this issue, wavering between the epistemological and metaphysical interpretations of *sabhava.* This is further evidenced by the qualification of *sabhava qua* cause as 'internal' *(ajjhattiko)* to a consciousness series, in contrast with that of *parabhava qua* condition as 'external' *(bahiro)* to that series. It appears that in the *Petakopadesa* the idea of *sabhava* does not go much beyond than this contrast between 'internal' and 'external'.

In fact, on certain occasions the couplet 'internal' and 'external' may even have a meaning more straightforward than that. We have already seen that the couplet 'internal' and 'external' features repeatedly in the *Nikdyas* as part of the characterization of the five *khandhas.* Therein any given person is the point of reference of whatever is external, whereas one's own experience is the point of reference of whatever is internal, and so one's own *khandhas* are internal, while those of other beings are external. Whereas in this case *bahira* and *bahiddha* are interchangeable, in the *Dhammasangani bdhira,* as noted above, is part of the couplet-*maft*'foJ and relates to a *dhamma-set* of a certain consciousness series. *Bahiddha,* though, is part of the *triplet-matikd* and simply means 'belonging to one's own experience', or 'personal' *(puggalikam).*

In this connection, Hamilton has suggested that *ajjhattika* and *bahiddha* should not be interpreted as implying an idealistic ontology, or in fact any ontology whatsoever. She relies on a convention found in the *Sutta-pitaka,* usually in contexts that are concerned with meditation, of using the terms 'internal' and 'external' to refer to oneself in contrast to others. Hamilton offers the example of the fundamental canonical texts on meditation, the *Satipatthana-* and *Mahasatipatthana-sutta* (M I 55ff. and D II 290ff. respectively), in which the two terms are used to indicate that the meditation exercises are to be practised both on one's own physical and mental faculties as well as on those of others.

I argue that the *Petakopadesa's* and the *Nettippakarana's* concept of *sabhava* in the sense of 'internal' is narrower than the general denotation of what marks one's set of things as opposed to someone else's: rather, it is used to distinguish the *dhammas qua* psycho-physical, short-lived events, and hence specifically refers to what is internal or external to a consciousness series. This interpretation fits in both with the first occurrence of *sabhava* in the *Petakopadesa,* as discussed above, and with its third appearance, within a passage concerned indeed with meditation.

In a section dealing with the nine successive attainments *(anupub-basamapattiyo),* the question raised is 'What is proficiency in meditation?' *(katamam jhanakosallam),* in reply to which a series of skills is offered. Among these skills is included 'skill in the *sabhava of jhana' (jhane sabhavakosallam).* Ñanamoli's translation of this phrase is 'skill in the meditations' individual essences', but what this skill in fact means is 'knowing which *jhana* one is in'. To know what distinguishes a certain *jhana* as opposed to any other conscious state, whether ordinary or meditative, requires a practitioner to differentiate and define each occurrence appearing in her consciousness, not merely to focus attention on her own faculties and states of mind as a point of reference rather than on someone else's.

The significance of the *Petakopadesa* and the *Nettippakarana* lies in their establishing the idea of an own-nature intrinsic to a consciousness series, as opposed to the other-nature that is external to that series.

Both texts entertain a notion of an own-nature essentially had by sets of *dhammas,* and do so more clearly and distinctly than the *Patisambhidamagga,* which may hint that they are posterior to it. Still the idea of own-nature emerging here is not worked out onto-logically, for what is insisted upon is that this particular nature defines what a given set of *dhammas* is; what it means to be *this* series of *dhammas* rather than *that.* Since human experience is seen as an ongoing flow of a consciousness stream made up of interlocking series of *dhammas,* an attempt is made to individuate this process by defining its constitutive *dhammas* in terms of their *sabhava.* The process itself, however, is not yet dissected into distinct phases, and *sabhava* does not yet determine what each and every *dhamma* is, either ontologically or epistemologically Let us now examine the apprehension of *sabhdva* within the framework of the *Buddhavamsa,* another para-canonical text comprising the *Khuddaka-nikdya.*

The Buddhavamsa

The mythically constructed biography of the Buddha includes, among other components, tales that trace the various lineages culminating in the birth and life of the 'historical' Buddha Gotama. While the Buddha's *jdtaka* lineage is constituted by events that took place in his previous lives, according to the Theravada he was also the successor of a series of Buddhas stretching far back into the past. The notion of this Buddha lineage is rooted in the *Mahdpaddna-sutta,* in which Gotama is the seventh in a series of former Buddhas, but the later Theravada has focused its attention on an extended set of twenty-four former Buddhas with Gotama as the twenty-fifth. The tradition concerning this lineage of twenty-four previous Buddhas, which both encompasses and adapts the lineage associated with the *Mahapadana-sutta,* is expressed in the *Buddhavamsa,* a text dated to the late second century or early first century BCE and that is one of the last additions to the Canon. Each of the *Buddhavamsa's* twenty-four stories relates an encounter between one of the former Buddhas and the future Gotama in one of his previous rebirths. In each case the future Gotama renews his commitment to the practice of the ten perfections and his vow to attain Buddhahood and in each case the Buddha in question predicts that in the future Gotama will achieve his goal.

In the *Buddhavamsa* the term *sabhdva* is mentioned twice. It first occurs in the story of Buddha Mangala, who is known for 'having shown people the own-nature *(sabhdvattam)* of conditioned phenomena'. The abstracted form *sabhdvattam* does not add much beyond the signification of *sabhdva* in the previously discussed texts. Once again *sabhdva* here signifies own-nature in its rather broad sense, referring to the nature of clusters of conditioned *dhammas.* In his commentary on this passage, Buddhadatta accordingly expounds *sabhdvattam* as 'the common characteristics of impermanence etc'.

The term *sabhdva* recurs on another occasion, where it has undergone an interesting elaboration. The context is Bodhisatta Sumedha's account of the ten perfections conducive to awakening. Having related these ten perfections Sumedha says: 'While I was reflecting on these principles *(dhammas)* having their own-natures, qualities and characteristic marks *(sabhdva-rasa-lakkhane),* the earth and the ten-thousand worlds quaked because of the effulgence of the *dhamma.* Compounding the category of *sabhdva* with *rasa* and *lakkhana,* the above statement anticipates the position of the latter as two of the post-canonical basic categories of *dhamma* exegesis and the primary role of *sabhdva* in the developed *dhamma* analysis as a categorial determinant. In addition to the doctrine of *sabhdva,* the commentarial method of *dhamma* exegesis is based upon a fourfold schema that assigns each *dhamma* a defining characteristic *(lakkhana),* a mode of manifestation *(paccupatthdna),* an immediate cause ('footing', *padatthdna)* and a quality *(rasa).* This method had already been anticipated by the *Petakopadesa's* use of the characteristic, manifestation and immediate cause of certain *dhammas.* The fourth aspect of analysis added in the commentaries is *rasa* as 'quality' in a narrow, technical sense. In the *Nikdyas* the term *rasa* usually means 'taste' or 'flavour'; the object sphere of the tongue *(jivhd),* that is, one of the six object fields corresponding to the six sense faculties *(sadyatana).* It is also used figuratively in the compound *vimutti-rasa,* the 'taste of liberation'. The *Patisambhiddmagga* employs the term *rasa* in a sense residing somewhere in between 'quality' and 'accomplishment'. This is shown in Treatise X, the topic of which are the 'fine extracts that are an elixir' *(manda-peyyam):* the extracts in question are the attainments constituting the *brah-macariya* life of a monk, among which are included resolution, exertion, non-distraction and so forth. The text states: 'That which is the accomplishment of meaning, of *dhamma* and of liberation is the elixir.' In this context, *rasa* acquires a qualitative sense denoting the achievement of the finest part of anything.

In the commentaries, though, *rasa* is endowed with the technical denotation of the unique capability or function of any single *dhamma.* The commentaries distinguish between two shades of meaning of this function: the first is *rasa* in the sense of 'action' *(kicca)* of the *dhammas* under discussion, namely, their contributory operation in conditioning other *dhammas;* the second is *rasa* in the sense of 'achievement' *(sampatti)* of those *dhammas,* that is, in the qualitative sense of the defining nature of those *dhammas,* whereby *rasa* is interchangeable with *sabhdva qua* 'own-nature'. For instance, when Buddhaghosa explicates the concept of virtue *(silo)* by analysing it according to its distinguishing characteristic, function, manifestation and immediate cause, he asserts:

Its function *(rasa)* is spoken of in the sense of action *(kicca)* and of achievement *(sampatti),* that is, as the undoing of misconduct and as the quality of being faultless. So what is called 'virtue' should be understood to have the nature *(rasa)* of uprooting misconduct as its function in the sense of action, and the nature *(rasa)* of being faultless as its function in the sense of achievement. For with regard to characteristic, etc., function is either called action or achievement.

The *Buddhavamsa* employs the terms *sabhdva, rasa* and *lakkhana* as ordinary and familiar aspects of the perfections of a Buddha. This usage indicates that the text presupposes the method of *dhamma* exegesis based on these concepts in a somewhat casual manner, building upon a conceptual schema that had already been well established by the time of its composition. Indeed in his commentary to the *Buddhavamsa,* Buddhadatta explains the compound *sabhdva-rasa-lakkhane* as follows: 'In the case of "own-nature, function and defining characteristic", the meaning is: "While he was reflecting on what is called *(sankhdta)* own-nature with its function and characteristic mark".' The commentator uses the term *sabhava* as if it were an accepted convention and, differently from its previous occurrences, here, for the first time it refers to one particular set of *dhammas* – the ten perfections making a Buddha, rather than to the totality of *dhammas* or to numerous classes of them working together. Likewise, the term *lakkha~a* now signifies a defining characteristic or a class-inclusion concept specific to each *dhamma,* whereas in its earlier appearances it denoted the universal marks shared by all the conditioned *dhammas*. The point is that this is the first instance in which *sabhava* determines, along with a *dhamma*'s characteristic mark and quality, what that particular *dhamma* is. In the present context it determines what each of the ten perfections is, and these perfections in their turn define what a Buddha is. Ye t no conclusions regarding the ontological status of each of the defined *dhammas* can be drawn from this usage of *sabhava.* The ten perfections are doctrinal concepts or principles, not existing 'entities'. Nothing necessarily implies that they exist by virtue of their *sabhava* and, in fact, they are not apprehended ontologically at all. The *sabhava* of each of the ten perfections marks it off from the remaining perfections; it is an epistemo-logical guideline that makes each *dhamma* knowable and discernable, rather than what testifies to its reality or actual existence.

The Milindapañha

Another para-canonical text employing the term *sabhava* is the *Milindapañha*. This text is a heterogeneous work of which the earlier and later parts are strikingly different in their style, indicating that it is not a unified product of one author. By comparing the fourth-century Chinese version of the text, which contains only the first part of the Pali equivalent, it has been deduced that the *Milindapañha* is, in fact, a collection of discrete texts. This first and earliest part of the work is quoted in the *Old Atthakatha* and must have been composed in India between 150 BCE and 200 CE. The four remaining parts can be traced very roughly: they are quoted in the *Atthakatha* and surely existed after the Canon had been settled into five *Nikayas*, but there is no evidence that they preceded Buddhaghosa.

Although the *Milindapañha* frequently employs the term *sabhava* (it features more than twenty times throughout the text), there is no semantic unanimity across its occurrences: despite its prevalence by the time this text was compiled, it had a fluctuant, context-depending meaning. On the majority of its occurrences *sabhava* denotes 'nature' in its broadest sense. To mention but two instances of this usage: in one passage solitary meditation (*patisallana*) is discussed and is said to be endowed with twenty-eight qualities, one of which is that 'it shows the nature of conditioned states'. Later on this nature is identified as 'ultimate empti-ness'. On another occasion the text reckons twelve kinds of people who do not pay respect, among whom is one 'who is inferior due to his inferior own-nature'. In this passage, and in several other places in the text, *sabhava* signifies the non-technical and somewhat vague term 'nature' (*pakati*) in the sense of 'natural disposition' or 'character'. In fact, on one occasion it is compounded with the very word *pakati:* discussing the nature of Buddhas, Nagasena proclaims that 'It is the nature and own-character *(sabhdva-pakati)* of Buddhas, of Blessed Ones, that only one Buddha appears in the world at a time. For what reason? Because of the omniscient Buddhas' grandeur of qualities. What is magnificent and different in the world your majesty, is one only.' I take the compound *sabhdva-pakati* as a *kammadhdraya,* whereby the two members reflect each other's meaning.

In all the preceding passages *sabhdva* denotes a broad range of meaning, is not predicated of particular *dhammas* and does not convey any ontological allusions. Yet on several occasions in the *Milindapañha* the term *sabhdva* is used in a narrower and more technical sense than mere 'nature'. For instance, in the opening of the section that deals with the dilemmas *(mendaka-pañha),* it is declared: 'In the teaching of the King of *Dhamma* there are speech that expresses indirectly, speech that is allusive and speech that is the literal truth *(sabhdva).'* In this context *sabhdva* denotes the qualitative sense of 'essence' signified by the term *rasa* when it figuratively refers to the finest, distilled part of anything, as we have already come across in the *Patisambhiddmagga.* On another occasion the text broaches the relation between the Tathagata and the *sangha,* whereby the following idea is said to have occurred to the Tathagata: 'The *sangha* is to be honoured by virtue of its nature *(sabhdva).* I shall honour the *sangha* by means of my property.' Once more, *sabhdva* may be taken here as tantamount to *rasa* in the figurative sense of the finest part of anything. And again, the same shift from this figurative sense to the narrower and more technical meaning of capability or function takes place here, whereby *sabhdva* is explicitly compounded with *rasa.* In this passage, Nagasena discusses with Milinda the fear of death and says to the king:

> Death, your majesty, is the cause of fear among those whc have not seen the truth [...] That, your majesty, is the power of the own-quality and own-nature *(sarasa-sabhdva)* of death, because of which beings with defilements tremble at death and are afraid of it.

This coupling of *sabhdva* and *rasa* is reminiscent of the *Buddhavamsa's* similar compounding the two terms along with *lakkhana,* the conceptual triad customary of the commentarial *dhamma* analysis.

The *Milindapañha* also employs *sabhdva* in connection with *lakkhana,* though it is uninformative as regards the distinction between them. For instance, assuming that both terms are interchangeable, in a section dealing with non-injury *(ahimsd)* Nagasena quotes the Buddha's statement that non-injury is approved by all Tathagatas as conducive to one's welfare, then tells king Milinda: 'This is the instruction and *dhamma* teaching, your majesty, for the *dhamma* has the defining characteristic *(lakkhana)* of non-injury; this is the statement of its own-nature *(sabhdva).'* The last occurrence of *sabhdva* worth mentioning with respect to this issue is one in which it features in the full compound *sabhdva-rasa-lakkhana,* insinuating the same meaning we encountered in the *Buddhavamsa.* Here the topic under discussion is the Buddha's instruction to the monks not to be given to delight in others' praises of him, of the *dhamma* or of the *sangha.* Nagasena then addresses King Milinda:

> The former statement, your majesty, was spoken by the Blessed One when he was illustrating correctly *(sabhdvam),* truly, as is the case, truthfully and as really is the own-nature, the quality and the defining characteristic *(sabhdva-sarasa-lakkhana)* of the *dhamma.*

Note that *sabhava* is mentioned twice in this sentence and that on its first occurrence it is used as an adverb in the sense of 'genuinely', 'correctly' or 'as it is'. This signification is one of the acknowledged meanings of *sabhava* recurring several times throughout the *Milindapañha.*

Now this sense of *sabhava* relates to an interesting doctrinal development. In the *suttas* the Buddha's teaching is referred to either by the Buddha himself or by others as that which is 'true' and 'real' in the ultimate sense, employing in this connection such qualifiers as *bhutam, taccham* or *tatham.* As part of the doctrinal systematization of Buddhist thought, however these qualifiers were gradually endowed with a metaphysical significance and became interchangeable with the term *sabhava,* so that by the time of the commentaries and sub-commentaries they were all connected with a realist ontology. What initially meant 'correct' or 'true' came to denote 'what is the case', 'real' and finally 'what there is'. We shall discuss this terminological expansion in the following section.

To sum up, the *Milindapañha* employs the term *sabhava* more frequently than any of the para-canonical texts we have previously explored which indicates that by the time of its composition the term had already gained currency and become regularly used. The text is heterogeneous and accommodates various senses of the term *sabhava,* albeit with little doctrinal elaboration. On the whole there is not much innovation in the *Milindapañha*'s use of *sabhava,* and nearly all its denotations mentioned had already been promulgated in prior texts. Moreover, no certain conclusion with regard to an ontological interpretation of *sabhava*,can be derived from this text. The *Milindapañha* uses this term in a looser manner than the previous works we have considered: *sabhava* here features in much less technical contexts and is not applied to the *dhammas* in their narrower, metaphysical sense acquired subject to the *dhamma* theory. The text does not see the *dhamma* analysis as its primary concern, nor does it take much interest in the ontological status of the *dhammas*. It was during the post-canonical period that marked changes occurred in this respect along with the commentaries' extensive use of the term *sabhava* and as part of the fixation of the *dhamma* theory. The following section traces the conceptual transformations involved in these doctrinal developments.

BUDDHIST DOCTRINAL THOUGHT IN THE ATTHAKATHÅ

From the Canonical Abhidhamma to the Pali Commentaries

The composition of the original versions of the commentaries in Old Sinhalese ended in the first century CE. These Sinhalese originals were eventually replaced by their Pali versions made in the fifth century CE. The commentarial period witnessed the attempts to explicate the theoretical position implied by the canonical Abhidhamma, and so in many cases the exegetical system manifests a move away from the standpoint found in the *Abhidhamma-pitaka*. Whereas the early Abhidhamma offers a mapping and analysis of the material found in the *suttas*, elaborating on it for consistency the commentaries seek to consolidate, fill in and explain that material. The commentarial attempt to reduce the oral tradition to a written body of knowledge, to interrelate the original, scattered teachings and to create an all-embracing, comprehensive and consistent theory in which every doctrine should find its proper place, shaped the changing nature of the resultant exegetical works. This change is reflected in the commentaries' introduction of new ideas that are at times remote from the scant indications of the original texts.

The paramount new ideas espoused by the commentaries are related to the changing meaning of the key concept *dhamma* and the harnessing of the term *sabhdva* for its explanation. These ideas draw on the already extant *dhamma* analysis, as developed by the early Abhidhamma and presented in the Abhidhamma canonical books, particularly the *Dhammasangani,* the *Vibhanga* and the *Patthana.* Since the *dhamma* theory analyses conscious experience into *dhammas,* the Abhidhamma treatises consist of innumerable *dhamma* lists and categorizations based on the assumption that each *dhamma* is to be known separately as well as in all its relations to other *dhammas.* The system, then, draws on the two complementary methods of analysis and synthesis. The analytical method dominates the *Dhammasangani* that supplies a detailed categorization of the *dhammas* forming the contents of one's consciousness. Later on, the *Dhammasangani* commentary expands the laconic definitions of these *dhammas* by employing the scheme, already anticipated by the *Petakopadesa,* of stating the characteristic, manifestation, immediate cause and function of each *dhamma* constituting the smallest psycho-physical unit, that is, a single moment of consciousness. The *locus classicus* of the synthetical method is the *Patthana,* which supplies a thorough account of the *dhammas'* conditional relations across the momentary thought process.

The framework emanating from the juxtaposition of the two methods accords with early Buddhist teaching of the middle way: it avoids both the eternalist view *(sassata-vdda)* which maintains that everything exists absolutely, and the opposite annihilationist view *(uccheda-vada)* which holds that things, having existed cease to exist. Moreover, at least in this early phase of its evolution the Abhidhamma is not so much a dogmatic system, but a conceptual framework assimilative of its preceding, scattered teachings. In this connection Gethin argues that the *Dhammasangani's* analysis of *dhammas* should not be taken as a closed system offering an enumeration of a final number of irreducible elements. Although the text enumerates particular numbers of items in various lists, these are not irreducible elements and in the final analysis it turns out that the lists are changeable and open-ended. This suggests that the canonical Abhidhamma is more exploratory in nature than is usually thought, aiming at an unlimited inquiry into the true nature of human experience. To some extent this state of affairs is also applicable to the commentarial outlook, as presented in the *Dhammasangani* commentary. It is true that the *Atthasdlini* seeks to provide an exhaustive analysis of all possible types of *dhamma* and to complete those *dhamma* lists left open by the original text, as evidenced by the phrase 'these or whatever others may occur'. Yet even in the commentary these so-called exhaustive lists often employ alternative definitions, so that the conclusions regarding the status of the *dhammas* they enumerate are, to some extent, merely tentative.

Nonetheless, the Abhidharma schools, the Theravadin Abhidhamma included, generally agree that the *dhammas* are knowable in an ultimate sense and are not further resolvable into any other constituent. The *dhammas* thus emerge as the final limits of the Abhidharma analysis of conscious experience. We have previously seen that the advent of the *dhamma* theory and its associated doctrines of atomism and momentariness gradually led the evolving Abhidharma schools into reifying experience, if in a different manner from the advocates of eternalism and the holders of substance metaphysics. This tendency to reify experience formed part of a broader process of terminological and doctrinal generalization, in which the concept of *svabhava* played a dominant role. It is within the Sarvastivada-Vaibhasika framework that one finds what may be reckoned the culmination of this process.

The Sarvastivada-Vaibhasika introduced a distinction between two fundamental types of existence: substantial or primary existence *(dravyasaf)* and conceptual or secondary existence *(prajñaptisai)*. The category of primary existence includes *dharmas,* namely, the irreducible components of the empirical world, whose existence is certain and independent of both conceptual analysis and physical fragmentation. Secondary existence, by contrast, is dependent upon mental and linguistic construction. Thus all things are either primary existents, *dharmas,* or secondary existents composed out of *dharmas*. Only *dharmas* have *svabhava* and can be primary existents, and obviously no *dharma* can be a secondary existent, but all existents are *sat*. The Sarvastivadins are renowned for arguing that the *dharmas* exist as past, present and future, but it should be noted that they conceived of *svabhava* as an atemporal category transcending the present moment and time in general. That is, the presence of a *svabhava* indicates that a *dharma* is a primary existent, a *dravyasat,* irrespective of its temporal status, namely, whether it is a past, present or future *dharma*. This temporal status is determined by the presence or absence of function *(karitra):* past and future *dharmas* have only their *svabhdva,* while a present *dharma* also has a function. That is, the distinction between the modes of existence of a *dharma* as past and future and a *dharma* as present corresponds to the opposition *sasvabhdvamdtradravya:: sakdritradravya.*

The Sarvastivada version of the *dharma* theory introduces a metaphysical dimension to the contemplation of *dharmas;* it paves the way for a distinction between substance and quality, and eventually results in a transformation of the *dharma* theory into a *svabhdva-vdda,* 'doctrine of particular nature'. According to this doctrine, each and every *dharma* is itself unique (though amenable to categorization), possesses its own defining characteristic *(svalaksana)* that marks only *dharmas* of its kind and is identified by its *svabhdva,* which here may be rendered 'ontological determinant', for it determines that the *dharma* consists in substantial reality *(dravya).* The exact difference between *svalaksana* and *svabhdva* is somewhat vague: the *Abhidharmakosabhdsya* equates *svabhdva* with *svalaksana,* setting it in opposition to the common characteristics *(sdmdnyalaksana)* that pertain to all conditioned *dharmas* (imperma-nence etc.). Moreover, on various occasions the same illustrations are given for both concepts: for instance, solidity is brought forward as the *svabhdva* and *svalaksana* of earth. But there is a remarkable difference between the two: the *svabhdva* is an ontological determinant of primary existence, although it does not have an ontological status and is not an ontological category in its own right. To have a *svabhdva* is to be a primary existent. Hence the *svabhdva* is the determinant of a *dharma* which is *dravya,* a substantially real entity, and is what defines a *dharma* as having primary existential status regardless of its temporal status. Now both *svabhdva* and *dravya* are used to describe the existence of a *dharma* recognized as a primary existent. The difference is that they characterize the reality of a *dharma* from two different perspectives: *svabhdva* refers to the *dharma*'s individual essence that distinguishes it from all other *dharmas. Dravya* refers to any primary existing *dharma* that so exists by virtue of its own individual essence, as distinct from those *dharmas* that exist merely as provisional designations *(prajñapti).* The *svalaksana,* on the other hand is an epistemo-logical, linguistic determinant of a *dharma:*

it is by means of its own-characteristic that a *dharma* becomes uniquely discernable, verbally definable and knowable. The *svalaksana* renders a verbal description unique to each *dharma* and makes it possible to refer to that *dharma* as distinct from any other *dharma.* The difference between *svabhdva* and *svalaksana* has also been explained by the fact that *svabhdva* is atomic and refers to the primary existence of a *dharma,* whereas *svalaksana* is regarded as the sensible distinguishing characteristic possessed by the atomic *svabhdva.* For instance, blue 'atoms' are the *svabhdva* of blue, while the perceptible blue colour as the unique, distinguishing characteristic these atoms possess is the blue's *svalaksana.* This explanation, though, implies that not only is *svabhdva* an ontological determinant, but that it also has an ontological status of its own.

Buddhological studies often give rise to the impression that, in the final analysis, the Sarvastivadin conception of *dharma* is what prevails in Buddhist thought. Bear in mind, though, that the Theravadins did not subscribe to the Sarvastivada metaphysics: they did not incorporate the Sarvastivada atomstic theory directly into their system, and rejected the claim that the *dharmas* exist as past, present and future. Most importantly for the present context, they did not use the category of *sabhava* to denote *dravya* and rejected the very Sarvastivada equation of a *dharma* with *dravya.* Ye t the Sarvastivadin metaphysics did leave its mark on the Theravadin position. Paul Williams argues that the position on the role of *svabhava* as positing primary existents is common to both the Sarvastivada and the Theravada:

> [T]he two schools disagree by implication on questions of temporal determination and ultimately on the possibility of reference to non-existents, but not over the primary status to be given to the entity which possesses the *svabhava.* For both it is the presence or absence of the *svabhava* which renders the entity a primary existent, and if the Sarvastivadin sees the Theravadin as destroying the opposition *sasva-bhavamatradravya::sakaritradravya* and thus rendering impossible the tenseless usage of our language and many of our everyday cognitive experiences, nevertheless the disagreement is epistemological and linguistic, not ontological.

As we shall see below, the Sarvastivada indeed influenced the Theravadin Abhidhamma version of the *dhamma* theory. This Sarvastivadin influence is embodied in the Pali post-canonical, commentarial literature, where the term *sab-hava* came to be excessively used for the sake of further elaboration on the nature of the *dhammas*. But would it be true to interpret the Sarvastivada and Theravadin Abhidhamma consent in terms of ontology? Were the later Abhidhammikas motivated by an interest in the ontological status of the *dhammas* as primary existents and did they employ the concept of *sabhava* for that purpose? Chapter has revealed that the Pali Abhidhamma does not take much interest in ontology, if by 'ontology' we mean the classical treatment of the question of being and exis-tence. My claim is that the Theravadin commentarial construal of *sabhava* derives from the canonical Abhidhamma *dhamma* analysis and that therefore *sabhava* is predominantly used for the sake of determining the *dhammas'* individuality, not their existential status. Even when the post-canonical texts introduce what may be rendered as a realist ontology, this ontology is bound up with the Abhidhamma analysis of consciousness, wherein *sabhava* is what determines the individuality of the *dhammas* as psycho-physical events as they appear in consciousness, not their existence *per se*. I agree with Williams that the disputes between the Sarvastivada and the Theravadin Abhidhamma are basically epistemological rather than ontological. My suggestion, though, is that the Abhidhamma's refraining from challenging the *dhammas'* ontological status demonstrates its indifference to and neutrality on ontological matters, not necessarily its assent to the Sarvastivadin notion of the *dhammas* as *dravya*.

While our reconstruction of the Abhidhamma *dhamma* theory and its derivative doctrine of *sabhdva* as centred on the philosophical problem of individuation is presented in Chapter 4, the next section recounts the Theravadin commentarial elaboration on the concept of *sabhdva* and its customary ontological interpretation.

The Concept of Sabhava in the Atthakatha

A recurrent definition of *dhammas* in the exegetical literature is: '*dhammas* are so called because they bear their particular natures'. An extended variation on this definition found in the *Atthasdlini* states that '*dhammas* bear their own particular natures. Alternatively *dhammas* are borne by conditions, or according to particular natures'. Does not the very use of the term *sabhdva* overstress the reality of the *dhammas* and imply that a *dhamma* is a discrete entity, a 'thing' existing in its own right? Moreover, do not these definitions amount to the admission of a duality between a *dhamma* and its *sabhdva,* between the bearer and the borne, thus implying a distinction between substance and quality - a duality which is at odds with the Buddhist doctrine of no-self?

It may be argued that to read such a duality into the recurrent definition of the *dhammas* as given above is to misunderstand it. Nyanaponika Thera remarks that this definition testifies only to the *dhammas* not being reducible to any other substantial bearers of qualities, and by no means implies that these *dhammas* themselves are such substances or bearers, nor that they are distinct from their particular natures or functions. In fact, the commentaries equate the *dhammas* and their *sabhdva.* The *Visuddhimagga* thus states that '*dhamma* means *sabhdva*'. Similarly, the *Mulatikd* on the *Dhammasangani* says: 'There is no other thing called *dhamma* apart from the particular nature upheld by it.' Moreover, as Karunadasa shows, the prevalent commentarial definition of a *dhamma* ought to be seen in the context of the logical scheme employed by the Abhidhammikas in defining the *dhammas.* This scheme consists of three main types of definition named after what they attribute to the definiendum: agency definition *(kattu-sddhana),* instrumental definition *(karana-sddhana)* and definition by nature *(bhdva-sddhana).* For instance, Sumangala's commentary to the *Abhidhammatthasangaha* expounds *citta* as follows:

Consciousness *(citta)* is that which is conscious; the meaning is that it knows *(vijdndti)* an object. [...] Or else consciousness is the means by which the associated *dhammas* are conscious. Alternatively, consciousness is the mere act of being conscious *(cintana).* For it is mere occurrence in accordance with conditions that is called 'a *dhamma* with its own particular nature' *(sabhdva-dhamma).*

The agency and instrumental definitions are deemed a figurative manner of speaking; conventions *(vohdra)* that are based on tentative attribution *(samdropana)* and employed for the sake of facilitating instruction in the Buddha's teaching. They endow a *dhamma* with a duality that is merely a mental construct, insinuating that a *dhamma* is a substance with inherent attributes, or alternatively an agent performing some action, while, in fact, it is a psycho-physical occurrence devoid of any such duality. By contrast, a definition in terms of the particular nature of a *dhamma* is recognized as valid in an ultimate sense, for it brings to light the true nature of a given *dhamma* in its impermanence and non-substantiality, and as a unique occurrence devoid of any duality. Having explicated *citta* as cited above, the *Abhidhammatthasangaha* commentary continues thus:

> In consideration of this, it is the definition of the particular natures of ultimate *dhammas* that is taken as absolute; the explanation by way of agent *(kattar)* and instrument *(karana)* should be seen as a relative manner of speaking. For a *dhamma's* being treated as an agent, by attributing the status of 'self to the particular function of a *dhamma,* and also its being [treated] in consequence as an instrument, by attributing the state of agent to a group of conascent *dhammas,* are both taken as a relative manner of speaking. The explanation in these terms should be understood as for the purpose of indicating the non-existence of an agent, etc., apart from the particular nature of a *dhamma.*

It is in the context of this explanatory apparatus, Karunadasa maintains, that the definition of a *dhamma* as that which bears its particular nature has to be understood. This definition is an agency definition, and hence it is merely provisional: the duality between *dhamma* and *sabhdva* is conventional, whereas in actual fact *dhamma* and *sabhdva* have two different senses referring to the same meaning. The *dhammas* are invested with the function of bearing their particular natures in order to convey the idea that there is no enduring agent behind these *dhammas.* They should also not be regarded as quasi-substances, for the extended definition, as mentioned above, states that a *dhamma* is that which is borne by its own conditions. This addition illustrates the impossibility of the occurrence of a *dhamma* without its own-nature: a *dhamma* with no *sabhdva* would be indeterminate and ineffable. That a *dhamma* may equally be defined as an agent bearing its *sabhdva* and as a passive object, that which is borne by its *sabhdva,* attests to the relativity and the conventional status of these two definitions: since both are equally applicable, neither is essentially true. This state of affairs reflects the interdependence between a *dhamma* and its *sabhdva,* and hence *dhammas,* as they really are in their true natures, should not be conceived of in terms of a oneway dependency of substance and attribute. A *dhamma* is an occurrence of a dynamic psycho-physical event under appropriate conditions and its *sabhdva* determines its individuality as distinct from any other such occurrence.

Nevertheless, despite all the qualifications imposed on the usage of the term *sabhdva,* the latter testifies to a striking doctrinal change in the exegetical literature. This change is complex and has to it several different aspects. The first of these aspects is embodied in the commentaries' usage of *sabhava* as a synonym for a *dhamma* and in their defining any given *dhamma* by virtue of its *sabhava.* That the equation of *dhamma* with *sabhava* becomes a regularly familiar notion in the commentaries is indicated by the fact that both terms are taken as interchangeable within a vast array of texts. As noted above, the *Visuddhimagga* proclaims that *dhammas* mean 'particular natures', and the sub-commentary to the *Dhammasangani* indicates that there is no other thing called *dhamma* apart from the particular nature borne by it. The same idea is expressed by such statements as 'The word *sabhava* denotes the mere fact of being a *dhamma*', or 'There is no such thing called "activity" apart from the *dhamma's* particular nature.' In the commentaries *sabhava* has a narrower sense than in the earlier para-canonical texts: no longer does it signify some vague 'nature', nor the nature of clusters of *dhammas,* but an atemporal category determining what each and every single *dhamma* is. The concept of *sabhava* is employed here for the first time as a determinant of a *dhamma's* individuality. Note that it determines *what* a *dhamma* is - what it means to be this particular *dhamma* rather than any other - and not *that* a *dhamma* is. As such the concept of *sabhava* attests to the Theravadins' interest in unveiling the nature of conscious experience: this, they presumed could be carried out by enumerating the possible types of those events constituting one's experience and by individuating them. To individuate the *dhammas* the Abhidhammikas had to provide a method for determining what any given *dhammic* instance of every possible event-type is and what makes it so, and for this purpose they used the concept of *sabhava.* It is my contention that this empirically based interest in conscious experience motivated the Abhidhammikas more than any possible concern with ontology, namely, with the question of the *dhammas'* being and existence - either their primary existential status as ultimately real experiential constituents or their temporal existence. Chapter 4 buttresses this claim by a close study of the canonical and post-canonical Abhidhamma's treatment of the problem of the *dhammas'* individuation.

The mature Abhidhamma's interest in conscious experience accords with the canonical Abhidhamma worldview, but the commentaries elaborate on and expound the concepts of *dhamma* and *sabhava,* while in the canonical and para-canonical texts neither concept is fully worked out. Moreover, this further systematization of the concept of *sabhava* ties in with the second aspect of doctrinal change manifested in the commentaries, namely the introduction of the idea of 'individual characteristic' *(salakkhana)* and its association with the *dhamma* theory. An alternative definition of *dhamma* prevalent in the commentaries states that *'dhammas* are so called because they bear their individual characteristics'. The commentaries draw a distinction between two senses of *lakkhana:* between the universal characteristics *(samanna-lakkhana)* of the totality of *dhammas,* on the one hand and the particular characteristic *(salakkhana)* of each and every *dhamma,* on the other hand. The former consist of the *tisankhatalakkhana:*

The characteristics of the *dhammas* are shown by the Blessed One as two on account of being general *(samanna)* and individual *(paccatta).* As for the materiality aggregate, the individual characteristic is pointed out, for the characteristic of materiality is not like that of feeling (*vedana*) etc., and hence it is called 'individual characteristic'. But feeling etc. have the characteristics of impermanence, *dukkha* and no-self, and hence those are called 'universal characteristics'.

The own-characteristic is comprehended through a process of sense perception that one experiences for oneself, whereas the universal characteristics are known through a process of reasoning. This concern with the *dhammas* as discrete, particular events distinguishable by unique marks is new to the commentaries, for the earlier texts mainly dealt with the *dhammas* as totalities or clusters working together and having various attributes in common, and did not associate these attributes with the concept of *sabhava.*

This association is promulgated in the commentaries. Thus, the *Atthasalini* observes: 'It is the particular nature or the generality of such and such *dhammas* that is called their characteristic.' The *Mulatika* comments on this point:

The own-nature of solidity [in the case of earth] or touch [in the case of contact] etc., is not common [to all *dhammas*]. The generality is the own-nature consisting in impermanence etc., which is common. In this connection [i.e. Dhs §], the characteristic of being skilful ought to be regarded as general because it is the own-nature common to all that is skilful. Alternatively, it is the particular own-nature because it is not shared by what is unskilful.

Along the same lines of thought, the *Paramatthamañjusa*, the *Mahatika* to the *Visuddhimagga*, clarifies this:

The *dhammas'* own-nature (*sabhava*) consists of their particular nature (*sako bhavo*) and common nature (*samano bhavo*). Therein by the former is meant the characteristic of solidity [with reference to earth] or of touch, etc. [with reference to bodily contact etc.]. By the latter is meant the common characteristics of impermanence, *dukkha* etc. What is called 'knowledge' has the characteristic of penetration in accordance with both of these, as was said: 'Knowledge has the characteristic of insight into the *dhammas'* own-natures.'

This assertion is reminiscent of the distinction drawn in Western philosophy between 'nature' and 'essence', as indicated above, and therefore *sabhava* in the sense of *sako bhavo* may be rendered here as 'individual essence', albeit this should be qualified to the epistemological denotation of essence. Bear in mind that essence singles out what necessarily determines an individual as that very item it is, whereas nature is a broader term and may be regarded as the sum total of the concurrent attributes an individual possesses. The commentaries, then, use the term *sabhava* to signify both the common nature that is generally predicable of *dhammas* in their totality and, when taken as equivalent to *salakkhana,* the narrower meaning of 'essence' - in its epistemological denotation -that is not predicable of any other *dhamma.* In this latter sense, to have a *sabhava* is to possess an essential characteristic individuating a certain instance of empirical occurrence as unique and distinct from any other instance of its type. 'What is called *salakkhana'*, so it is argued 'is the *sabhava* that is not held in common by other *dhammas.'*

Note that this is a point on which the Theravada and the Sarvastivada-Vaibhasika differ. In the Sarvastivadin framework, as we have seen above, the *svabhdva* is an ontological determinant of primary existence, of a *dharma* being a *dravya*. The *svalaksana*, on the other hand is an epistemological, linguistic determinant of a *dharma* as that which is discernable, definable and knowable. The Theravadins do not seem to hold such a distinction: *salakkhana* and *sabhava* are both taken interchangeably as epistemological and linguistic determinants of the *dhammas:* as what renders any given *dhamma* distinguishable and definable. This understanding may have been influenced by the Indian Grammarians *(Paniniyas)* and logicians. In ordinary Sanskrit *laksana* means a mark, a specific characteristic or evidence that enables one to identify the object or objects indicated *(laksya)* as distinct from others. The Grammarians employ this pair of terms in a slightly different sense: the *sutras* that embody the rules of grammar are called *laksana*, and these indicate the forms that are grammatically correct, that is, *laksya*, so that the incorrect forms are excluded. This is also connected with the logicians' use of the same pair of terms in the sense of 'definition' and 'definiendum' respectively. Here *laksana* may be rendered as a 'definition through characterization' that differentiates a certain concept or logical category Matilal explains in his discussion of the Indian theory of definition:

If a specific evidence, say *a*, is what allows us to ascertain that something is *A*, *[...]* then *a* would be a defining character of *A*. In other words, with the help of *a*, we would be able to differentiate *A* from what is not *A*, and a definition sentence could be given as: '*A* is what has *a*.' This notion of *laksana* must have been insinuated into the Theravadin exegetical system, thus affecting the use of the term *salakkhana* and its identification with *sabhava* in the sense of a *dhamma's* distinguishing definition. This is evinced in the *Visuddhimagga*. For instance, in discussing the contemplation of the body's impurity Buddhaghosa says:

In the place where the bloated sign of impurity *(uddhumatakam asub-hanimittam)* has been laid down, one registers any stone, or ant-hill, or tree, or bush or creeper, each with its own sign and object. Having done that, he characterizes *(upalakkheti)* the bloated sign of impurity by its having a defining own-nature *(sabhdvabhdvato)*.

This is further explained thus:

Having thus registered [each with its] own sign and object, it should again be brought to mind that it has a defining own-nature, its own state of being bloated which is not held in common by anything else, since it was said: 'he defines *(vavatthapeti)* it by its having a defining own-nature.' The meaning is that it should be defined according to its own-nature *(sabhava)* and own-quality *(sarasa),* as 'the bloated'.

Seen in the light of this exegetical usage of the term *lakkhana,* inasmuch as *sabhava* is identified with *salakkhana,* its dominant function is that of an episte-mological and linguistic determinant of the *dhammas* as individuals, rather than an ontological determinant of the *dhammas* as primary existents. The Theravadin Abhidhamma' employment of *sabhava* in connection with *salakkhana* attests to its interest in assigning any given *dhamma* a characteristic that is applicable solely to it, and which is referred to by a unique verbal description. *Sabhava* is therefore neutral to the question of the existence of the defined *dhammas* as real entities. I discuss this epistemological aspect of *sabhava* in Chapter 4.

Nevertheless, the later Abhidhammikas and Theravadin commentators were led into drawing metaphysical conclusions from the foregoing epistemological doctrine of *sabhava.* In tandem with the interpretation of *dhamma, sabhava* and *lakkhana* at the level of epistemology and language, the post-canonical texts accommodate another line of thought about these concepts - one that seems to introduce ontology into the Abhidhamma system. The commentators indeed qualified the usage of the term *sabhava,* rejected substance metaphysics and its associated substance-attribute ontological model, and apprehended the *dhammas* as psycho-physical events. Yet the overall picture painted by the main commentaries accommodates another motif, namely, the reality of the *dhammas.* Consider, for instance, the *Atthasalinfs* explanation of the *Dhammasangani's* distinction between the categories of *citta* and *cetasika:*

When the first of the great skilful *cittas* of the sense-sphere arises, at that time the fifty and more *dhammas* that have arisen by way of factors of *citta* are indeed ultimate constituents *(dhamma)* in the sense of self-existents *(sabhava).* There is nothing else, whether a being, or an entity, or a man or a person.

This statement alludes to the Theravada debate with the Puggalavada. As recorded in the *Kathavatthu,* the Puggalavadins claimed that 'The person is known in the sense of a real and ultimate fact.' The Theravadins emphatically refuted this claim, but in doing so they implied that only the *dhammas* are known in the sense of a real and ultimate fact. This means that the *dhammas* are not further resolvable into any other kind of underlying substrate; that they are the ultimate limits of the analysis of conscious experience. This may lead to the conclusion that within the confines of human experience there is no other actuality apart from the *dhammas*. As noted by Gethin, the force of *sabhava* in the above *Atthasalini*'s statement appears to focus not so much on the essential nature of particular *dhammas*, but on the fact that there is no being or person apart from *dhammas*; that *dhammas* alone are what exist. The *dhammas* that once used to refer to propositions, doctrines or principles, which need not be conceived of ontologically, are here acknowledged as primary existents – the ultimate constituents of one's experience. Moreover, the evidence for the very existence of each such constituent is its *sabhava*: the *sabhava* indicates that its respective *dhamma* does not depend on any other item for its existence. *Dhammas* are self-existents; this is the meaning of their upholding their *sabhava*, that is, they uphold their own-nature and thus their self-existence. This implies that not only does any given *dhamma* represent a distinct, knowable and nameable fact about the experiential world, but it also comes to represent in its own right a distinct instance of empirical occurrence that is not shared by any other *dhamma*. In this context *sabhava* may be rendered as 'own-essence'. Unlike the earlier occurrences of *sabhava* as essence in the sense of a *dhamma*'s individuator, here it acquires an ontological significance. On this line of thought the *sabhava* provides a causal account of its associated *dhamma*' s mode of being: rather than categorizing a given *dhamma* by explaining the intension of its individuality within its domain, it explains what constitutes this individuality and thus why that *dhamma* exists as a particular event, as an actual individual. It is then found to be the cause of this existence.

This idea is not an organic development or a natural outgrowth of the Nikaya mindset, or even of the early Abhidhamma. To judge from the sermons documented in the *suttas*, the Buddha never claimed that the *dhammas* are the only realities or primary existents, though some of his statements may have lent themselves to such an interpretation. In the *suttas* the Buddha's teaching is referred to either by the Buddha himself or by others as that which is 'true' and 'real' in the ultimate sense, employing such qualifiers as *bhutaµ*, *tacchaµ* or *tathaµ*. For instance, in the *Po tthapada-sutta* we find Potthapada stating that 'The ascetic Gotama teaches the path which is real and true, namely, the way things are and the way they work.' Along with the doctrinal systematization of Buddhist thought, these qualifiers came to be connected with the term *sabhava*. We have already encountered the use of *sabhava* in the sense of 'true' or 'genuine' within the context of the *Milindapañha*, where it is not yet endowed with an ontological bearing. The commentators took this denotation of *sabhava* one step further and invested it with an ontological dimension. Referring to the above statement of the *Po tthapada-sutta*, the commentary explains that *bhuta* means 'occurring according to own-nature (*sabhava*)', and that *tacchaµ* and *tathaµ* are synonyms for this. The sub-commentary then moves towards an ontological interpretation, rendering 'occurring according to own-nature' as 'existing according to ultimate individual essence'. The *Visuddhimagga* commentary also embodies the same shift towards realism and ontology. While Buddhaghosa equates *dhamma* with *sabhava* in its sense of 'own-nature', which does not necessarily have an ontological significance, the *Mahdttkd* invests this equation with ontology. *Sabhdva* is now not only an epistemological determinant of a *dhamma's* distinct nature, but also attests to the *dhamma's* real existence; it is an ontological determinant and may accordingly be rendered as individual essence at the level of ontology:

> The act of becoming *(bhavana)*, which constitutes existingness *(vijja-mdnatd)* in the ultimate sense, is essence *(bhava)*; it is with essence, thus it is an individual essence *(sabhdva)*. The meaning is that it is possible in the true sense, in the ultimate sense. For these are called *dhammas* because they bear their own individual essences.

Similarly, the *Mulatikd* on the *Dhammasangani* glosses the meaning of *sabhdva* in the compound *sabhdvarasalakkhana* as 'it is with essence, namely definite existence (*aviparitatd vijjamdnatd*)'. This compound thus means 'defining *rasa* with its existence'.

The commentators, then, first endow the final products of their analysis with the status of ultimate facts, but from this they draw the conclusion that the *dhammas* are also ultimately real existents. If the Buddha's *Dhamma* accords with how things ultimately are, if grasping his teaching means 'seeing things as they really are' *(yathdbhutadassana),* and if the *dhammas* are the building blocks of the way things ultimately are, then to know the *Dhamma* is to understand things in terms of ultimately real, that is, existing, *dhammas*. This doctrinal shift must have had several distinct stages: the phrase 'seeing things as they really are' initially indicated 'comprehending the Buddha's teaching completely', that is, fully grasping the four noble truths. Later on it gained a stronger metaphysical bearing and began to signify 'understanding how things operate' and 'what is the case'. Finally the phrase was ontologically interpreted as 'knowing what there is'.

The move towards realism and an ontological conception of *dhamma* and *sabhdva* is inextricably related to another crucial development in the commentaries, namely, the fixation of the mature theory of momentariness. We have noted that the origins of the theory of momentariness lie in the Pali canonical sources and its explicit beginning is found in the Abhidhamma texts, including the *Dhammasangani,* the *Patthdna* and the *Kathdvatthu.* Analysing the psycho-physical processes described by the *suttas* at the micro-level of their constitutive phases, the canonical Abhidhamma focuses on the *dhammas* as evanescent events. Note that at this stage the listed *dhammas* signify short-lived occurrences that come to pass on certain occasions *(samaya),* then pass away on others. Along with the introduction of the doctrine of momentariness the concept of *samaya* is gradually replaced by that of *khana,* but the temporal dimensions of the moment remain unspecified. The commentaries, however, espouse the full-fledged theory of momentariness: here, based on the threefold scheme of sub-division of a moment, each and every phenomenon is dissected into three distinct instants of origination *(uppddakkhana),* dissolution *(bhangakkhana)* and endurance *(thitikkhana).*

The establishment of the mature theory of momentariness is closely connected with the commentarial interpretation of the concept of *sabhdva* along ontological lines. As part of the reification of the *dhammas,* the *sabhdva* of any given *dhamma* comes to be seen as constitutive of a *dhamma's* endurance-moment and as the point of reference of its two other sub-moments.These instants are now understood as the phases of the actual existence of that momentary *dhamma. A dhamma* is here unequivocally assigned an ontological status and the very fact of its possession of *sabhdva* is evidence for its existence throughout the three sub-moments. This is illustrated by the commentarial definitions of the three times, namely past, present and future: 'In the triplet of "past", the word "past" means having passed beyond its own-essence, or beyond the origination-moment etc. "Future" means not yet having reached those two, and "present" means having arisen conditioned by this or that cause.' Thus, before a *dhamma* eventuates it does not yet obtain a *sabhdva* and when it ceases it is denuded of this *sabhdva.* As a present occurrence, though, while possessing its *sabhdva,* it exists as an ultimate reality and its *sabhdva* is evidence of its actual existence as such.

The *Visuddhimagga* further testifies to this doctrinal development on various occasions, as shown, for instance, in its following claim with respect to the twelve *dyatanas:*

Here all formed bases should be regarded as having no provenance and no destination. For they do not come from anywhere prior to their rise, nor do they go anywhere after their fall. On the contrary, before their rise they had no individual essence, and after their fall their individual essences are completely dissolved. And they occur without mastery [being exercisable over them] since they occur in dependence on conditions and in between the past and the future.

The *dyatanas,* then, exist as realities in between their origination and cessation moments. In this connection, Karunadasa notes that 'the kind of existence implied here is not past or future existence, but present actual and verifiable existence *(samvijjamdnatd).* This emphasis on their actuality in the present phase of time rules out any association with the Sarvastivadins' theory of tri-temporal existence.' Another evidence of the shifting ontological notion of *dhamma* and *sabhdva* is found in the *Visuddhimagga* chapter dealing with various kinds of recollections *(anussati)* as subjects of meditation. There, with reference to mindfulness of breathing, the phase of breathing in and out is explained as contemplation of impermanence. It is then observed:

Herein, the five aggregates are the impermanent. Why? Because their essence *(bhdva)* is rise and fall and change. Impermanence is the rise and fall and change in those same aggregates, or it is their non-existence after having existed; the meaning is, it is the break-up of produced aggregates through their momentary dissolution since they do not remain in the same mode.

To identify impermanence as the *bhava,* namely, the essence of conditioned *dhammas* – in this case the five aggregates – is not a new idea. The innovation is that this *bhava* of impermanence is now tied in with the theory of momen-tariness and the denotation of *dhammas* as real existents, for this imperma-nence is identified as the *dhammas'* non-existence after having existed as ultimate realities.

Commenting on this passage, the *Mahatika* repeats the idea that the five aggregates are called 'impermanent' because their essence are their emanation, cessation and continuous change. It then proclaims:

The meaning is that their individual essences (*sabhava*) have rise and fall and change. Herein, conditioned *dhammas'* arising owing to causes and conditions, their coming to be after non-existence, their acquisition of an individual self (*attalabha*), is 'rise'. Their momentary cessation when arisen is 'fall'. Their changedness due to ageing is 'change'.

That is, *sabhava* determines the rise, fall and change of the *dhammas,* and 'rise' means the phase of their actual existence as ultimate realities. The commentary even goes as far as naming this phase 'the acquisition of a self (*atta*)'. The commentary to the *Abhidhamma-matika* repeats this idea, stating that '"To arise" means to reach beyond the origination-moment etc. by having manifestation, or else to obtain a self'. Finally, the *Anutika* on the *Dhammasaðga~i* explicates the meaning of '*dhammas* arisen' thus:

The meaning of '*dhammas* arisen' is having the state of a *dhamma* that is being grasped (*gahita*), a *dhamma* that is occurring (*vattamana*). Since what is called 'an arisen *dhamma*' is that which has reached the origination-moment etc., which upholds its own-essence and is upheld according to conditions, the meaning of 'the essence of *dhammas* arisen' should be understood as having the state of being present (*paccuppannabhavo*).

The commentaries' employment of the term *sabhava* in connection with the doctrine of momentariness and subject to the *dhamma* theory assigns it new significance that is removed in spirit not only from the Buddha's 'original' teaching, but also from the early Abhidhamma.

To sum up, a close investigation into the concept of *sabhava* in relation to the *dhamma* theory shows that Buddhist thought underwent a remarkable doctrinal change. We are now in a position to observe that the difference between the earliest strata of Buddhist teaching and the canonical Abhidhamma is primarily epistemological, not ontological. It consists in the shift from a process-based to an event-based approach to the analysis of sentient experience. This shift challenged criteria for distinguishing every possible event presenting itself in consciousness and for specifying what makes it the very particular it is. Aiming at this objective, the Abhidhammikas developed the *dhamma* categorizations and, in the transitional, para-canonical texts, broached the category of *sabhava*. Ye t the early Abhidhamma *dhamma* analysis also intends to ascertain that every psycho-physical event is knowable and nameable, and that the words and concepts employed in the systematic discourse that is thus developed uniquely define their corresponding referents. In this respect the *dhamma* analysis, as we shall see in the next chapter, paves the way for conceptual realism – a worldview that is based on the notion of truth as constituted by a correspondence between our concepts and statements, on the one hand, and the features of an independent, determinate reality, on the other hand. Conceptual realism does not necessarily have implications for the status of this reality as externally existing. But to espouse such a position is to make a noteworthy move away from the earliest Buddhist teaching.

If Pali Buddhism was, in the final analysis, led into adopting metaphysical realism and introducing ontology into its framework, then these developments are the product of the later systematization of Buddhist thought that took place during the exegetical period. In the commentaries the early Abhidhamma inclination towards conceptual realism is strengthened: the developed *dhamma* theory and the doctrine of *sabhava* emerge as an abstract, atemporal discourse representational of all possible instances of encountered phenomena. The post-canonical Abhidhamma steps further away from the *suttas* and from the canonical Abhidhamma likewise, reckoning the final units of its analysis, the *dhammas*, to be the ultimate, independently existing constituents of experience. Here emerges the idea that the phenomenal world is, at bottom, a world of *dhammas qua* individuals. It may be suitable to describe this scheme an 'ontological model', but in the Buddhist context this rendition is not neatly matched by the customary meaning of ontology in Western philosophy. If the concept of *sabhava* has any onto-logical bearing, then this is markedly different from the idea of ontology as the branch of philosophy that is concerned with being and what there is. Rather, ontology here resides between the realms of psychology, soteriology and language, for the Theravadins apply the *dhamma* analysis to their investigation of consciousness as part of their sophisticated meta-psychological system.

5

Individuals Revisiting the Abhidhamma Dhamma Theory

The preceding chapters have dealt with the various doctrinal developments, refinements and shifts of emphasis undergone by the canonical and post-canonical Abhidhamma as part of the systematization of Buddhism and of its consolidation from an oral teaching to an institutionalized tradition (*sasana*). We have seen that the doctrinal transition from the Sutta mindset to the Abhidhamma worldview is best understood in terms of a change in epistemological attitude and metaphysical foundation (albeit both lines of thought belong to the category of process philosophy), and that at the hub of this change lies the question of what a *dhamma* is. While in the Sutta period the *dhammas* served as guidelines for construing sentient experience based on an anti-substantial conceptual scheme, within the Abhidhamma framework the *dhammas* emerged as particulars – distinct, evanescent constituents of experience – and were gradually assigned a growing metaphysical dimension in the form of their *sabhava*.

To grasp the significance of this metaphysical shift we must account for the philosophical motivation underlying the Abhidhamma vision as embodied in the *dhamma* theory. This, I demonstrate in this chapter, is rooted in the problem of individuation, and specifically in the Abhidhamma's attempt to individuate one's mind from the standpoint of its event metaphysics. Inspired by Peter Strawson's seminal book *Individuals*, the present chapter first explicates the concept of an individual and introduces Western philosophy's approach to the problem of individuation.

The complex problem of individuation involves several questions, two of particular relevance to the Buddhist material are the question of the intension of individuality and the question of the principle or cause of individuality. The second division of this chapter shows that the early Abhidhamma *dhamma* analysis, as presented by the *Dhammasaðga~i* and the *Vibhaðga,* focuses on the intension of the *dhammas'* individuality. I explore the philosophical meaning of a theory of categories and explain why it befits individuation of particulars. In this context I discuss the ancient Indian Grammarians' notion of categories and the Va i fesika categorial theory as sources that are likely to have interacted with the Abhidhamma *dhamma* analysis.

The third division of this chapter presents the developed, post-canonical Abhidhamma as preoccupied with the question of the principle of the *dhammas'* individuality and shows that the Theravadins broach *sabhava* as this principle. In this connection I invoke the concept of *lakkha~a* and the relation of individu-ation to definition. I then explain how the developed Abhidhamma event-based analysis of the consciousness process (*citta-vithi*), the doctrine of *sabhava* and the theory of momentariness are all interconnected and subject to the interest in the principle and the cause of the *dhammas'* individuality. Lastly, I address the Abhidhamma's individuation of *nibbana* and account for its developed fourfold *dhamma* typology.

THE PROBLEM OF INDIVIDUATION

In his book *Individuals* Strawson explores what he calls 'descriptive metaphysics', namely, that branch of metaphysics of which purpose is to describe the structure of our thought about the world in an attempt to lay bare the most general features of our conceptual scheme. This scheme, Strawson argues, is based on the category of particulars and necessitates methods of their identification as well as criteria for their individuation. By 'particulars' is meant specific persons, occurrences, material objects, places and things to whom or which a unique reference may be made by certain expressions: proper names, proper nouns, descriptive phrases beginning with the definite article and expressions compounded of these. Once the reference is understood, the particulars in question can be identified. The class of things in general that can be identified and referred to Strawson calls the class of individuals. Whenever something can be introduced into a proposition and brought under some principle of collection along with other things, that thing assumes the role of an individual, logical subject. For Strawson only some individuals are particulars: following Kant, particulars are empirical and uniquely situated within a spatio-temporal matrix in which unity is an inseparable feature of our conceptual scheme. The class of individuals is broader and embraces non-particulars: qualities, properties, propositions, numbers, relations, facts and species. The point is that we think of the world as containing particulars and of the world's history as made up of particular episodes; and we think of these particular things and occurrences as included within our common discourse, as items we can identify and about which we can talk. As Strawson puts it, particulars are the paradigm of logical subjects, or rather, 'the fundamental objects of reference'.

Particulars are therefore fundamental to our conceptual scheme, to the way we cognize and interpret encountered phenomena. This implies that particulars are effective conceptual instruments for explicating human experience: in fact, every explanation of such experience necessarily involves particulars. Drawing on these assumptions, Strawson further claims that a certain category of particulars is especially basic to our identification of other categories of particulars, namely, the category of material bodies. These basic particulars are such that 'as things are, it would not be possible to make all the identifying references which we do make to particulars of other classes unless we made identifying references to particulars of that class, whereas it would be possible to make all the identifying references we do make to particulars of that class without making identifying reference to particulars of other classes.' Strawson emphasizes that the term 'basic' is strictly taken in terms of particular identification; that he does not wish to say that non-basic particulars are in any sense less real than the basic, material ones. Ye t he does admit that it would seem 'unobjectionable' to say that basic particulars are also 'ontologically prior' to other types of particulars in our conceptual scheme. Such a concession leads to ontological reductionism that not only sees everything as reducible to basic particulars, but also holds that the former conceptual state of affairs obtains because basic particulars are the ultimate, existing 'building blocks' of reality.

Nevertheless, even in its stronger, ontological version the main thrust of a theory of particulars hinges not upon the notion of existence but of *individuation*. The reason is that in order to include a given type of particulars within our conceptual scheme and its implied ontology, and in order to say something of metaphysical significance about their existence, one must first be able to say what exactly these particulars are and what makes them so. One must know some individuating fact, or facts, other than that X was the particular being referred to. Strawson explains:

> To know an individuating fact about a particular is to know that such-and-such a thing is true of that particular and of no other particular whatever. [. . .] One who could make all his knowledge articulate would satisfy this condition for particular-identification only if he could give a description which applied uniquely to the particular in question and could non-tautologically add that the particular to which this description applied was the same as the particular being currently referred to.

The recourse to individuation is necessary because the definition question 'What does it mean to be a particular thing of that kind?' is prior to the ontolog-ical, population question 'What is there?' In proving the existence of certain particulars one has not yet made any commitment with respect to the nature of those entities. An existential proof does not involve a theory about the nature of entities of that kind, and until such a theory is given it would be impossible to determine whether or not, in establishing the existence of these items, there has been established something of true metaphysical importance. What must be shown is not just that there is such-and-such a particular, but also that it comprises a unique category that no other already admitted existent truly belongs to. What is necessary for determining this singularity, then, is a categorization of the items that constitute the empirical world. Such a categorization will consist in a theory about what it is to be a particular of any given kind (P). In the course of saying what this is, the categorial theory – in distinction from a mere characterization of particulars – will reveal how items of that kind (Ps) stand in relation to members of other kinds and whether or not the Ps are among those members of other kinds. This engenders the metaphysical convictions (i) that each and every particular has a unique nature that accounts for its individuality; (ii) that this nature determines the particular's status within our conceptual scheme and its implied ontology; and (iii) that this unique nature can be defined and communicated.

Here it should be noted that one cannot directly attribute Strawson's view of a plurality of particulars to the Abhidhamma, for the latter by no means allocate material bodies the role or the status Strawson does – a difference that essentially stems from the fact that Strawson's understanding of particulars is laden with the fundamental notion of substance, while the exemplary particulars the Abhidhamma is concerned with, namely, the *dhammas*, are psycho-physical events couched in anti-substantialist terms. Another complexity may result from the application of Strawson's idea of *basic* particulars to the Abhidhamma framework, but for the time being we shall defer the question of whether the *dhammas'* primacy is solely conceptual or perhaps also ontological until later in this chapter, after having clarified the philosophical problem of individuation and its treatment in the canonical Abhidhamma. These difficulties notwithstanding, it is primarily with respect to Strawson's recourse to individuation that I appropriate his concept of particulars.

As for individuation, this should not be conflated with identification: the question of identity consists in asking whether something can be referred to as the same thing at different times, and this is quite unlike asking what makes an object precisely what it is rather than any other. W.V.O. Quine has discussed the logical primacy of identification over existence: before we say that a so-and-so is present we must ask whether this is the same so-and-so as that and whether one such thing is present or two. He has coined this primacy 'No entity without identity'. By the same token, the logical primacy of individuation may be rendered as 'No entity without individuality'. This also calls to mind Donald Davidson's remarks on the nature of events and event-description: 'Before we enthusiastically embrace an ontology of events, we will want to think long and hard about the criteria for individuating them.'

Davidson's statement is equally applicable to whatever entities constitute the world according to one's conceptual scheme – be they substances, propositions, processes or events. I argue that the problem of individuation underlies the development of the Abhidhamma event-oriented epistemology and its later metaphysical vision of the *dhammas*. To provide a comprehensive account of human experience, the Abhidhammikas had to establish an apparatus for the individua-tion of one's mind. This is what the *dhamma* theory and its subordinate doctrine of *sabhava* are intended for.

Before we turn to the complexity of individuation, a terminological clarification is due. In what follows the term 'individuals' denotes the class of things in general that can be identified and uniquely referred to, material and immaterial alike. Whatever is individual is also singular and particular, though not necessarily vice versa. Singularity is the opposite of plurality, while individuality is the opposite of universality. Even universals are singulars, for they are not aggregates, but they are certainly not individuals. Particularity has no appropriate opposite in this context, and hence there is little advantage in distinguishing between particularity and individuality. I shall use 'individuation' to signify the process by which an individual acquires its inner constitution that renders it as such, and 'individuality' to denote this constitution. The problem of individuation, then, is concerned with individuality, with that which makes an item what it is. Individuality is often regarded as interchangeable with nature, but nature normally refers to the characteristics that are common to things of various kinds. It can be specific or generic: the specific nature consists of the characteristics that distinguish a thing from a larger group of things and make it part of a smaller such group (e.g. rationality in humans). The generic nature is shared by several species and makes their members belong to a larger group distinct from other larger groups (e.g. having a body in humans). By contrast, what sets a thing apart from all other things, including those falling with it under the same group, constitutes the thing's individuality. A consideration of X's specific nature will focus on how and in what respects X is the same as other particulars – for example, on what renders X indistinguishable from other human beings and distinguishable from non-human beings. A consideration of X's individuality will focus on how and in what ways X is unique; on what distinguishes X from any other particular, whether human or not. It is only when 'nature' is used in this less prevalent sense of 'own nature' that it may be taken as equivalent to individuality. The clusters of philosophical issues concerned with generic or specific natures are named 'the problem of universals', whereas those concerned with individuality are termed 'the problem of individuation'.

In his two volumes *Introduction to the Problem of Individuation in the Early Middle Ages* and *Individuation: An Essay on the Foundation of Metaphysics*, Jorge Gracia has provided a comprehensive investigation into the problem of individu-ation in medieval and early modern philosophical literature. The following discussion relies on these two sources.

The problem of individuation involves several questions, the most prominent of which are:

1 The intension of individuality: what it means to be this very particular and no other, what the nature of an individual is.

2 The discernibility of individuals: how we distinguish individuals, what is the cause or principle by which we become aware of an individual as an indivisible unit numerically distinct from everything else.

  The first question is logico-epistemological, for it concerns the clarification of the concept of individuality; the second question is purely epistemological, as it pertains to the conditions for the discernibility of individuals.

3 The extension of individuation: whether there are any entities that possess individuality and exactly which these are.

4 The ontological status of individuation: whether there is some distinction in reality between individuality and the individual's nature, and what the basis of that distinction is.

5 The cause or principle of individuation: what, in the internal constitution of an individual, makes it the very item it is.

This latter question should not be conflated with the issue of numerical differentiation between individuals that have many properties in common. Even if there existed just one individual, there would still arise the problem of accounting for the individuality of that single individual. The last three questions are metaphysical: they involve the description of reality and the status of individuality in it.

In Western tradition all the questions regarding the problem of individuation have been formulated within the framework of substance metaphysics and answered in view of the substance-attribute ontological model that it begets. Consider the treatment of the intension of individuation: here much effort has been put into explicating the meaning and true nature of individual substances. To apprehend what an individual is, what it means to be a particular item rather than any other, has been equated with knowing what it means to exist as an individual substance. Let us examine more closely how this idea came to pass.

THE INTENSION OF INDIVIDUALITY

What is an Individual?

It was Plato who made the distinction between universal and individual central for ontology. His answer to the question 'What is real?' denied particular, sensible objects reality in its full sense and ascribed that reality to transcendent, universal Forms. Forms (also rendered as Ideas) are the true natures all things participating in the same class have in common and in virtue of which those things are what they are. Holy things, for example, are such because they are instances of the Form Holiness. Forms alone can be the object of genuine knowledge. By contrast, the sensible particulars of everyday experience are said to imitate or copy the Forms and be knowable by mere belief or opinion. Plato relegates them to the realm of appearance, subjectivity and relativity.

In the *Philebus* Forms are said to be at once one, many and unlimitedly many: one, insofar as they are a genus; many, insofar as the genus consists of many species; and unlimitedly many insofar as the species subsumes unlimitedly many individual members. Aristotle adopts this division of things into genera, species and individuals, but rejects Plato's metaphysics of transcendent Forms and turns the Platonic priority relation between Forms and individuals on its head: he assigns the individuals an ontological priority. Although he accepts that without the universal there is no genuine knowledge, he argues that our employment of universal names does not require a corresponding universal Entity transcending the particulars in which it is instantiated. Every epistemic inquiry begins with concrete particulars of the empirical world, and seeks to account for some encountered state of affairs whose essential structure is made up of instantiations of universal natures. Hence, no universal can exist without being individualized by its inherence in this or that empirical individual: there is no Wisdom, for example, other than the wisdom instantiated in individual subjects in the everyday world. This equally applies to species and genera: neither 'animal' nor 'man' exists apart from individual animals and individual men.

Aristotle is the first to use the term 'individual' in its technical sense of a singular, particular item. This usage originated from a literal translation of the Greek word *atomon*, which had already been used to denote indivisible magnitudes. In the *Categories* Aristotle glosses 'individual' as 'that which is numerically one', in contrast to the universal, which is 'the one about the many'. The members of a genus can be divided into their species to the extent that they lack specific unity, and a species can be divided into its subjective members to the extent that they lack numerical unity. These, when distinguished according to numerical difference, are indivisible individuals. In the *Categories*, then, an individual is the indivisible, subjective part of a species. Although in this treatise Aristotle assumes the existence of individual non-substances, such as properties and quantities (e.g. the individual property of 'paleness', say, of Socrates), still he speaks of individuals as if they were the concrete particulars of ordinary experience: tables, horses, trees and human beings. He further declares that individual objects alone can be reckoned as primary substances, because they underlie everything else. Individual substance is the preponderant of the ten categories enumerated in the *Categories*, and the one that is assigned a logical, epistemological and ontological primacy. For Aristotle, then, the extension of 'individual' is restricted to a primary substance and its intension is 'an indivisible, primary substance'.

This Aristotelian notion of individual substance was adopted by Boethius (*c*.480–524 CE) and by him passed down to the medieval scholastics, whose views on this matter have been preserved in philosophical discourse to the present day. The scholastics elaborated on Aristotle's legacy, formulating a standard, fivefold definition of individuality: a substance's individuality consists in its instanti-ability, impredicability, indivisibility, numerical distinction and identity, that is, its capacity to remain the same through time and under change. If a primary substance is to be an individual then it must be unique, distinguishable and identifiable. This sense of an individual, as demonstrated by Strawson's denotation, is preserved in contemporary philosophy. It is also fundamental to the Abhidhamma *dhamma* analysis.

The main argument in this chapter is that the Abhidhamma metaphysics concerns not so much the ontological status of the *dhammas* as primary existents, but first and foremost their status as individuals. To individuate something is uniquely to distinguish it from all other things; it is to specify what that thing is by clarifying its true nature. This issue is epistemological, but it has ontological implications: the individuation of a certain item is bound up with the conditions for bringing that item, or an item of its kind, into being. On the Western, substance-attribute ontological model substances are the ultimate genera of what there is, or of what may be referred to by categorial designations, and hence the phrase 'what it is' must be a variant of the term 'substance'. It is easy to see why this would be assumed when the category of substance is assigned an ontological and epistemological primacy.

Substance metaphysics, however, is not the only possible type of metaphysics: equally tenable is a metaphysical system in which processes rather than substances best represent encountered phenomena. The problem of individuation may well ensue from such a system, though one would then ask what the nature of individual occurrences that make up experience is and what in experience individuates each such occurrence, not what the nature of a substance is or what in objects makes them substances *qua* individuals. Buddhist thought has thrived on such an anti-substantialist, processual outlook: the *dhammas* that the Buddha discusses and that the early Abhidhamma categorizes are not the Aristotelian primary substances, but mental and physical occurrences, whether processes or events. The Abhidhamma's shift from analysing human experience in terms of processes to analysing it in terms of events led to the view that each and every phenomenon is an interlocking complex of momentary, psycho-physical events that are distinguishable and identifiable. If this account of human experience is to be adequate and warranted, then it must be grounded in a theory of the nature of this experience. If *dhammic* events are individual objects of thought, the question is in what sense they are so and what makes a certain *dhamma* instance different from any other instance of its kind. The present chapter shows that the Abhidhamma *dhamma* analysis purports to establish a theory of individuation of one's mind, specifically of those events arising in the mind as it progresses along the path to awakening. Here, too, there arose a distinction between the intension and the principle of individuation. In the following sections we shall see that the early, canonical Abhidhamma is primarily concerned with the problem of the intension of individual *dhammas*, whereas the post-canonical Abhidhamma focuses on the question of the principle of the *dhammas'* individuality.

We now turn to an examination of the canonical Abhidhamma position as gleaned from the *Dhammasaðga~i* and the *Vibhaðga*.

THE CANONICAL ABHIDHAMMA AND THE INTENSION OF INDIVIDUALITY

The Dhammasakga

The *dhammas* reviewed by the *Dhammasaðga~i* always prove to be factors of *citta* in the broad sense of psycho-physical events that present themselves in one's consciousness. In fact, the term *citta* is used here in two different senses: first, as one of the eighty-one conditioned *dhammas* that is a name for the bare phenomenon of consciousness of which essential characteristic is the cognizing of an object; second, as a term for a given combination of consciousness and its accompanying mental factors. Although *citta* as bare consciousness is a single *dhamma* and a discrete category, it can never be experienced as such in its own origination moment, for, according to the Buddhist intentional model of consciousness, consciousness is always directed to some particular object. Any given consciousness moment cognizes its specific object by means of certain mental factors. *Citta,* therefore, always occurs associated with its appropriate *cetasikas*: mental factors that.perform diverse functions and that emerge and cease together with it, having the same object (either sensuous or mental) and grounded in the same sense faculty.

Any given consciousness moment – any assemblage of *citta* and *cetasika* – is divided according to various classification schemes and falls under a certain broad category of consciousness. Fixed by the post-canonical Abhidhamma, this analysis is based on the *Dhammasaðga~i*'s schema of *dhamma* analysis, particularly in its application to consciousness as prescribed in Book I, the *Cittuppadaka~da,* which for this purpose utilizes the triplet-couplet *abhidhamma-matika* and a number of other variables. At this point it would be useful to turn to the analysis of consciousness as given in the commentarial literature. From here it may be easier to approach the origin and significance of the early, canonical Abhidhamma notion of the intension of individuality.

The developed Abhidhamma system describes eighty-nine basic types of consciousness. These are divided according to various guidelines, the most fundamental of which reveals a fourfold hierarchy according to the four planes (*bhumi*) of consciousness. The first three planes are also qualified by the term *avacara* that means 'a sphere of action or movement', 'scope', or 'moving in the sphere of'. The sphere frequented is the plane of existence (also called *bhumi*) that, according to Buddhist cosmology, is designated by the name of its appropriate, characteristic sphere of consciousness, that is, the sensuous, the form and the formless consciousness spheres (*kamavacara-*, *rupavacara-* and *arupavacara-citta* respectively) that correspond with the sensuous, the form and the formless planes of existence respectively. A particular consciousness sphere encompasses those *citta* types that are typical of the corresponding plane of existence and which act in, or frequent that plane by tending to arise most often there. Although consciousness of a particular sphere is not necessarily unique to the corresponding plane (for instance, form and formless-sphere *cittas* may arise in the sensuous plane), a sphere of consciousness is typical of the plane that shares its name and the actively skilful or unskilful *citta*s of a particular sphere tend to condition rebirth into the corresponding plane of existence.

Thus at the bottom level of this hierarchy there are the fifty-four types of sensuous-sphere *citta* – a broad category characteristic of the normal state of mind of human beings, but also of other beings in the realms of the five senses, such as hell beings (*niraya*), animals, hungry ghosts (*petti-visaya*), jealous gods (*asura*) and the lower gods (*deva*). Next there are the fifteen classes of form-sphere *citta*, followed by the twelve classes of formless-sphere *citta*. Both these categories characterize the state of mind of divine beings collectively known as Brahmas, as well as of ordinary beings when attaining the five *rupajjhanas* and the four formless attainments (*arupasamapatti*). Each *jhana* is defined by way of a selection of associated mental factors called the *jhana* limbs (*jhanaðga*) that, of the variety of mental factors associated with each *jhana* consciousness, distinguish the specific *jhana* from the others and induce the process of concentration absorption (*appa~a-samadhi*). The first *jhana* contains five factors: initial directing thought, sustained thought, joy, pleasure and one-pointedness of mind (*vitakka, vicara, piti, sukha, cittass' ek'-aggata*). The four higher *jhanas* are attained by successively eliminating the grosser *jhana* factors and by refining the subtler factors through deeper concentration. The factors of *vitakka, vicara* and *piti* are removed in the second, third and fourth *jhanas* respectively, while in the fifth *jhana sukha* is replaced by equanimity (*upekkha*). The *rupajjhanas* are so called because they are normally attained while in meditation by concentrating on a material object as a contemplation device (*kasi~a*), such as the four great elements, the four colours blue, yellow, red and white, light and limited space. The four formless attainments, which allow for the further refining and stilling of the mind and are presented as essentially modifications of the fourth *jhana*, are the bases of boundless space, of boundless consciousness, of nothingness, and of neither-con-ceptualization-nor-non-conceptualization (*akasanañcayatana, viñña~añcay-atana, akiñcaññayatana, nevasaññanasaññayatana*). Finally, there are the eight kinds of supra-ordinary or transcendent (*lokuttara*) consciousness: these have *nibbana* as their object and are experienced only at the time of attaining the four paths and their respective four fruits, namely, stream-attainment (*sotapatti*), once-return (*sakadagamita*), non-return (*anagamita*) and *arahant*-ship.

This fourfold hierarchy is organized in accordance with the first triplet of the *abhidhamma-matika* into skilful (*kusala*), unskilful (*akusala*) and indeterminate/ undeclared (*abyakata*) types of *citta*. The undeclared class is twofold, comprising *cittas* that are resultant (*vipaka*) and those that are purely activity (*kiriya*). Various other variables operate within these broad categories, though not all of them are equally significant in each category. Germane to our present objective are the method by which the Abhidhamma categorizes *citta* and the status of the categories engendered. These are embodied in the categorization of sensuous sphere *citta*:

Kusala-citta The skilful sensuous-sphere *citta* is eightfold according to whether it is accompanied by and associated with happiness (*somanassa*), equanimity (*upekkha*), knowledge (*ña~a*) and instigation (*saðkharika*).

Akusala-citta Unskilful consciousness pertains to the sensuous sphere alone and is threefold according to its being rooted in greed (*lobha*), hatred (*dosa*) or delusion (*moha*). There are twelve types of unskilful *citta*: eight are rooted in greed and are distinguished according to whether they are associated with happiness or equanimity, accompanied by wrong view *(ditthi)* and instigated or uninstigated. Two types are rooted in hatred: accompanied by unhappiness *(domanassa)* and associated with aversion *(patigha),* they are distinguished according to whether they are instigated or uninstigated. The remaining two types of unskilful *citta* are rooted in delusion: accompanied by equanimity they are associated with either doubt *(vicikicchd)* or restlessness *(uddhacca).*

Vipdka-citta This is consciousness that results from previously active skilful or unskilful *citta.* At the sensuous sphere there are sixteen kinds of skilful resultant and seven kinds of unskilful resultant *citta.* These are further divided according to being either motivated ('with root-cause', *sahetuka)* or unmotivated ('without root-cause', *ahetuka).* Six *dhammas* are regarded as *hetus* in the sense of motives: greed hatred delusion and the opposites of these three, namely, non-attachment, friendliness and wisdom. Thus, a motivated resultant *citta* has greed hatred etc. as its cause, whereas an unmotivated *citta* is devoid of a *hetu* as its cause. Eight types of skilful resultant *citta* are unmotivated: these include the modalities of cognitive awareness *(cakkhuvinnana, sota-, ghana-, jivha-, kdya-* accompanied by pleasure), the mind element *(manodhatu)* that is a receiving *(sampaticchana)* consciousness, and the element of mental cognitive awareness *(manoviññdnadhdtu)* that is an appraising *(santtrana)* consciousness and can be accompanied by either happiness or equanimity. Eight kinds of skilful resultant *citta* are motivated: these parallel the unmotivated resultants, but are distinguished from them by mirroring actively skilful *citta* according to its association with feeling, knowledge and instigation. The seven unskilful resultant kinds of *citta* are unmotivated only. They mirror the respective skilful motivated resultants, except that body discrimination is here accompanied by bodily pain and the appraising consciousness is of one kind accompanied merely by equanimity

Kiriyd-citta Kiriyd is a technical term unique to the Pali Abhidhamma, and already features in the *Dhammasangani* and the *Vibhanga.* Cousins notes that the term *kiriyd* denotes a type of mentality that does not take part in the *kammic* process. *Kiriyd-citta* is a class of consciousness that is neither productive of any result in the future, and hence is not actively skilful or unskilful, nor is it resultant from previously active skilful or unskilful *citta:* it is neither *kamma* nor *vipdka.* This type of consciousness normally applies to the state of mind of the *arahant* and is 'intended to designate the spiritual sensitivity of a man of developed wisdom, who responds to every situation with appropriate activity without partiality of any kind'. There are eleven types of sensuous-sphere *kiriyd-citta.* They, too, are distinguished according to their being motivated or unmotivated. The motivated ones mirror their respective types of actively skilful *citta* and are unique to the *arahant's* mind. The unmotivated ones are essential to cognition and are experienced by all beings in ordinary consciousness: these are the *citta* that adverts to the five 'sense doors' and the *citta* that adverts to the 'mind door'. Thus there are altogether fifty-four types of sensuous-sphere consciousness.

Each of the next two broad categories of form and formless-sphere *citta* embraces skilful, resultant and *kiriya* types of consciousness. The category of skilful form-sphere consciousness includes five types of *citta,* distinguished according to the number of *jhana* factors with which they are associated. The skilful formless-sphere consciousness is divided into four types, distinguished according to their association with the four formless attainments. The form and formless-spheres resultant and *kiriya* types of consciousness correspond with their respective types of skilful *citta* (*kiriya* occuring only for *arahants*). Finally the transcendent consciousness consists of eight types of *citta:* four skilful are experienced at the time of attaining the four paths, and four resultant when attaining the respective four fruits.

The schema of eighty-nine categories of *citta* was organized by the commentarial tradition, but, like the developed *dhamma* categorization in general, is gleaned from the *Dhammasaðga~i*. Hence the principles underlying the practice of categorizing the *dhammas*, and consciousness specifically, are already found in the early Abhidhamma, if only implicitly. The *Cittuppadaka~da* of the *Dhammasaðga~i* analyses the varieties of *citta* and is structured according to the first triplet of the *abhidhamma-matika*. The first part inspects the skilful states of consciousness, the second one the unskilful states and the third one the undeclared states. On the whole, the variables operating within these three broad categories are later adopted by the commentarial tradition.

The *Dhammasaðga~i* does not enumerate all existing *dhammas*, but rather analyses those mental occurrences that appear in one's mind conditioned by one's progression along the path to awakening. Each such occurrence represents an interlocking complex of phenomena made up of the appropriate type of *citta*, a number of necessary *cetasikas* and various kinds of material phenomena. All these components must therefore be identified and distinguished. The *Cittuppadaka~da* investigates the nature of the appropriate types of consciousness and their accompanying mental factors, whereas the second division, the *Rupaka~da,* scrutinizes those material phenomena that are a species of *dhamma,* namely, *rupino dhammas*. Divisions I and II elaborate on the nature of the *dhammas* that are skilful and produce good *kamma,* those that are unskilful and produce bad *kamma,* and those that are undeclared and produce no *kamma*. This constitutes the first triplet of questions in division III, the *Nikkhepaka~da,* which further categorizes the *dhammas* by systematically exploiting the *matika*'s numerous variables. Consider, for instance, a few of the questions asked in the first chapter: 'What are the *dhammas* that are impure and defiling?' In addition to the three roots, the answer also includes 'the defilements that are associated with them, the four mental *khandhas* when these are associated with them, and whatever bodily, speech or mental act originate from them.' Other questions are: 'What are the *dhammas* that are to be abandoned by mental cultivation (*bhavana*)? And by insight?'; 'What are the *dhammas* the causes of which are to be abandoned by mental cultivation?'; 'What are the *dhammas* that are inferior, mediocre or excellent?';

'What are the *dhammas* that are bound up with what is wrong?' The lengthy list of questions multiplies the number of possible *dhamma* types almost indefinitely. These, albeit they all fall into one of the broad categories of skilful, unskilful or undeclared, differ from one another in their quality and intensity – an issue we shall immediately address. What the *Nikkhepaka~da* summarizes, then, is, the entire treatise as an inquiry into the distinctions between instances of *citta* based on the differences in their relative strength or intensity. More than 'an inquiry (not necessarily exhaustive) into the concrete, or, as one might say, the applied ethics of Buddhism', to quote C.A.F. Rhys Davids, this book is, first and foremost, soteriological: it reveals the ways in which consciousness operates and fuels its continuation into the future, and hence it is but an elucidation of the noble truths of the origin and cessation of *dukkha*.

Rather than an inventory of the *dhammas* that exist 'out there', the *Dhammasaðga~i* is, at bottom, an investigation into the constituents and workings of the mind. The *Dhammasaðga~i*'s *dhamma* typology yields a manual, as it were, of whatever objects of thought that may possibly present themselves in consciousness only on those occasions that are significant within the context of the Buddhist path to awakening and for the practice of mental cultivation. The *dhamma* analysis is therefore by no means a closed, exhaustive theory. The text does not intend to offer a final list of the actual existing *dhammas* in their totality, but account for the true nature of those basic kinds of *dhamma* that make up ordinary consciousness as opposed to the awakened mind of Buddhas and *arahants*.

As observed in Chapter 3, it was the task of the commentary to furnish the *dhamma* analysis with those *dhammas* that the *Dhammasaðga~i* had merely mentioned as 'others'. Ye t even in the *Atthasalini* the purpose is to fix all possible *types* of *dhammic* occurrences and not all possible *dhamma* tokens. It would be impossible to give a final number of the actual *dhammas* themselves, for the same *dhamma* type can vary considerably, even infinitely, so much so that it may subsume countless, phenomenologically distinct instances. The Abhidhamma texts show that the *dhamma* categorizations are merely presented as basic schemes for practical purposes of exposition. In fact, even the developed division into eighty-nine classes of *citta* is not regarded as ultimate: the post-canonical literature acknowledges an alternative schema of 121 types of *citta,* which results from a division of the transcendent *citta* into forty sub-types. The point is that the *dhamma* categorizations are not meant to be final or absolute: the tradition, from as early as the *Dhammasaðga~i* onwards, deliberately supports the proliferation of categorization schemes and the multiplication of the *dhamma* types generated by them. In the *Abhidhammavatara,* for instance, Buddhadatta proclaims that once additional variables pertaining to the sensuous sphere beyond the customary ones are taken into account, then the eight types of actively skilful *citta* can be divided into 17,280 distinct categories. It thus follows that the corresponding eight types of resultant *citta* can similarly be divided into a very large number of types.

This method is not mere scholastic proliferation: in view of the Abhidhamma pragmatic interest in mental cultivation, it emerges that the inflation of types of *citta* and the apparent openness of the *dhamma* lists are intentional and aim at the postulates of impermanence and of no-self. The *dhamma* lists are not to be read as a catalogue instructing us about the ultimate entities we would come across as inhabitants of our world. In fact, the full recitation pattern (or 'portion of recitation', *bha~a-vara*) is given only for the first type of *citta* presented and it is unclear just how many *citta* types there are, let alone how many actual *dhamma* tokens there are, for obviously there are more than the eighty-nine major *citta* types and infinitely many different *dhammas*. The *dhamma* lists should rather be meditated upon and hence revealed to act out the idea that there are no ultimate, irreducible entities, because all experienced phenomena – their constitutive *dhammas* inclusive – are always reducible to other phenomena upon which they depend for their occurrence and are always amenable to further division. As noted by Gethin, this is a reminder of the richness and subtlety of experience, as well as a challenge to perceive and investigate that richness and subtlety for oneself. By creating ever more complex divisions of *citta* and *dhamma* the Abhidhamma texts intend to avoid too fixed a view of things. The Buddha's teaching suggests that the fundamental problem of human existence results from emotionally and intellectually grasping at and fixing the world of experience. In order to put an end to this problem we have to undermine and break up the apparently solid and static world that we make up for ourselves, thus seeing it as it really is: inherently impermanent and insubstantial. This, Gethin claims, is what the Abhidhamma lists, which are born out of *vibhaðga*, 'analysis' or 'breaking up', are meant for:

> Sometimes the texts suggest the world is to be analyzed and seen in terms of the five aggregates, or the twelve sense-spheres, or the eighteen elements; sometimes in terms of wholesome, unwholesome and indeterminate dhammas [. . .] In offering these different methods the texts seem to want to remind one that when the world is broken up into parts, these parts are not to be mistaken for inert lumps; they are moving parts and what is more they are parts that continuously change their shape and colour depending on the perspective from which they are being viewed. [. . .] Try to *grasp* the world of the *Dhammasaðga~i*, or the Patthana, and it runs through one's fingers. In short, the indefinite expansions based on the *matikas* continually remind those using them that it is of the nature of things that no single way of breaking up and analyzing the world can ever be final.

The early Abhidhamma *dhamma* categorization has, however, another pressing significance that points to the very heart of the intension of individuation, namely, the question of what a *dhamma* is. The *dhamma* analysis prescribed in the *Dhammasaðga~i* is more than a mere catalogue of what *dhammas* there are according to their kinds. The attempt is not to reveal the absolute number of *dhammas* in their totality, but to know fully what goes on in the mind when one tries to train it. If the person is but the sum total of processes that makes her up, and if the consciousness process is seen as a temporal series of distinct consciousness moments, 'then when an ordinary being *(puthujjana)* is experiencing wholesome consciousness, what at that moment distinguishes him or her from an *arahant?'* This concern emanates directly from the concerns of the *Nikayas,* but differently from the Sutta worldview the Abhidhamma shifts the emphasis from asking 'How does the mind work throughout the transition from ordinary consciousness to the awakened mind?' to 'What is the nature of one's mind at every moment of that transition?' If the latter question is to be answered adequately, a condition that needs to be satisfied is that the operating *dhammas* that make up one's mind must be identifiable and distinguishable: what mental forces, what *kammic* qualities make up this process, and exactly how do they differ from one another? To answer these questions the first step would be to account for the intension of individuality, namely, for what it means to emerge as a distinct *dhamma* that presents itself in one's consciousness. This question is predominant in the early, canonical Abhidhamma.

We have seen that the Western approach to the question of the intension of individuation has been to absorb the concept of individuality completely within the all-embracing bosom of a substance, substituting 'individual substance' for 'individual'. The early Abhidhamma, by contrast, answers this question in terms of the Buddhist process-oriented approach to sentient experience. Shifting from process to event-oriented metaphysics, as well as from an empirically oriented postulate of impermanence *(anicca)* to a schematization of experience-in-time construed in terms of moments *(khanika-vdda),* the Abhidhamma focuses on the large-scale process of the path to awakening and zooming in, identifies its constitutive events. It divides the entire process into the processes operating within it, categorizes these sub-processes according to their different types and analyses each of these into the fleeting events that originate on that occasion. The *Cittuppadakanda* of the *Dhammasangani* well represents this practice.

The *Cittuppadakanda* distinguishes the *dhammic* events constituting different varieties of consciousness. Each type of *citta* is analysed by way of what the commentary calls three 'great sections' *(mahd-vdra):* the section that determines what *dhammas* contribute to the *citta* under discussion *(dhamma-vavatthdna),* the section on groups *(samgaha)* or items *(kotthasa),* and the section on emptiness *(sunnatd).* A comprehensive elaboration of all the three sections is given only in the case of the first type of skilful sense-sphere *citta.* The first section simply lists fifty-six *dhammas* that occur at a single instance of this type of consciousness: contact, feeling, apperception, volition, consciousness, applied thought, sustained thought, joy, pleasure, one-pointedness of mind and numerous other *dhammas,* ending with awareness, attention, calm, insight, exertion and balance. Then there follows a 'word-analysis' *(pada-bhdjaniya):* of each of the fifty-six *dhammas* it is asked what it is on that occasion and each is defined in its turn. At times the definition also refers to the appropriate conditions for the *dhamma's* emergence on that specific occasion. For instance, to the question 'What on that occasion is feeling?' the reply is:

The pleasing mentality, the pleasurable mentality that, on that occasion, is born of contact with the appropriate mind-consciousness element; the pleasantness, the pleasure that is experienced and has arisen from contact with thought; the pleasant, pleasurable sensation arisen from contact with thought - this, on that occasion, is feeling.

In this way all the fifty-six *dhammas* that make up the first type of sensuous-sphere *citta* are defined.

The second section classifies the fifty-six *dhammas* according to the following items: the *khandhas,* the spheres, the elements, the nutriments, the faculties, the *jhdna* factors and the path factors. Those *dhammas* that do not fall into any of the above items are reckoned as single factors. Then it is asked of each of these items what it is on that occasion and each is again analysed into its constitutive *dhamma* assemblages. Some definitions are interchangeable with those given in the first section, but in others the *dhammas* are newly expounded. To get a sense of the intricacy of these concentric levels of analysis consider, for instance, the treatment of the *khandha* of mental formations *(samkhdra)* on that occasion: this is broken down into fifty *dhammas,* some of which are not mentioned in the first section, such as the fear of sin *(ottappam),* serenity of body and mind *(kdya-, cittapassaddhi),* their wieldiness *(kdya-, cittakammahhatd)* or their fitness *(kdya-, cittapdguññatd).* This analysis is then repeated in the section on emptiness, wherein similar questions are put forward regarding each of the previous sets. Here the emphasis is laid on the idea that the type of *citta* in question is a combination of these phenomenal sets and nothing more; that there is no enduring entity underlying the *dhamma* assemblages. Gethin indicates that the various groups or sets brought out in the *kotthdsa-* and *suññatd-vdras* are directly related to the correspondences between some of the fifty-six *dhammas* given by the preceding section of word analysis. For instance, the word analysis of *vitakka* presents it both as *a jhdna* factor *(vitakka)* and a path factor *(sammd-samkappa);* one-pointedness of mind *(cittass' ekaggatd)* is seen as at once a *jhdna* factor *(cittass' ekaggatd),* a faculty *(samddhindriya),* a power *(samddhi-*

bala) and a path factor *(sammd-samddhi).* The sections on sets and on emptiness reiterate this multiplicity of aspect that the fifty-six *dhammas* possess. A consideration of the *Cittuppddakanda* treatment of the remaining seven types of skilful sensuous-sphere *citta,* as well as of the skilful form-sphere, formless-sphere and transcendent types of *citta,* reveals that the above multi-level analysis repeats in each case, yielding a copious categorization of the varieties of *citta* arising throughout the progression along the five *jhdnas* of the form sphere, the four formless attainments, and the eight paths and fruits of the transcendent consciousness. The same principles of analysis are applied to the remaining basic categories of *citta:* the unskilful, the resultant and the *kiriyd.* In what sense, then, does the early Abhidhamma *dhamma* analysis confront the question of the intension of individuality?

The pivotal point is that this analysis illustrates that any actual occurrence of consciousness consisting of an assemblage of *citta* and *cetasika* is unique. The *Dhammasangani's* repetitious question 'What is such-and-such a *dhamma* on that occasion?' is directed to the intension of the *dhammas'* individuality, that is, what a particular, individual *dhamma* is. The text shows that any moment of consciousness may be similar in many respects to some other occurrence within that series of consciousness moments, but it is not identical with any other; it is the specific result of a singular complex of conditions that can never be exactly replicated. Although all possible *dhammas* fall into a finite number of event-types, within each such category there may be infinitely many different *dhammas,* for even the same *dhamma* can vary considerably.

There are various examples of this principle. For instance, the *dhamma* of one-pointedness of mind contributes to several different types of consciousness, but on each occasion it is distinguishable from every other instance. This is how the *Dhammasaðga~i* defines this *dhamma* when it is involved in the skilful sensuous-sphere consciousness: The endurance, stability, steadfastness of mind that, on that occasion, is the absence of distraction, balance, unperturbed purposefulness, calm, the faculty and the power of concentration, right concentration – this, on that occasion, is one-pointedness of mind.

In its treatment of the section of skilful consciousness the *Atthasalini* accordingly glosses *cittass' ekaggata* as a synonym for concentration (*samadhi*). One-pointedness of mind, though, is also involved in the constitution of the unskilful types of *citta*. Just as concentration facilitates moral action, so it is essential to effective immoral action. If the mind is not distracted, the commentator remarks, the murderer's knife does not miss and the theft does not miscarry. The *Dhammasaðga~i* renders one-pointedness of mind involved in the first type of unskilful *citta* (rooted in greed, accompanied by happiness, associated with views and uninstigated) exactly as in the abovementioned case of skilful consciousness, substituting 'wrong concentration' for 'right concentration'. Nevertheless, the definition of this same *dhamma* when contributing to the eleventh type of unskilful *citta* (rooted in delusion, accompanied by equanimity and associated with doubt) is quite different: it includes 'the persistence of mind occuring on that occasion', but omits the remaining synonyms and qualifiers formerly given, 'concentration' inclusive. Buddhaghosa explains in what sense one-pointedness of mind now differs from its previously mentioned instances. He indicates that it is not always appropriate to call this *dhamma* 'faculty of concentration' (*samadhindriya*), for it is sometimes too weak to warrant that name:

> In the exposition of one-pointedness of mind, because this [*dhamma*] is weak, and because only the degree of endurance [necessary] for the occurrence of *citta* is found here, therefore one term alone, 'endurance of mind', is stated, without the terms 'stability', etc. For that reason, in the outline [of this eleventh *citta*], too, 'the faculty of concentration', etc., are not mentioned.

To broach another example of the variability of one and the same *dhamma*, the root of non-hatred (*adosa*) is equated with loving kindness (*metta*) only in some of the *citta* types in which it partakes. Non-hatred is necessarily included in all the five *jhanas*, but loving kindness involves happiness, and hence it cannot be present in the fifth *jhana*. Similarly the complete balance of mind *(tatra-majjhattata)* is reckoned as neutral feeling or equanimity *(upekkha)* only in the *fourth jhana*, although it also occurs in the first *three jhanas*. These and other examples are discussed by Gethin, but one example is particularly worth mentioning here in greater detail: the groupings of the faculties and the powers *(indriya; bald)*.

The distinction between the otherwise identical lists of faculties and powers *(saddha, viriya, sati, samadhi* and *panna)* is made with reference to their relative strength or intensity: the powers are explained as essentially the faculties made strong. Elsewhere the faculties are understood in the sense of predominance *(adhipati),* the powers in the sense of being unwavering or unshakeable *(akampiyatta).* Now this distinction - just like the entire *dhamma* categorization -makes sense only if the strength of the *dhammas* varies. It is only with regard to consciousness that has a certain strength or intensity that one can draw the distinctions the *Dhammasangani* makes. Underlying the treatise's method is the fundamental notion of what the *dhammas* really are: not static contents of the mind and certainly not substantial elements, but basic forces that collectively arise and present themselves in consciousness for a short while before they fall away to be followed by some other such assemblage of forces. *Dhammas* are the diverse capacities or capabilities of mental events, and hence in order to define what an individual *dhamma* is one must determine what it does. The distinction between different instances of the same *dhamma* is made on the grounds of some difference in the quality and intensity of the *dhamma*'s operation *(pavatti).* Actively skilful and unskilful *dhammas* produce future *kamma* and are also distinguishable by the intensity of their *kammic* outcome, but even *dhammas* that do not produce *kamma,* such as those that constitute *kiriya citta,* still operate and are distinguishable in virtue of their relative strength of operation.

In parallel with this principle, the fourth chapter of the *Cittuppadakanda* analyses the skilful types of *citta* pertaining to the first three spheres in terms of their degrees of efficacy. Each *citta* is marked off according to whether it is of low, medium or excellent efficacy and whether its dominant influence - one of the four bases of meditational success or power *(iddhi-pdda),* that is, the desire to act *(chanda),* vigour *(viriya),* thought *(citta)* or investigation *(vimamsa)* - are of low, medium or excellent strength. The commentary clarifies that this threefold gradation refers to the *citta's* relative efficacy or intensity of *kamma.* Since the analysis of skilful *citta* is a paradigm for the categorization of consciousness in general, one may assume that the same rationale is also applicable to the other broad categories of consciousness, excepting *kiriya citta.* This shows that the Theravadins regard every instance of *dhamma* as distinguishable from every other instance, even in cases where they seem to be essentially identical. If we compare an instance of one-pointedness of mind in the eleventh unskilful *citta* with its other instances in the skilful resultant sensuous-sphere *citta,* then there is no difference in this *dhamma*. Still each of these instances is phenomenologically distinguishable from the others owing to subtle *kamma*-based variations in the *dhamma*'s operation within its own series and outside of it. A certain *dhamma* instance of a given *citta* type may fulfil its capability differently from some other *dhamma* instance of the same type, so that these two *dhamma* tokens would behave as two singular, phenomenologically distinguishable events.

To summarize, the *Dhammasaðga~i* not only delineates which *dhammas* qualify for inclusion in the categorization of primitive event types, but also shows that each *dhammic* instantiation or exemplification of those event types is a unique individual and provides a method of distinguishing any such individual *dhamma* as that particular instance. Any given consciousness moment is understood as falling into a certain broad category of *citta,* the number of categories depending on how many variables are taken into account. These variables engender differences in the quality, degree and intensity of the *dhammas*' operation, by virtue of which any given *dhamma* is not only numerically distinguishable from any other, but also individually distinguishable (note that individuation should not be conflated with numerical difference). These manifold distinctions 'must be understood as in some sense inherent to the very nature of any *actual* instance of a *dhamma,* and they, in addition to spatio-temporal location, distinguish that particular instance from other instances'.

The *Dhammasaðga~i* testifies to the early Abhidhamma emphasis on the logico-epistemological question of the intension of individuation. The text repe-titiously asks: 'What is such-and-such a *dhamma* on such-and-such an occasion?' in an attempt to provide a method of defining a *dhamma*'s individuality; of stating what it means to occur as this particular event subject to a given set of conditions. As Piatigorsky remarks, '*What* was thought of or meditated upon was far more important than *how* something was thought of or meditated upon. The object of thinking prevailed over modes of thinking.'And it is this dependence of 'how' on 'what' that led to the idea that different events taking place within one and the same 'field of thinking' might have been presented to the thought of the investigator as discrete occurrences or series of occurrences. Viewed in this light, each of the three broad *citta* categories (skilful etc.) embraces several basic types of *citta* – categories themselves. These second-order categories, such as 'the first type of skilful sensuous-sphere *citta*', are designating names that refer to certain patterns or modes of occurrence by which psycho-physical events present themselves in one's mind. The events instantiated in each type of *citta* are third-order categories themselves, each of which designates a distinct type of event embracing innumerable phenomenologically distinguishable individual instances. For example, 'one-pointedness of mind' is a categorial name referring to an event of a certain kind that is instantiated in infinitely many unique instances individuated on account of some difference in their operation and efficacy.

Indeed the *Dhammasaðga~i'* s *dhamma* categorization enables one to distinguish any given *dhamma* as instantiating one of the *dhamma* types: it does so by assigning that *dhamma* a categorial name that reflects what essentially it is based on the fact that it shares the same defining characteristic that is common to all instantiations of its kind. In this respect the *dhamma* analysis works similarly to other systems of categorization. This analysis, however, is not merely a theory of types, but would be better rendered as a theory of individuals, for the concept of *dhamma* is closely related to the conceptually cognate notion of *sabhava qua* an individuator of a particular *dhamma* token. Although all possible *dhammas* fall into a finite number of categories or event types, within each such category there are countless different *dhamma* tokens, for – given the notion of *dhammas* as objects of thought and as the diverse capabilities of mental events – even the same *dhamma* can vary infinitely, because as an object of thought it would be seen as different when involved in different instances of 'rise of thought'. Piatigorsky explicates this point as follows:

One ought to be aware of a clear methodological difference between our own and Buddhist approaches to the idea of 'a different object'. For, given all varieties and variations, we would call an object 'different' because of its *objective* difference (or differences) from other objects. While from the Buddhist point of view, it would be seen as different, in principle at least, when present in *another situation of thought*, and/or *another state of consciousness* (i.e.

dharma). That is, we may say, that to an Abhidharmist, any object of another thought (or even another moment of thought) would be another object, for this mere reason.

Before we appraise the exact relation between categorization and individuation, let us review the treatment of the intension of individuation in the *Vibhaðga*.

The Vibhakga

When the *Dhammasaðga~i* and the *Vibhaðga* are considered together it emerges that the two works are mutually dependent. The *Vibhaðga*'s scope is shaped by a perspective different from the *Dhammasaðga~i*'s and includes only several of the topics that are outlined by the *abhidhamma-matika,* but it retains the same principles of *dhamma* analysis. The *Vibhaðga* contains eighteen chapters, each of which examines a different topic, in most cases by means of three modes of analysis arranged in three distinct sections: Suttanta Analysis (*bhajaniya*), Abhidhamma Analysis and Interrogation (*pañhapucchaka*) – a section that shows in detail how each of the terms used ought tc be defined within the framework of the *Dhammasakga~i*'s triplets and couplets. The list of the eighteen analyses is regarded as a separate *matika* and is based on an early Saµyutta method of compiling *sutta* material according to the following lists: (i) the five aggregates; (ii) the six sense faculties; (iii) the twelve links of the dependent co-origination formula; (iv) the four applications of awareness; (v) the four right endeavours; (vi) the four bases of success; (vii) the five faculties; (viii) the five powers; (ix) the seven factors of awakening; (x) the noble eightfold path. This meta-list is the kernel of such canonical Abhidhamma works as the *Vibhanga* and the *Dhatukatha* and is termed by modern scholarship 'the core *matika*'.

An examination of the *Vibhanga's* core *matika* reveals that the text inquires into the processes that make up an ordinary mind vis-à-vis an awakened mind: *vibhangas* 1-6 deal with the processes that bind one to *samsdra,* while *vibhangas* 7-16 analyse the skilful processes that liberate one, with the last two *vibhangas* revisiting miscellaneous topics that have implicitly arisen in the preceding sections. Much of the *Vibhanga's* material assumes the *Dhammasanganis* method: the Interrogation sections employ the triplet-couplet *matika* in their *dhamma* analysis and the

Abhidhamma Analysis sections closely follow the *Dhammasangani's* structure, asking of each phenomenon or process what it is then dissecting it into its operating *dhammas.* Each such analysis yields a definition of the process in question, specifying what mental forces and qualities constitute it, the nature of these mental forces and qualities, and the conditions for their emergence. Moreover, the Abhidhamma Analysis sections draw on the *Dhammasangani's citta* categorization. This is evidenced in the sixth *vibhanga,* which opens with a *matika* indicating 144 variations of the dependent co-origination formula, built up systematically around sixteen basic variations, each of which is further subject to nine variations. The subsequent exposition then applies each variation in turn to the various *citta* types as given in the *Cittuppadakanda.*

The *Dhammasangani* equally assumes the *Vibhanga* core *matika,* especially in the sections on sets and emptiness, which derive their *dhamma* groupings from the core *matika.* Gethin has observed that the *Dhammasangani* treats the core *matika* in terms of the *abhidhamma-matika,* whereas the *Vibhanga* treats the *abhidhamma-matika* in terms of the core *matika.* The Abhidhamma method is thus informed by the interaction of the two lists. This textual exchange, though, also reflects the early Abhidhamma preoccupation with the intension of the *dhammas'* individuality. The following representative case, whose principles feature throughout the *Vibhanga's* Abhidhamma Analysis sections, buttresses this claim.

The Abhidhamma analysis of the aggregate of consciousness *(vinnana)* presents it in its various aspects according to numerical arrangement. The aggregate of consciousness is said to be singlefold as associated with sense contact; twofold as accompanied or not accompanied by a root; threefold as skilful, unskilful and neither-skilful-nor-unskilful; fourfold as belonging to the four spheres; fivefold as associated with the five controlling feeling faculties; sixfold as the six modalities of cognitive awareness; sevenfold as the first five modalities of cognitive awareness plus the element of mental cognitive awareness (mind-consciousness-element) and the mind-element; eightfold when adding to the above tactile cognitive awareness accompanied by pleasure and pain; ninefold when instead adding the element of mental cognitive awareness that is skilful, unskilful and neither-skilful-nor-unskilful; and tenfold when combining the last two divisions. Then there follows a lengthy series of intricate variations on the above numerical divisions, the majority of which are based on the triplet-couplet *abhidhamma-matika*. For instance, when analysed with reference to the couplets, the aggregate of consciousness turns out to be twofold in many respects: as associated with or dissociated from a root; as that which is not a root but is accompanied by a root; as that which is neither a root nor accompanied by a root; as ordinary and transcendent; as the object of the attaching dispositions (*asava*) or that which is not their object; as associated with or dissociated from the defilements; as that which is dissociated from the defilements but is their object, and so on and so forth. These elaborations become even more complex once additional variables are taken into account. The aggregate of consciousness is found to be twentyfold, then thirtyfold, and eventually simply 'manifold', wherein it is not clear how many distinguishable varieties it possesses.

Not only does the *Vibhaðga* employ the same principles as the *Dhammasaðga~i dhamma* analysis, but it also hovers over the question we have previously identified as intrinsic to the *Dhammasaðga~i*. The *Vibhaðga,* too, seeks to account for the ordinary mind as opposed to the *arahant*'s awakened mind. It therefore sets up a manual of the events occuring in one's consciousness when one follows the path to awakening: from ordinary, unawakened mind to a critical point where 'waking up' is understood to be near, so that it is only a matter of time until the occurrence of final, perfect awakening. The *Vibhaðga*'s *dhamma* lists are, again, expository categorizations of mental and physical events. They illustrate that an essentially the same *dhamma* is, in fact, a category of event of a certain kind, marked by the diversity of its innumerable instances. Like the *Dhammasaðga~i*, the *Vibhaðga* focuses on the intension of a *dhamma*'s individuality. It is structured around the question 'What is such-and-such a *dhamma*?' and prescribes a method of explicating what it means to originate as this particular event rather than any other, either of the same type or of other types.

In summary, the early Abhidhamma account of the intension of the *dhammas*' individuality is a categorial theory that enables its users to distinguish and define any given *dhamma* taken to be significant for mental cultivation. So far I have stressed that this concern is logico-epistemological and follows directly from the

Nikayas. Ye t the Abhidhammikas invest it with a metaphysical vision that paves the way for conceptual realism and leads to a significant move away from the Sutta worldview. Conceptual realism presupposes that we are, by and large, capable of understanding the world, and that the notion of truth consists in a correspondence between our concepts and statements, on the one hand, and the features of a determinate reality, on the other hand. The Abhidhamma's undertaking of the *dhammas'* individuation is not concerned with the ontological status of any external reality, although it does have implications for the reality of those *dhammas*, since it assumes that every *dhamma* is necessarily an individual of a kind and is not further resolvable into any other kind of thing; that the *dhammas* are the ultimate limits of the analysis of experience. The Abhidhamma categorial theory distinguishes the different ways in which we can call up the *dhammas* as subsistent individuals for discussion. Moreover, it assumes that every *dhammic* event occuring in one's consciousness is knowable and nameable. This conceptual realism with regard to individual *dhammas* implies realism with regard to their kinds – *dhammas* are the only kinds of thing there are and each kind is signified by a categorial designation, a concept of a distinct sort or kind of individuals.

In adopting this position the early Abhidhamma is likely to have been influenced by the contemporary Brahmanical schools, the Nyaya-Vaifesika specifically. This requires us to survey the philosophical significance of categories, their exact relation to the problem of individuation and their construal in the contemporary Indian philosophical milieu. To these issues we now turn.

THE CANONICAL DHAMMA ANALYSIS AS A CATEGORIAL THEORY OF INDIVIDUALS

On Categories and Categorizations

If something is to be a distinguishable individual then its proper nature must be determined. To establish the nature of a particular individual one must, first, ascertain that things of its kind, and only they, compose a unique category, and second, distinguish within that category the individual from other members of its kind. What is required, then, is a categorial theory of the particulars constituting the domain in question, be it the empirical world or one's consciousness. But how does a categorization differ from classification and why is it an appropriate means for individuation?

Aristotle was the first to have used the term 'category' in the sense of an ultimate genus's name (e.g. 'quantity'), or of what that name signifies, that is, the ultimate kinds of being. To elucidate the meaning of Aristotle's categories it has become customary to turn to an early treatise within the *Organon*, which, by its very title, *Categories*, seems to unfold this matter. The treatise opens by presenting a list of ten categories: substance, quantity, quality, relation, place, time, position, state (possessing or having), activity and passivity. Although Aristotle's doctrine of categories is ubiquitous in his writings, nowhere does he attempt to justify these ten categories – a vacuum that has led generations of scholars into offering logical, grammatical and metaphysical interpretations of their nature.

It is generally accepted that Aristotle's doctrine of the categories concerns the question 'What is being?', that it aims at providing a systematic account of the fundamental kinds or modes of being, and that it sorts out every existent into one such irreducible kind. Commentators tend to identify the categories with the types enumerated, but the categories may also be the truth conditions for basic assertions (ways of being true about something), or else classes of categorial expressions signifying the various items grouped under such headings as 'substance', 'quality' or 'quantity'. It is also possible that the categories are not classes at all, either of entities or of expressions, but predicates that apply to either of them. The latter suggestion is supported by the fact that the doctrine of the categories is supplemented with a semantic theory. This has to be so, because being is thinkable only when it manifests itself in language. The sole possible definition of being that Aristotle offers in the *Metaphysics* is, accordingly, the observation that 'being can be said in many ways' and 'in many senses'. The *Categories* prescribes the different ways of calling up subsistent beings for discussion by assigning them predicates; the basic ways of saying something about any given object according to its diverse modes of *being expressed* by a cat-egorial designation. A thing's different categorial names bring it up in capacities that may each be distinguished in one and the same subsistent thing. We may refer to an object, for instance, by saying that it is a substance (e.g. a tree), a quality of something (green), a quantity of something (the size of two feet), etc. Still any reference thus made is always to a substance, and hence categorization brings together language and ontology.

In the *Categories* Aristotle presents a fourfold semantic diagram of 'the things named': individual substances (e.g. 'this man'), individual non-substances (properties and quantities, for example, Socrates's being pale), general substances (species and genera, the kinds into which subjects fall) and general properties (e.g. the generic name 'knowledge'). Aristotle, though, withholds ontological status from non-substantial universals and at the *Metaphysics* VII even claims that genera and species, namely, substantial universals, do not exist apart from indi-viduals. Hence the *Categories'* underlying semantics can be accommodated by a world of individuals only, for the above division of things is reducible to two types of existents: individual substances and individual non-substances. To be an item in a category is, in the first instance, to be an individual: a non-recurrent particular, whether substantial or non-substantial. Moreover, since the investigation into substance is centred on the population of primary substances, the world of the *Categories* is essentially a world of concrete, sensible particulars.

Now it is impossible to pin down an individual by progressively specifying its properties, for properties are, by definition, general: they can apply to an indefinitely large number of individual instances. To ascribe a property to a thing is to classify it by its comparison with other similar things. A class subsumes members that are characterized by some similarity in respect of which they fall under that same class (e.g. 'table', 'sparrow'), and it is therefore unnecessary to observe each individual in a class. The characteristics that distinguish a thing from a larger group of things and make it part of a smaller such group construct its specific nature. But the specific nature is not an individuator: it is always a contingent fact that the complete set of a thing's properties will be sufficient to individuate it. We have no conclusive assurance that any group of properties has one, and only one, instance, let alone that every set of all the properties of some individual has that individual as its unique instance. Classification is thus incompatible with a statement of uniqueness. Rather, the class concept is adequate to account for plurality and diversity; it amounts to a unification in terms of some common nature, to an ordering of things that fall into it in their totality. The totality formulas of the *khandha, ayatana* and *dhatu* are, for this reason, classifications: they sort out all the *dhammas* in their totality into three groups, each of which is characterized by the *tisaðkhatalakkha~a*. If one's purpose, however, is to account for a thing's individuality, then one would have to provide a categorial theory of that type of thing, not totality formulas and classifications. This is why the Abhidhammikas needed the *dhamma* categorizations and, later on, the developed fourfold *dhamma* typology. Motivated not only by a concern with the totality of what there is, but also by an interest in the individuality of each and every *dhammic* instance in one's consciousness, they had to account for what an individual *dhamma* is, and for this purpose the extant totality formulas were found to be wanting.

By contrast to the class concept, the category concept allows one to explain singularity. Whereas the members of a class are marked by a specific nature they all have in common, a category embraces diverse items that display the same pattern of affirmation, or the same mode of being, though each is distinguishable on account of its own particular nature. One prevailing approach to offeing a cate-gorial theory of individuals in Western scholastic philosophy is called 'the blueprint approach'. On this approach, the categorization of an individual substance within the complex makeup of things is reached by providing a blueprint for bringing that individual, or an individual of its kind, into being. Just as a recipe in a cookery book lists ingredients and their modes of combination, so the blueprint for an individual substance would account for the constituents of that item and the modes of unification whereby those constituents encompass a distinct kind, a category.

Our exploration of the *Dhammasaðga~i* and the *Vibhaðga* reveals that when confronted with the question of the *dhammas'* individuality the early Abhidhamma, too, developed a categorial theory. This theory lends itself to interpretation in accordance with the blueprint approach to individuation, though with one significant exception: it is rooted in a process-based, event metaphysics and is subject to the Abhidhamma soteriological constraints. It does not provide a blueprint for bringing into being enduring individual substances, but rather for the occurrence of evanescent individual events in one's consciousness. The *dhamma* categories are therefore names designating 'modes of rise', or 'modes of occurrence' that may proceed at different levels of generality: they may account for each *dhamma* type that originates (e.g. what the origination of one-pointedness of mind means), or else for particular individuals (e.g. what it is for a particular instance of one-pointedness of mind to partake in the first type of skilful sensuous-sphere *citta*). The *Dhammasaðga~i* and the *Vibhaðga* prescribe a method of distinguishing any given *dhamma* according to its modes of being expressed by a categorial designation. Here, too, the same *dhamma* may be brought up by different categorial names, and these indicate diverse capacities – unique *kammic* qualities and intensities – that distinguish any instance of that *dhamma* from any other instance of the same kind.

The Abhidhamma notions of the *dhammas'* categorization and individuation were developed in an Indian philosophical milieu: they were probably moulded by intellectual exchange with the Sarvastivadins and the Brahmanical schools, specifically the Grammarians and the Nyaya-Vaifesika. We shall now look in this direction.

CATEGORIES IN INDIAN PHILOSOPHY

The Linguistic Origins of Categories

The Vaisesika set up the most inclusive categorial system in classical Indian metaphysical discourse, but the idea of categorization and the term *padartha,* the Sanskrit rendering for 'category', date as early as the ancient Grammarians' (Vaiyyakaranas) analyses of language into its various components. *Padartha* literally denotes a referent, that which stands for the meaning of a word but it also signifies a predicament, that is, the character or status assigned by a predication, and within classical Nyaya framework, a basic issue or a topic of discourse; sixteen such topics are enumerated at the beginning of the *Nyayasutra*. In discussing the etymology of Vedic words, Yaska's *Nirukta* (fifth century BCE?) presents a fourfold categorization of the parts of speech *(pada)* into nominal words *(nama),* verbs *(akhyata),* prefixes *(upasarga)* and particles *(nipata).* The term *padartha* features in this early text on one occasion: the context is an analysis of prefixes, wherein the Grammarian Gargya is quoted as saying that prefixes have various different referents *(padartha).* It is then explained that the change in the meaning of the noun or the verb to which prefixes conjoin is the referent inhering in those prefixes and which they utter. Yaska, however, does not identify the ultimate meaningful constituents of Sanskrit - a task left to the later Grammarians, foremost of whom is Panini.

Sutra 1.2.45 in Panini's *Astadhyayi* recognizes three meaningful linguistic entities: verbal roots *(dhatu),* nominal stems *(pratipadika)* and affixes *(pratyaya).* Taking 'stem' to refer to both verbal roots and nominal stems, this means that for Panini only stems and affixes have meaning, while words and sentences have at best meanings that are derived from these constituents. In contradistinction to Panini, Patañjali, in the first *Ahnika* of the *Mahabhasya* (second century BCE), embraces Yaska's categorization of the parts of speech as prescribing the ultimate meaningful linguistic constituents, proclaiming that 'Words are fourfold only. The four kinds of word are noun, verb, prefix and particle.' In the second *Ahnika,* though, Patañjali presents a different fourfold typology of words according to their referent: (i) words that refer to arbitrary proper nouns *(yadrcchasabda);* (ii) words that refer to an attribute or quality *(gunasabda);* (iii) words that refer to an action or motion *(kriyasabda);* and (iv) words that refer to a genus or generic property *(jatisabda).* Whatever is meaningfully expressible falls into one of these four categories. Significant for our present interest is the fact that categorization of words from the point of view of their referents would necessarily have relevance not only to semantics but also to ontology. This connection between semantics and ontology as embodied in a categorial theory becomes apparent from the time of Patañjali onwards.

To begin with the first category, Patañjali distinguishes two possible referents of proper nouns: generic form, or configuration *(akrti),* and individual substance *(dravya).* This distinction is found in his discussion of part of a *varttika* in the first *Ahnika,* which reads *siddhe sabdarthasambandhe.* Analysing this as *siddhe sabde 'rthe sambandhe ca* and rendering *siddha* as 'eternal' *(nitya),* Patañjali glosses the compound in the *varttika* as stating that a word its referent and the relation between the two are eternal. To be eternal, he continues, the referent would have to be a generic configuration, not an individual substance. The latter is perishable, but the *akrti* is common to many individuals, and hence even though it may be destroyed with one individual, it continues to exist in others. In tandem with this statement, however, Patañjali proclaims that *dravya* in the sense of substrate, or the stuff out of which a thing is made, can also be considered eternal: the shape of a lump of gold for example, may be altered in various ways into a variety of jewels, but the gold itself remains the same. Hence he settles on neither *akrti* nor *dravya* as the exclusive meaning of a word. Patañjali considers *akrti* and *jdti* synonymous: preceding his commentary on the abovementioned *varttika* is a passage in which he ascribes to Panini the idea that a word's referent may be both a generic form and an individual substance, and where he uses *akrti* and *jdti* interchangeably. The two terms, though, do not yet denote a universal in the sense of an abstract entity or a class-notion that makes up various particulars members of a single class, but rather the visible form by which the members of a class are recognized.

The term *dravya* has its own history of semantic intricacy. Narain remarks that in Panini's *Astadhyayi* the term *dravya,* on one of its three occurrences *(sutra* 5.4.11), denotes substance, but that the latter concept is also expressed by such terms as *sattva, adhikarana* and *bandhu.* It is a different *sutra,* though, that may clarify Panini's and the later Grammarians' apprehension of *dravya* in the sense of substance. As Matilal observes, Helaraja, Bhartrhari's commentator (*c.* tenth century CE), claims that in order to understand the Grammarians' notion of substance it is necessary to analyse Panini's rule prescribing *ekasesa (sutra* 1.2.64). *Ekasesa* is a grammatical operator by which two or more words refering to two or more substances are reduced to one word in its dual or plural inflection as appropriate. In his *Varttika,* Katyayana (third century BCE?) comments that Panini's prescribing this *ekasesa* operation is motivated by the idea that each nominal word is a proper name or a singular term refering to one individual substance at a time. A substance, then, is that which is distinguishable by its nominal signifier.

Moving on to thè *Mahabhasya,* here, referring to conceptual developments in the early, scarcely documented history of the philosophical systems and summarizing centuries of earlier debates in the history of Indian theories of language, Patañjali is aware of different senses of both *dravya* and *akrti* as well as of corresponding variations in the relationship between these two terms. On the one hand he recognizes *dravya* as substance *qua* the substratum *(adhikarana)* of attributes, that in which attributes inhere; it is the underlying stuff, the shapeless -albeit determinate - material of which things are made, while *akrti* here means the particular and transitory form such material may assume. On the other hand he employs *dravya* as a substance in the sense of an individual: a particular, concrete entity that has its generic identity or class membership owing to a permanent generic form *(akrti)* intrinsic to it. For Patañjali's linguistic and semantic approach, this second sense of substance is more significant and he attempts to explain it in various ways. First, by attribute he primarily intends the sensory qualities (colour, sound, taste etc.), and defines substance as what is essentially different from these qualities. On another occasion he refers to substance as a bundle of attributes (*gu~asamudaya*); a conglomeration or assemblage of qualities. According to a third definition substance is the permanent, enduring core of things: while attributes emerge and disappear, substance is what remains unchangeable; it does not lose its essence (*tattvaµ*), that is, its being (*bhava*), when different attributes come to be associated with it. Interestingly, this definition suggests that what Patañjali intends by substance as an individual is, in fact, *svabhava qua* own-nature; that which is unique to a particular individual and accounts for its peculiarities (as opposed to *jati*); what makes it distinguishable from any other individual, either of the same or of a different kind. I argue below that while the Vaifesika doctrine of categories is coloured by the Vaifesika apprehension of substance in the sense of a substratum, the Abhidhamma *dhamma* categorization places at the forefront the concepts of individual and of *svabhava,* albeit these are subject to the Buddhist postulate of impermanence and to its anti-substance metaphysics.

As for the remaining two linguistic categories, Patañjali's most comprehensive definition of *gu~a* or attribute is found in two verses that read thus: 'Attribute is what abides in substance (*sattva*), perishes, is to be found in a variety of genera, is a predicate, is not produced by action, and is essentially different from substance.' The category of *kriya*, or action, is explicated with reference to its instantiation in activity (*iha*), movement (*cesta*) and operation or exertion (*vyapar a*).

The tradition of grammatical thought as documented in the *Mahabhasya* provides significant counterparts for Vaifesika metaphysics: as we shall see presently, each of Patañjali's four categories of the meaningful parts of speech has its analogue in the Vaifesika categorial theory. Ye t despite its grammatical correlations and linguistic implications, the Vaifesika theory is not a grammatical or linguistic theory, and the school's approach to categorization is remarkably different from the *Mahabhasya*'s . Our present concern, though, is with the interrelations between the origins of the Vaifesika metaphysical categorial theory and the Abhidhamma *dhamma* theory. As this relation may have sprung from, or at least been mediated by linguistic and grammatical circles, let us now consider the doctrinal exchange between Buddhist thought and early Indian theories of language.

Bronkhorst adduces textual evidence of Patañjali's acquaintance with Buddhist doctrine, and even suggests that Patañjali may have borrowed his philosophical ideas about the nature of composite linguistic units and their ontological status from the canonical Sarvastivada. First, he points to *Mahabhasya* passages which attest to Patañjali's familiarity with the Buddhist postulate of impermanence and its later elaboration in the form of the doctrine of momentariness. For instance, a passage in the commentary to Pa. 4.1. reads as follows: 'Activity is constant, for nothing in this world remains in its own identity even for a moment. Either it rises for as long as it should rise, or it is destroyed.'

Second, Bronkhorst discusses the possibility that Patañjali's understanding of the nature of linguistic entities relies on the Sarvastivadin notion of linguistic *dharmas*. We have already come across Patañjali's analysis of the *varttika* that reads *siddhe fabdarthasaμbandhe*, where he concludes that a word, its referent or denoted object, and the relation between the two are eternal, thus implying that a word is an independently existing, eternal entity. Patañjali also acknowledges two sorts of linguistic entity, namely, *var~asaμghata* and *padasaμghata*, but it is not clear which of the two designates a word. Discussing the single *Mahabhasya* passage in which the expression *padasaµghata* is used, Bronkhorst mentions the conventional interpretation that *padasaµghata* means 'a collection of words', but then introduces an alternative interpretation: *padasaµghata* is a non-technical synonym of *pada* used primarily by non-grammatical circles, and which Patañjali employs in the sense of a single word as an indivisible entity. On this assumption *var~asaµghata* would refer to a single speech sound conceived of as a single, indivisible entity; what collects sounds, uniting all the constituent elements of a single sound so as to form one sound. A correct interpretation of *var~asaµghata* and *padasaµghata*, Bronkhorst suggests, could be gleaned by examining the canonical Sarvastivadin linguistic *dharmas:* specifically *vyañjanakaya* and *padakaya/namakaya*. These are subsumed under the Sarvastivadin category of 'factors dissociated from thought' (*citta-viprayuktasaµskar a*), and initially named single sounds and single words conceived of as single, indivisible, existing – albeit momentary – entities. The Sarvastivadin doctrine of momentariness implied that words and sounds, because they are extended in time, could not have real existence. The Sarvastivadins solved this problem by postulating that words and sounds had real existence as separate, linguistic *dharmas*. Assuming that Patañjali's *var~asaµghata* and *padasaµghata,* on the one hand, and the Sarvastivadins' *vyañjanakaya* and *padakaya,* on the other hand, are related concepts, it is difficult to determine who borrowed from whom, and chronological considerations cannot provide any conclusive answer. Ye t since *var~asaµghata* and *padasaµghata* play no role in Patañjali's discussions and are introduced as examples only, and because they represent a concern with ontological questions which do not otherwise characterize Patañjali's work, Bronkhorst concludes that Patañjali derived his ideas concerning *var~asaµghata* and *padasaµghata* from the Sarvastivadins. This derivation, though, was probably indirect, which may explain the differences between Patañjali's and the Sarvastivadin Buddhists' views, foremost of which is the fact that for Patañjali the word is eternal, for the Buddhists momentary.

Another issue indicative of the doctrinal interrelation between Patañjali and the Sarvastivadins, which we shall here note only in brief, is the resemblance between the Sarvastivadin notion of *dharma* as *dravya* and Patañjali's understanding of *dravya* as an individual substance (excepting the latter's eternality): a particular, concrete entity which keeps its distinctive identity through change and has its attributes and qualities. Moreover, this notion is reminiscent of Patañjali's distinction between *sphota* and *dhvani:* a word or phoneme (*fabda*) is *sphota,* that is, a permanent, independently existing entity, whereas sound *dhvani,* is that word's actual, ephemeral and changing manifestation when uttered; it is the *sabda's* quality. The idea is that the variability due to utterance by different speakers under different circumstances belongs to the audible part of speech, while *sphota* is the invariable sound-pattern, what remains constant and unaffected. Patañjali, then, acknowledges an independently existing word-entity, an essence-possessing substance distinct from the changing 'noise' that characterizes it when uttered on different occasions.

Our present concern, though, is with the Theravadin Abhidhamma. The affinity between the Grammarians' ideas and the Abhidhamma is subtler than that between the former and the Sarvastivada-Vaibhasika, and was probably transmitted into the Pali texts via Sarvastivadin sources. One notable example of this intellectual exchange, already discussed by P.S. Jaini, is the correspondence between the Vaibhasika *samskdra* of *namakaya* and the Theravadin *dhamma* called *namapannatti.* The term *paññatti,* which we may provisionally render as 'concept', features in the Pali *suttas* with reference to designations, names or concepts that are themselves unreal albeit used in everyday discourse. The idea of *pannatti* is further developed in the canonical Abhidhamma. *Pannatti* forms one of the *abhidhamma-matika* couplets and is defined in the *Dhammasangani* as follows:

> What are the *dhammas* that are *paññatti?* A definition, a designation, a concept, a current term, a name, a denomination, the assigning of a name, a manner of speaking, a letter, a phrasing on this or that *dhamma* -these *dhammas are pannatti.* All *dhammas* are nameable.

The commentary elaborates on this salient closing point:

> One single *dhamma* encompasses all *dhammas,* and all *dhammas* fall into one *dhamma.* How so? This *ndmapaññatti* is a singular category encompassing all *dhammas* belonging to the four spheres. There is no being, no conditioned phenomenon that may not be designated by a name.

This is remarkable evidence of the conceptual realism creeping into early Abhidhamma framework. Conceptually, *dhammas* are the ultimate units of categorization, analysis and distinction of experience, so that each and every phenomenal occurrence, each *dhammic* event, is knowable and nameable: it is regarded as a discernible object of knowledge and assigned a unique name expressing its proper nature. This notion would pave the way for metaphysical realism, whereby *dhammas* alone are what ultimately exists, and rather similarly to Leibniz's monadology, to have primary existence is to be the bearer of a singular definition; to be uniquely describable and differentiated from any other entity. The Abhidhamma tendency for conceptual realism points to the Nyaya-Vaisesika, according to which system all objects are characterized by existence, knowability and nameability, as a source of doctrinal influence, although such influence may have been mediated by the Sarvastivada-Vaibhasika. Let us now turn to the Vaisesika categorial theory.

The Developed Indian Categorial Theory: the Vaisesika

We have already referred to the Vaisesika atomistic theory and to the list of categories *(padartha)* presented at the opening of the *Vaisesikasutra:* substance *(dravya),* attribute or quality instances *(guna),* motion or action-moments *(karma),* universal *(sdmdnya),* individuator *(visesa)* and inherence *(samavdya).* In the *Vaisesikasutra* the enumeration of all substances, attributes and motions precedes the definitions of these three categories - a structure that, as Halbfass notes, attests to the Vaisesika's cosmologically and ontologically oriented approach to categories, which is markedly different from Patañjali's linguistic approach.

We have also come across the significance of the majority of these categories throughout this study, for they concur with the fundamentals of the substance-attribute ontological model as previously explained. The Vaisesika ontology is rooted in a substance metaphysics that, conjointly with a realist outlook, engenders a plurality of independently existing particulars. The Vaisesika system lists the ultimately existing substances, incorporating them - both in their permanent form as eternal, indivisible atoms *(paramdnu)* and as impermanent, destructible compounds of atoms - in a more comprehensive enumeration of types of entities, namely, the six *paddrthas.*

The first *padartha,* substance, is ninefold embracing earth, water, fire, air, ether *(dkdsam),* time, space, self *(dtman)* and mind *(manas).* The first four are primary, material, elemental substances: they consist of irreducible, invisible and permanent atoms *(paramdnu).* The encountered world in its entirety is made up of composite substances, that is, imperishable compounds of atoms that conglomerate and separate but in themselves remain permanent. Thus the identity of a substance through time is based on the identity of its constitutive atoms. Ether, space, time and self are immaterial, that is, non-atomic, unitary, all-pervasive, indestructible substances and a receptacle for material phenomena. The self, of which there is a plurality, is permanent and eternally existing. Mind countless, infinitely small atoms of which populate the world is considered as an unconscious instrument transmitting perception to the self, albeit being distinct from it. Mind is deemed material, although its atoms do not combine to produce composite substances as the other physical substances do. Substance is next defined as that in which attribute and motion inhere and as the common cause of substance, attribute and motion, that is, of all constructed phenomena.

The number of attributes varies slightly in different texts. Prasastapada's classical list includes twenty-five attributes, of which the following ten are *murtaguna* inhering in material substances: colour *(rupa),* taste *(rasa),* odour *(gandha),* touch *(sparsa),* proximity *(paratva)* and distance *(aparatva)* - (priority and posteriority in space and time), gravity *(gurutva),* fluidity *(dravatva),* viscidity *(sneha)* and speed *(vega).* Ten *amurtaguna* inhere in immaterial substances: intellect *(buddhi),* pleasure *(sukha),* pain *(duhkha),* desire *(iccha),* aversion *(dvesa),* endeavour or volitional disposition *(prayatna),* merit *(dharma),* demerit *(adharma),* effect or ability *(bhavana)* and sound *(sabda).* The remaining five *ubhayaguna* inhere in both material and immaterial substances: number *(samkhya),* dimension *(parimana),* separateness *(prthaktva),* conjunction *(samyoga)* and disjunction *(vibhagd).* Attribute is defined as that which inheres in a substance, possesses no attributes itself, and is not the cause of conjunctions and disjunctions because of its being dissociated from them. It is a property-particular, such as a particular shade of green colour that by its inherence in one substance is distinct from the green contained in another. Since substances in themselves have nothing that allows their discrimination, attributes enable us to classify substances into kinds and to differentiate them as numerically distinct particulars. Some attributes inhere in one individual substance but some, such as conjunction and number, may inhere in several entities jointly and simultaneously.

Motion or action is of five types: moving upwards, moving downwards, contraction, expansion and simple locomotion. It exists momentarily and inheres in material substances alone. Each action-moment inheres exclusively in one substance, does not itself possess attributes, and is the constitutive cause of conjunctions and disjunctions. The category of action furnishes the basis for the changing object: the only changes in the cosmos are changes in the arrangements and the positions of attributes and of atoms, and it is action by virtue of which atoms and their assemblages adhere together and rearrange. Hence action is significant in the causal mechanism of conjunctions and disjunctions - two attributes that, in turn, are crucial to the explanation of qualitative change. Unlike attributes that are static (albeit not necessarily permanent or coeval with their substrates), motion is dynamic and momentary. Yet attribute and action alike are particulars endowed with an ontological status, although they exist as individual realities only insofar as they inhere in substances.

Inherence is a relation of two distinguishable entities that cannot occur separately. Being a relation of container to contained it also indicates an order of dependence: the contained provides unity and identity, the container the reality of the entity. Unlike the relations of conjunction and disjunction, inherence is permanent. It is essential both to the organization of the Vaisesika categories and to the ontological priority of substance, for it is the one omnipresent principle that accounts for the fact that the encountered world is a world of concrete objects rather than of isolated constituents.

The fully developed Vaisesika view of universals is that they are real, independent, timeless and ubiquitous entities which inhere in a plurality of substances, attributes and motions. In the *Vaisesikasutra,* however, the term *samanya* signifies recurrent generic properties, such as substantiality *(dravyatvam),* whiteness etc., which account for the fact that numerically distinct substances may be identified as members of the same class and be referred to by an identical concept. The various sorts of *samanya* fall into a hierarchical series: cowness, for instance, is a genus relative to a particular cow, but is a species relative to the more inclusive genus of substantiality. It is thus stated that the essences of substance, attribute and action may be viewed as both general and particular. The highest, most inclusive universal is existence (*bhava*), which inheres in all substances, attributes and motions. Thus we are told that 'Existence is a universal only, for it generates nothing but recurrence [or inclusion, i.e. inclusive awareness, *anuv®tti*].' Lower, specific universals (*samanyavifesa*) produce exclusion and distinction as well as inclusion. We may then say that universals are limits on the degree of the atoms' possible distinction and change: one thing *a* can become another thing *b* if and only if a universal is instantiated in both *a* and *b*, namely, if *a* and *b* are of the same type. The universal inheres in a plurality of objects and, having the same form in all, brings the idea of itself in any one. Unlike the attribute in which it is instantiated, nothing is instantiated in the universal. That is, it is not a locus of inherence; it is not an object. For this reason, and also because the universal is independent of its substrates, it is eternal.

Particularities are factors of individuality which, like universals, are eternal and inhere in substrates without themselves being inhered in. By contrast to universals, though, each particularity inheres exclusively in one substrate. Particularities therefore reside only in substrates that are eternal, non-composite substances, namely, the individual atoms, souls and minds, and the unitary substances ether, space and time. We have seen above that attributes differentiate but do not necessarily individuate; they do not account for what it means to be this very entity rather than any other, nor for what makes it so. Now since the scope of *vifesa* is extended over the eternal substances alone, we may say that this category is not concerned so much with the numerical differentiation of encountered existents in general or with their identity, but rather with the individuation of those existents that are eternal substances. *Vifesa,* then, points to the question of what the true nature is of a given primary existent and of what makes it the very particular it is.

The Vaifesika notion of substance, then, is remarkably different from that of Patañjali. As mentioned above, by *dravya* Patañjali primarily intends substance in the sense of an individual *qua* a bundle or a collection of qualities. A collection depends upon the collected elements, and hence a substance depends upon the qualities it collects. By contrast, in the Vaifesika system of categories, qualities, actions and even generic properties (universals) inhere in substance, and the substance is said to be the substratum of these properties. Moreover, the relation of inherence by which these properties are tied to the substance is a real relation, and hence for the Vaifesika substance as a substratum is not a mere bundle of qualities, but a real, systematic whole having a structure of its own and which is, by definition, independent of its qualities, motions etc.

Let us now move on from the specificity of each of the above categories to their overarching meaning as the basis of a categorial theory. What distinguishes a cat-egorial system from other taxonomies? Indian philosophical literature abounds with lists, enumerations, catalogues and classifications, and the Vaifesika doctrine of categories is no exception in this respect. As Ganeri notes, though, taxonomies are cheap, for there are many ways of dividing objects into groups. The choice of one particular way of dividing from the others is the selection of an ontology. Ganeri thus suggests that, since the *padarthas* are given rather than chosen for all but the original compilers of the *Va ifesikasutra*, one should focus on the tradition's methods of rationalization and revision, that is, on how the predetermined list of *padarthas* is made sense of and modified in accordance with the principles by which it is rationalized. In the case of classical Vaifesika the *padarthas*' later rationalization is even more pressing an issue, for in the *Va ifesikasutra* a complete list of all the six categories referred to by the term *padartha* is found only in one single *sutra* which is probably a later interpolation.

We have seen that, linguistically, categories prescribe the basic ways of calling up subsistent beings for discussion and in this sense establish the basis for meaning and reference, but also that categorization is therefore inevitably bound up with ontology. Indeed a consideration of the later Vaifesika rationalization of the categories shows that for this school the dominant connotation of the predetermined list of the six *padarthas* is ontological rather than linguistic.

Already in the *V a i fesikasutra* existence (*bhava*) is acknowledged as the highest, most inclusive universal. The text, though, considers *bhava* and *satta*, that is, being and reality, as interchangeable, for the statement succeeding to the above assertion reads thus: 'Reality (*satta*) accounts for our application of the notion "real" (*sat*) to substances, qualities and motions, and is something different from the members of these three categories.' The *Va ifesikasutra*, then, implies that whatever exists falls into the categories of substance, attribute and action. Moreover, in both their modes of existence -- as eternal, indivisible atoms and as impermanent, destructible compounds of atoms – substances are real substrates of real attributes and real motion or action-moments. *Bhava/satta* accounts for the fact that all substances, attributes and motions are referred to as real in thought and speech. 'It circumscribes', Halbfass explains, 'the totality of entities at the cosmological level of enumeration and classification, and it is added to these entities as if it were an enumerable, cosmological entity itself.'

By the time of Candramati's *Dafapadarthafastra* (fifth century CE?) – a treatise that survived in Hsüan-tsang's Chinese translation – a terminological change occurred, as the term *satta* is here used to refer to the universal inhering in the first three categories. Candramati identifies his *satta* with Ka~ada's *bhava*, presenting reality/existence as the highest universal and a separate *padartha*, while class-properties like substantiality, whiteness etc. are subsumed under the category of limited, specific universal (*samanyavifesa*). The *Dafapadarthafastra* is one of the only two independent works belonging to the later period of classical Vaifesika. The second independent work is Prafastapada's compendium of categories, the *Pa d arthadharmasaμgraha*. Prafastapada became the Vaifesika's most influential systematizer and his compendium is the most authoritative presentation of the classical system and its ontology.

Prafastapada interprets reality, *satta*, as a generic property comparable to, though more extensive than other universals, thus bringing reality/existence, generic properties (e.g. 'blueness') and the generic class-properties (substantiality etc.) under one category of universal (*samanya*). He therefore distinguishes between two kinds of universal: ultimate (*parasamanya*) and non-ultimate (*aparasamanya*). Reality is the ulṭimate universal because it produces only inclusion and because of its wide domain of instances: all particular, cosmologically distinct entities (*sat*) are regarded as *satta*. Generic and class-properties as well as their inseparable inherence in particulars are recognized as real in the sense of their being mind-independent, but their reality is non-ultimate owing to its restricted extension and because these universals produce not only inclusion but also distinction (*vyav®tti*). In addition to *satta* and *bhava* Prafastapada introduces several other ontological notions not found in the *Va ifesikasutra*. The first is the second-order concept of *astitva*, 'is-ness', also rendered as actuality or objectivity. Unlike *satta/bhava, astitva* applies not only to the first three categories of substance, attribute and motion, but also to the other three categories of universal, particularity and inherence. As a common denominator of all six categories, *astitva* is coordinate with knowability (*jñeyatva*) and nameability (*abhidheyatva*). It is therefore attributable to whatever is an enumerable and classifiable world-constituent, including reality, *sattaa,* itself; any nameable world ingredient 'is there' insofar as *astitva* can be ascribed to it. Prafastapada also broaches two other notions of being in order to distinguish existents from generic class-properties and universals: he characterizes substances, attributes and motions as having *sattasambandha,* 'connection with reality', universals, particularities and inherence as having *svatmasattva,* 'reality by virtue of one's own-identity'. Any cosmologically distinct 'real' (*sat*) is the substrate (*afraya*) of *satta* and the logical subject (*dharmin*) of *sattasambandha*. The latter is a temporal condition connecting a particular entity with the eternal, immutable universal *satta;* it ascertains that entity's presence and that *satta* is actually present in it. Unlike in the case of the first three categories, the existence of universals, particularities and inherence does not consist in their connection with reality but in their own-identity or essence.

A perusal of the classical Vaifesika construal of the six *padarthas*, as Halbfass summarizes, reveals that these categories are regarded as the most comprehensive units of enumeration, the ultimate divisions of reality and the most fundamental correlates of thought and speech. The totality of all particular, enumerable 'reals' is subsumed under the reified *satta* universal, which is, in turn, integrated into the ontological meta-category of *astitva*. The categories are thus intended to establish a basis for a system of enumeration; an exhaustive inventory of all world constituents within the limits of *astitva*. Although the Vaifesika doctrine of categories may be understood as analysing the concrete objects of our experience in an attempt to form a theoretical basis for our philosophical discussion, in the final analysis the categories are not mere cognitive-linguistic projections, but existents that are the direct correlates of our perceptions and conceptualizations; the referents of whatever is knowable and nameable. 'The Nyaya-Vaifesika philosophers believe', as Matilal puts it, 'that if we can analyze and classify the concrete objects of our experience in this manner into substance, quality and action, we would achieve a satisfactory explanation of "what there is", i.e., an explanation of what is meant when we say, "that object exists".'

The Vaifesika pluralistic realism and atomistic theory are grounded in a substance-attribute ontology that posits an objective reality in which all constituent substrates are objects of knowledge and are communicable through linguistic expressions. Its categorial theory focuses on the ontological question of being, that is, 'What is there?', rather than on the question of individuation, 'What is it?' The works of Prafastapada's commentators, such as Vyomafiva's *Vyomavati* (ninth century CE?) and Fridhara's *Nyayakandali* (991 CE), attest that central to classical Vaifesika self-understanding is the idea of a comprehensive meta-enumeration yielding an all-inclusive inventory, not only of particular types of entity but of whatever has the character of being. The six *padartha*s distinguish whatever existents there are; they are modes of existence. Exceptional in this respect is the category of particularity, *vifesa,* which does account for what a given existent is in distinction from any other existent of its kind. Nevertheless, *vifesa* – residing exclusively in the permanent, non-composite substances – is a category that individuates primary existents alone. That is, for classical Vaifesika primary existents alone possess individuality and the category of *vifesa* enables its users to ascertain that something is a primary existent. Hence in this context individuality, to borrow Quine's words regarding identity, is 'of a piece with ontology'.

In this respect and in its reliance on substance metaphysics the Vaifesika categorial theory parts from the early Abhidhamma

dhamma analysis. Ye t the Abhidhamma idea of *dhamma* categorization and its admission of conceptual realism evoke the Vaifesika system, or at least its early origins, as a source of doctrinal influence. This influence becomes clearer in the mature, post-canonical Abhidhamma, which explicitly inclines towards realism and reification of the *dhammas*. Moreover, in this later period the Abhidhamma focuses on a different aspect of the problem of individuation, namely, the principle or cause of the *dhammas'* individuality. The next sections clarifies what this issue involves and examines its treatment in the Theravadin commentarial literature.

THE PRINCIPLE OF INDIVIDUALITY

What Makes an Individual what it is?

Following Aristotle, the scholastics regarded the identification of principles and causes as the primary function of a scientific investigation. Thus the question of the cause or principle of individuation, that is, 'What is the cause of something's being an individual substance?', or 'What makes an individual the very item it is?', attracted the utmost attention of Western medieval authors and has exclusively been understood as 'the pure problem of individuation'. For Aristotle, knowledge (*epistéme)* is explanatory: to know something is to grasp its constituting principle; to comprehend *why* something is or has happened. This implies that a definition, as the term features in Aristotle's writings and later pervades the works of his scholastic heirs, is causal and real rather than nominal: it does not convey the linguistic meaning of a word but rather the cause of what that word refers to. Hence an investigation into the notion of individuality ought to reveal the internal, structural component that is its cause. Emphasized here is the metaphysical foundation of individuality in individuals themselves. The position adopted with respect to this question will depend to a large extent on the intension of individuality and the ontology adhered to. On a substance-attribute ontological model the pivotal issue is the inner structure of an individual: what feature in it ontologically constitutes it as such.

The concern with the principle of individuation can be traced to Aristotle's *Metaphysics*. In this treatise Aristotle denies that universals really exist, and hence individuals can no longer be reckoned as the ultimate, indivisible parts of species and genera. Aristotle, though, continues to maintain that properties exist and recognizes that an ordinary object of experience cannot be what underlies individual properties, because the object, by definition, includes properties and thus cannot be what makes them the properties of a single individual object. Aristotle here asks what underlies an individual substance. He calls this underlying principle the 'whatness' of things, an essence. The essence that is formulated by a definition is equated with the substance of each thing. It is this 'substance of a substance' that is regarded as an individual. In the *Metaphysics*, then, 'individual' refers to the principle that accounts for the individuality of ordinary individual substances – an internal, structural component in virtue of which its associated substance is the very particular that it is. Chapters 4–6 of *Metaphysics* VII analyse the internal structure of substance into form, matter and the compound form-and-matter. For instance, the matter of a bronze statue is bronze and its form is the shape of its outward appearance. Form is the substance's internal organization or structure that determines its capacity to behave or function in a characteristic way as it does. Aristotle chooses form as the essence and the cause of a substance's individuality, although it is far from clear how the form satisfies the conditions he lays out for 'essencehood'.

Aristotle's conception of form is but a theory of essential individuation, one of the various theories of individuation developed by the medieval scholastics and by modern philosophers. The difficulty with this theory is that we only have an individual object because it has its own unique form or individual organization, which ought not to be shared by other objects. The way in which an object has an essence must be essentially different from the way in which it possesses any of its qualities. Ye t forms, ways of being organized, dispositions or capacities – detailed as their specification is – can be had by several objects. An alternative theory is that of bare particulars: this holds that substances must contain something in addition to their characteristics, a bare particular that is the bearer of the characteristics co-present with it. A bare particular, while possessing the characteristics associated with the substance, confers individuality upon it, for it alone is unique to that substance. Still, bare particulars are only cognizable with reference to their characteristics. To avoid this difficulty the scholastics brought up theories of characterized particulars, such as the theory of accidental individuation. Accidents are the contingent characteristics that are separable from an essentially characterized particular and that may change while the latter remains numerically the same, such as the colour, shape or texture of my desk. If neither the essential constituents of a particular substance nor the set of its essential characteristics properly account for its individuality, then its accidents must function as individ-uators. Ye t if individual substances can share their essential characteristics, why should they not share their contingent ones?

The principle of individuation, then, has not properly been accounted for. All the above theories are flawed, while others that are not mentioned here conflate individuation with numerical difference. All these theories have failed because the principle of individuation is not only supposed to account for the individuality of a substance, but itself must be unique and non-instantiable: it ought to be an individual. This means that in individuating a form, essence, an accident or whatever else is regarded as the principle in question, we need to go beyond the object if the latter is to be an individual substance. We cannot individuate essences etc., on the basis of the objects of which essences they are, for the objects themselves are to be individuated by the essences. Karl Popper notes that essence can be described by a definition, but a definition must not use accidental universals or individual terms. From this he draws a conclusion that equally follows when taking into account other possible principles of individua-tion: individuals themselves cannot be defined, only the kinds to which they belong. This means, Popper explains, that in order to provide a unique characterization of an individual something else must be used, such as its spatio-temporal relations to at least one other individual. Michael Frede indicates that temporal relations teach us about an individual's history, and that even if all the essences of a given kind were completely identical we could still distinguish between them on the basis of their histories. For example, it should be sufficient to suppose that an essence can have a history to the extent that it can be instantiated in different matter at different times. It is possible to distinguish between various essences of the same kind on the basis of their histories, and between various essences of the same kind at a given moment on the basis of the present stages of their histories.

The question of the principle of individuation becomes relevant only within a realist context, for if it is held that there are no substantial realities that undergo change in order to become individuals, then there is no need to identify the principle or cause of such a change. The question, however, may well emerge within the context of conceptual realism and from the processual perspective of an event metaphysics. Thus one may ask not only what in objects individuates them as enduring substances, but rather what in experience individuates the occurrences that constitute one's mind. The following section portrays the post-canonical Abhidhamma event metaphysics as centred around the principle of the *dhammas'* individuality. What I have set out to show in this section is that the Abhidhammikas grappled with the difficulty of going beyond the *dhammas* in order to individuate them by exploiting their temporal relations and by appropriating the theory of momentariness.

The Post-canonical Abhidhamma and the Principle of Individuality

The commentarial period saw the advent of new doctrinal developments based on the extant canonical Abhidhamma material, foremost of which was the entwining of the already prevalent sense of a *dhamma* as an individual – a distinct psycho-physical, short-lived event of which dimension is not fixed – with the doctrines of *sabhava* and of momentariness. This engendered the notion of a *dhamma* as a single consciousness-moment encompassing three distinct sub-phases of origination, endurance and dissolution. Each such momentary event was then equated with and defined in virtue of its particular nature, *sabhava*. Previously we saw that in the commentarial literature the term *sabhava* is narrowed down and no longer signifies either a generic or specific nature, the sum-total of characteristics that distinguish a certain type of *dhamma*. Rather it denotes a structural constituent that is essential to a *dhamma* and that enables us to fathom why that *dhamma* possesses the characteristics it has. *Sabhava* is what determines the *dhamma*'s internal organization or disposition, which make it behave in a certain way or fulfil a specific function. We are now in a position to say that *sabhava* is the principle and cause of the *dhamma*'s individuality; what makes the *dhamma* the very particular it is rather than any other individual of the same kind.

This is demonstrated by the exegetical statement that 'there is no such thing called "activity" (*kiriya*) apart from the *dhamma*'s individual nature', and by the recurrent definitions of a *dhamma* as that which bears its *sabhava*, or alternatively as that which is borne by conditions in accordance with its *sabhava*. The meaning is that no *dhamma* occurs as indeterminate, having no individuality. Any given consciousness-moment originates with its unique imprint, bearing its particular 'genetic capacity' that determines its disposition to act in a certain way, its specific function within its series in the consciousness process. This idea is also expressed by the prevalent commentarial fourfold schema of defining a *dhamma* based on its distinguishing characteristic (*lakkha~a*), manifestation (*paccu-patthana*), immediate cause (*padatthana*) and function (*rasa*). This schema exhibits the individuality factors unique to a *dhamma*; its disposition to present itself and act in a certain way. The commentaries no longer ask 'What is such-and-such a *dhamma*?', nor do they make innovative alterations of the extant *dhamma* categorizations. Whereas the canonical Abhidhamma emphasizes the intension of individuation and asks what an individual *dhamma* is, the commentaries ask what in the inner structure of any given *dhamma* makes it the very particular it is. They seek the cause of a *dhamma*'s individuality and broach *sabhava* as this cause. The emphasis is shifted to the metaphysical foundations of individuation, to its basis in experience.

Now there is a close connection between being an individual – being distinguishable, determined and definable – and existing. Individuality may be logically prior to existence, but the very fact that we can pose the question of being means that the condition for every question is that being *per se* exists. We could not think if not starting from the principle that we are thinking something. It has thus been argued that nothing could be an individual if 'exists' were not predicable of it, though this existence does not necessarily refer to the individual's objective actuality, but to its being the subject of a propositional affirmation. Related as they are, however, being and individuation consist in two different questions, as evidenced by the distinction between existence and essence respectively. Moreover, although essence may be an ontological determinant, it is not an ontological category in itself. We have already seen that in the para-canonical Pali texts *sabhava* signifies a *dhamma*'s own-nature and plays the role of an individuator, while in the later, quintessential commentaries *sabhava* emerges as the cause of a *dhamma*'s certain mode of being and may be rendered as own-essence. We now ought properly to distinguish between the epistemological and ontological denotations of *sabhava*-as-essence.

Aristotle points out that we can ask two questions of every simple thing: 'Is it?' and 'What is it?' If the questions refer, for instance, to a certain man, the reply to the first question would be: 'Yes, it has existence', to the second: 'A person, he has an essence called "humanity".' The latter answer is the object's definition. In both the *Topics* and the *Metaphysics*, a definition is said to be the statement indicating the essence of its definiendum: the essence is that which makes something precisely what it is, and there is an essence only of those things the formula of which is a definition. 'Essence' here signifies an individuator and its thrust is epistemological: it explains, without an appeal to anything else, why its object is this very individual; it is what determines the true nature of its object. The distinction between existence and essence is the subject of a continuous, fervent dispute among the medieval scholastic metaphysicians. Boethius had provided considerable impetus for those later discussions by maintaining that in any composite entity its being and what it is are not one and the same. Among the scholastics of the high Middle Ages Thomas Aquinas is a leading advocate of the distinction between existence and essence. In his *De Ente et Essentia* (*c.*1254) Aquinas enunciates the necessity of a distinction between existence in the sense of 'isness' (*esse*) and essence in the sense of 'whatness' (*quidditas*). He renders essence *qua* quiddity as 'What is signified by the definition expressing what the thing is', namely, that in virtue of which a thing is what it is and nothing else. This implies that existence is a principle of being: that by reason of which an entity actually exists. Essence, by contrast, is a principle of individuation: that on account of which an entity is the particular thing it is and enjoys quidditative content.

The notion of essence, though, might have a stronger, ontological bearing. When Aristotle, as mentioned above, equates form with essence to denote the cause of a substance's individuality, the essence explains not only why this individual substance is that which is, but also why it exists as an actual, determinate individual.

Essence is here an ontological determinant, though not of existence *per se* but of a certain mode of existence: primary existence as an individual substance, that is, certain and non-dependent existence. The difference between essence as an epistemological individuator vs. ontological determinant of primary existence is later expounded by Locke, who distinguishes 'nominal essence' from 'real essence'. Possessing a nominal essence justifies the attribution of a particular name to an entity. A real essence is a prerequisite for the recognition of any nominal essence: it renders an extra-sensory substratum that makes sensory experience possible.

The very idea of essence is undoubtedly removed in spirit from the earliest Buddhist teaching and is remote even from the early Abhidhamma. The impetus behind the Madhyamaka criticism of the Abhidharma metaphysics lies in the Madhyamaka dissolution of the ontology of essence. Ye t the Madhyamaka criticism is more apposite with respect to the Sarvastivada-Vaibhasika than to the Theravada Abhidhamma. We have already seen that for the Sarvastivada all existents are *sat*, but only *dharmas* are *svabhava*-possessing and can be primary existents. To have a *svabhava* is to exist as a *dravya* and be included under one of the categories of the Sarvastivada ontological table. Paul Williams clarifies that in a second-order world of momentary phenomena like that postulated by the Sarvastivada, where there is no question of shared characteristics, what determines an instance of a *dharma* x rather than of y would be a unique definition. *Svabhava* is the principle applicable solely to a particular *dharma*, which renders its unique verbal description. But to have a unique definition is the result of having a unique characteristic (*svalaksa~a*), and this necessitates being a primary existent: primary existence is necessary for linguistic reference. *Svabhava* – albeit not itself a real essence -- is therefore an ontological determinant and a cause of primary existential status.

It is true that on various occasions Pali exegetical literature, too, contains passages that may separately be interpreted to suggest the idea of *sabhava* as a *dhamma'* s ontological determinant. Ye t this ontologically laden meaning of *sabhava* is not directly attributable to the Abhidhamma. Having repudiated the Sarvastivada conception of *dharmas* as *dravya*, from the Theravadins' perspective *dhammas* are not spatio-temporal point-instants, but rather consciousness moments, or, more correctly, the capacities and capabilities of mental events. Accordingly, the Theravadins do not normally use *sabhava* to indicate primary existence, but an individual definition unique to a *dhamma*. The point is that for the Theravada Abhidhamma *sabhava* predominantly plays as an individuator in its quidditative sense. Quiddity, as a definition expressing what something is, is categorically opposed to the ontological denotation of essence as 'the substance of a substratum'. Quiddity need not entail a substratum, although a substratum ordinarily entails in addition to itself some sort of quiddity. Formulated as a definition, the *sabhava* requires that there always be something to which it could refer, but it does not necessitate the existence – either secondary or primary – of any particular spatio-temporal instantiation of the *dhamma* defined. Equating *sabhava* with *salakkha~a*, the Theravadins usually regard both categories as an epistemological, linguistic determinant: to have a *sabhava* is to be knowable and nameable, that is, possess a unique definition. In harmony with this view certain post-canonical texts introduce the idea of a '*sabhava*-language' (*sabhava-nirutti*): a language of uniquely refering names, so that for each *dhamma* there is a corresponding name properly signifying it.

Nonetheless, here linguistic considerations pave the way for realism and ontology. *Sabhava* is an atemporal determinant of the *dhamma*'s individuality, not its temporal status. This category thus facilitates the construction of a *dhamma* categorization based on a tenseless use of language, for which Paul Griffiths has coined the term 'denaturalized discourse'. A denaturalized discourse is, first, normative, in that it seeks to establish the foundations (e.g. ideas, sensibilia) of any instance of knowledge. Second, it is typically regarded as universal, as applicable to all subjects irrespective of time and place. Third, it is abstracted from a natural language, intending to clear up the ambiguity and polysemy inherent in ordinary language used in everyday contexts. Functionally a denaturalized discourse intends to elucidate what truly exits. The Abhidhamma *sabhava*-language is an instance of a denaturalized discourse, albeit one that draws on a metaphysics quite different from that which has fostered such a discourse in Western tradition. It reduces the complexity of experience and the ambiguity of everyday language to a list of terms mirroring what ultimately exists in experience – a list that, given the syntax of the Pali, is entirely verbless.

Another indication of the 'ontologization' of *sabhava* is that the latter is not only supposed to account for a *dhamma*'s individuality, but itself emerges as a singular, non-instantiable individual. We have an individual *dhamma* only in virtue of its own particular *sabhava,* which cannot be shared by other *dhamma* instances of the same kind. For example, it is the *sabhava* of this particular instance of one-pointedness of mind that makes it what it is rather than any other instance of one-pointedness of mind within that consciousness-series. The commentaries display this idea by identifying both *dhamma* and *sabhava* as denoting the mere fact of originating as a *dhamma*. Embracing this stance, the developed Abhidhamma steps further away towards a realist attitude, reifying the *dhammas* as the irreducible, actual entities on which the phenomenal world rests. What is stressed is not so much the nature that is unique to a given *dhamma,* but the recognition that the encountered world is a world of individuals; that in the final analysis *dhammas* alone are what exist. Here the developed Abhidhamma notion of *sabhava* is plainly ontological: *sabhava* is not merely the individuator of its *dhamma,* but also its ontological determinant as a primary existent and an individual in itself.

If *sabhava* is an individual, then it must be distinguishable and identifiable. This is what the equation of *sabhava* with *salakkha~a* allegedly satisfies, for it implies that any *sabhava* is uniquely signified by a respective definition. But here crops up the same vexing difficulty that haunts the Western theories of individuation: linguistic recurrence precludes *sabhava* from qualifying only one single spatio-temporal instantiation of its *dhamma*. However detailed a verbal specification of *sabhava* we offer, it is always possible that more than a single *dhamma* could have this *sabhava.* As Popper tells us, individuals themselves cannot be defined. Thus, in individuating a *sabhava* we must go beyond its *dhamma,* for the latter itself is to be individuated by the *sabhava,* and hence it cannot account for its own cause of individuation.

We saw that one solution to this difficulty is to distinguish the principle of individuation on the basis of its history. In the context of the developed Abhidhamma this means first to distinguish between different instances of the same kind of *dhamma* on the basis of their temporal position within their consciousness series, and second between different instances of the same kind of *dhamma* at a given moment on the basis of the phases comprising each such consciousness-moment. This, I argue, is attempted by entwining the notion of *sabhava* with the developed theory of momentariness. The mature Abhidhamma does not merely analyse the processes described in the *suttas* into their comprising events, but takes each and every phenomenon as momentary and dissects it into three distinct phases of origination, endurance and dissolution. The threefold subdivision of a moment facilitates the rapprochement with realism and ontology, for the *sabhava* is equated with the endurance-moment of its *dhamma* – a phase that attests to the latter's existence throughout the three sub-moments. But what kind of ontology is this? Within the Abhidhamma framework ontology is not so much an inquiry into what exists *per se*, but into what constitutes the consciousness process and the awakened mind. The scope of this ontology falls between psychology and soteriology.

The description of the consciousness process (*citta-vithi*) is set out in Buddhaghosa's works, the *Visuddhimagga* and *Atthasalini* specifically, and is summarized in the manuals of Buddhadatta and Anuruddha. The theory of the *citta-vithi*, however, is not a product of the commentarial period: it is rooted in the canonical Abhidhamma and is well established in the old Sinhalese commentaries. Thus the *Dhammasaðga~i* shows that fully fledged cognition takes place at subsequent stages of the consciousness stream as a function of various mental faculties. This work gives a fairly static account of mental and material phenomena as they occur at particular moments. The elaborate theory of the *citta-vithi* accounts for their occurrence over a series of such moments. Two types of process are described: five sense-door process (*pañcadvara*) and mind-door process (*manodvara*). This theory and its relation to the theory of momentariness have been discussed by a number of scholars. The point I wish to stress here is that the theory of *citta-vithi* – albeit displaying what in the absence of a better terminology we may render 'Abhidhamma ontology' – embodies the Abhidhamma pragmatic concern with psychology. It also hints at the position of soteriology within the Abhidhamma framework. The reason is that the systematic account of the consciousness process is not meant to specify what exists *per se*, but what goes on in one's consciousness. The higher one progresses along the hierarchy of the four planes, the more complex the states of consciousness become, involving more mental factors. Still more significant are the qualitative differences that individuate one's mind: for instance, transcendent *lokuttara* consciousness may never involve those unskilful tendencies and defilements that still exist potentially and might occur at any moment of skilful *lokiya* consciousness. Accordingly, Gethin expresses the concern of the Abhidhamma as follows: 'If consciousness is understood to consist of a temporal series of consciousness moments each having an individual object, then when an ordinary being (*puthujjana*) is experiencing wholesome consciousness, what at that moment distinguishes him or her from an *arahant*?'

The attempts of the later Abhidhamma theoreticians to individuate the awakened mind are bound up with their construal of *nibbana* and with their espousal of the fourfold *dhamma* categorization into *citta, cetasika, rupa* and *nibbana*. The following and concluding section revisits these two issues.

On Nibbana, Individuation and the Fourfold Dhamma Categorization

No certain account of the nature of *nibbana* can be obtained from the *Nikayas*, as their main force is to shy away from any commitment on this issue and they use the term *nibbana* in several different senses. First, *nibbana* is the particular event that happens at the moment of awakening, specifically the extinction of the three fires of greed, hatred and delusion – an event that is the same for all who attain awakening and that the early texts call *nibbana* or *parinibbana* interchangeably, although the Pali idiom is a verb: *parinibbayati*, 'he or she *parinibbana*-s'. This sense seems to be part of an extended metaphorical structure that embraces enlightenment and its opposite, alluding to the three fires in the Brahmanical tradition. Second, *nibbana* signifies the experience of being without greed, hatred and delusion, namely, what is realized at the moment of enlightenment and is then applied throughout an enlightened person's present life. Thus at the moment the Buddha gained insight into the nature of *dukkha*, its arising, its cessation and the path leading to its cessation, he experienced a complete 'blowing out' of the three fires and the cessation of all the defilements (*kilesa*). He continued living motivated entirely by generosity, friendliness and wisdom, although the fuel of life, the five aggregates in a metaphorical structure, still remained – a state known in the commentarial tradition as '*nibbana* with a remainder of clinging' (*sopadisesanibbanadhatu*). When the remainder of clinging had been exhausted, the Buddha was not reborn into some new form of life, but rather *parinibbana*-d. In this third sense *nibbana* is the extinction of the five *khandhas* on the passing away of Buddhas and *arahants* as well as the state they experience after death, both termed '*nibbana* without a remainder of clinging' (*anupadisesanibbanadhatu*). Ye t some texts may equally support the view that *nibbana* amounts to some metaphysical absolute; a reality that makes sentient experience possible, but which cannot in itself be part of experience. Renowned in this respect is one of the Buddha's 'inspired utterances' (*udana*) concerning *nibbana*, which may be read as implying transcendental idealism:

There is, monks, an unborn, an unbecome, an unconstructed, an unconditioned (*asaðkhata*), without which the resultant born, become, constructed, conditioned could not be known. But because there is, monks, an unborn, an unbecome, an unconstructed, an unconditioned, the resultant born, become, constructed, conditioned can be known.

Nibbana is indeed the ultimate religious goal and the final release from all unsatisfactoriness and impermanence, but like all other phenomena it is *anatta*, not-self, and cannot be the liberated state of any self. Nor can it be properly described, for it is *atakkavacara*, inaccessible to discursive thought, and since it defies neat categorization it can only be referred to by way of negation: it is neither temporal nor spatial, neither mind nor matter. In the first 'inspired ùtterance' regarding *nibbana*, which is also one of the most complete statements on *nibbana* to be found in the Pali Canon, the Buddha refers to it as a domain (*ayatana*) of experience in which neither the elements that make up physical phenomena nor the most subtle consciousness types of the formless-sphere take part:

There is, monks, a domain where there is no earth, no water, no fire, no wind, no sphere of infinite space, no sphere of infinite consciousness, no sphere of nothingness, no sphere of neither-conceptualization-nor-non-conceptualization; there is not this world, there is not another world, there is no sun or moon. I do not call this coming or going, nor standing, nor dying nor being reborn; it is without support, without occurrence, without object. Just this is the end of unsatisfactoriness.

Such an appeal to ineffability is, of course, very common in religion: Steven Collins shows in his exploration of nirvana and narrative in the Theravada tradition that this appeal must eventually be made in relation to any concept of final salvation, for any form of eternal life is unimaginable. The attitude is rarely, however, quite so consistent and uncompromising as in the case of the Buddhist *nibbana*.

The traditional 'problem' of *nibbana* concerns the exact nature and ontological status of *nibbana* as the final condition of Buddhas and *arahants* after death, and as the ineffable realm revealed at the moment of awakening. But no such account of *nibbana* can be obtained from the *Nikayas*, as the question of what happens to the Tathagata after death is one of the problems the Buddha is said to have set aside, rejecting the very terms in which it is couched. Indeed the early texts contain materials that can be interpreted to suggest that *nibbana* is both some form of blissful, eternal super-existence, or extinction of the five aggregates. But even those passages that allegedly support a metaphysical or annihilationist interpretation of *nibbana* never do so unequivocally: these are merely hints and suggestions, not unequivocal declarations. The point is, however, that the tradition is aware of the apparent ambiguity resulting from these contradictory passages. This ambiguity is not due to carelessness or because the tradition could not make up its mind on that subject. Rather, it stems from the middle way dialectic of early Buddhism and is intended to avoid what the tradition considers the two basic wrong views: the annihilationist view and the eternalist view (*uccheda-vada/sassata-vada*).

The path set forth by the Buddha is meant to prescribe how to live the spiritual life, not satisfy intellectual curiosity where this would not be profitable. Accordingly, much can be said especially metaphorically, in praise of *nibbana* to encourage the seeker: we find frequent references to it as 'the country of No-Birth', that which is 'a wonderful ancient city where men of old had gone', that which is pure, unafflicted sublime, and so on. But beyond this the Buddha did not wish to go, and the *Nikayas* never depart from this position: there must be nothing so concrete said of *nibbana* as to encourage attachment or dogmatic convictions; *nibbana* is the cessation of craving, so obviously to crave *nibbana* obliterates its very meaning. The result is that if one were to accept that the above Nikaya extracts indicate a common Buddhist heritage concerning *nibbana,* then one would have to acknowledge that inasmuch as they are common they are vague. The texts put much more effort into explaining the dynamics of experience in *samsara* than the nature of *nibbana.*

This state of affairs undergoes a striking change in the Abhidhamma literature. The Abhidhamma position is already clearly formulated in the *Dhammasangani:* here the term *nibbana* does not feature in the main body of the text but is substituted by the compound *asankhata-dhatu,* 'unconditioned element', namely, that which is independent of relations of causal conditioning. This is not a matter of mere wording, but an indication of the Abhidhamma's attempts to dispel the obscurity clouding the nature of *nibbana,* concretize it and specify its status in actual experience. In pursuing this endeavour the Abhidhammikas must have realized that they could not accommodate the unconditioned element within the extant taxonomies of sentient experience, the analysis into the five *khandhas* specifically. Seeking an alternative formula to account for the unconditioned they found the *dhatu* totality formula suitable for this end.

The phrase 'unconditioned element' derives from the *Bahudhatuka-sutta,* where it is one of a series of explanations as to how a monk is *dhatu-kusala,* 'skilled in the elements'. Bear in mind that *dhatu* always refers to the distinct elements of cognition: a visible object is experientially distinct from an auditory object, from the organ of sight, from consciousness of sight, etc. Just as the analysis into the eighteen *dhatus* is intended to facilitate insight into personal identity as not-self, the purpose here is presumably to distinguish conceptually the unconditioned element of enlightened experience. As Cousins explains, in the Abhidhamma framework the mind is defined as momentary and intentional in nature; a given mental event involves the knowing by a single mind of a single object. The enlightenment experience was defined as the moment in which a transformed and hence transcendent mind in association with the mental structuring of the path, takes as its object the element *(dhatu)* which is unconstructed *(asankhata),* i.e. its basis is an experience of an aspect of reality which is uncaused and which does not construct new mental and physical events. Yet this aspect somehow acts as the support for the transformed and newly harmonious balance of mental events.

The term *asankhata,* which we have already come across in the *Uddna,* occurs on its own in the *Nikayas:* in the *Asankhata-samyutta* it is defined as the destruction of greed hatred and delusion, while the *Anguttara-nikdya* adds that it is free of the characteristics of the conditioned: arising, ceasing and change of what is present. *Sankhata* is a participle stemming from the root *sam-kr,* which means 'to shape', 'arrange together' and 'consolidate', but far more frequent is the verbal form *sankhara,* ordinarily rendered as 'mental formation', 'construction' or 'conditioning factor'. *Sankhara* is an activity, especially volition, which enables something to come into existence or to maintain its existence - it fashions or forms a thing. As one of the five *khandhas, sankhara qua* mental formation is what underlies all encountered phenomena and which gives impetus to the process of conditioning that fuels the sequence of rebirths. *Nibbdna* alone is *asankhata,* independent of mental formation, and is therefore totally different from phenomenal experience in its entirety Just as the *dhdtus* are distinct elements of cognition, the unconditioned and the conditioned are distinct and exclusive objects of experience.

The *Nikkhepakanda* of the *Dhammasangani* analyses the unconditioned element in accordance with the *abhidhamma-mdtikd.* Following the Nikaya dialectic, it provides a wealth of information about what the unconditioned element is not: it is neither skilful nor unskilful, associated neither with feeling nor with cognition, neither resultant nor giving result, does not require any object, is not classified as past, present or future, and so on, in accordance with the *mdtikd's* couplets and triplets. This in itself does not add much to our sense of *nibbdna.* The point is that the text articulates what the unconditioned element is totally different from, namely, the five *khandhas.* In the *cuantara-duka's* couplets *sankhata/asankhata* and *sappaccaya/appaccaya* the first term is explained with reference to the five *khandhas,* whereas the second term relates to the unconditioned element alone. This recurs in the *Mahantara-duka,* in the first three couplets of which the first term again refers to the five *khandhas,* while the unconditioned element is posed in opposition to these. Since *nibbdna* without remainder of clinging is the complete cessation of the five *khandhas,* the unconditioned element is totally different from the *khandhas,* and hence also excludes the mind-body complex: nothing that is predicable of this complex is attributable to the unconditioned element. Even more striking is the fact that the above three *Mahantara-duka* couplets - with/without an object; *citta/not-citta; cetasika/not-cetasika* - are but a different arrangement of the four fundamental categories of the later Abhidhamma: *rupa, citta, cetasika* and *nibbdna.* The *Dhammasangani* here anticipates the idea of *nibbdna* as a distinct category of Buddhist thought, thus taking a consequential step beyond the *Nikayas'* elusive approach to the nature and status of *nibbdna* within Buddhist conceptual scheme.

Here for the first time *nibbdna* is conveyed by a positive qualification: since both the conditioned and the unconditioned are subsumed under the wider category of *dhamma, nibbdna* is a *dhamma,* an object of mental cognitive awareness about the intension and status of which questions can be raised. *Nibbdna* is an object of thought among other *dhammas:* it is not a special object of thought, but a special *dhamma*. Accordingly, it is said to be the only thing that does not belong to the five *khandhas*, yet belongs both to the sphere of mental data (*dhammayatana*) and to the element of mental data (*dhammadhatu*). Although inaccessible to discursive thought, it is an object of thought; though not a thought (*na citta*), it is a *dhamma*, and though not a *saðkhatadhamma*, is *asaðkhatadhamma*. *Nibbana* in this context is established as *sui generis:* it is the one and only unconditioned *dhamma*, and hence it excludes whatever makes up experience as we know it, all temporal and spatial relations, and all other *dhammas* that may appear in consciousness. Ye t this is not because *nibbana* is a-*kammatic* (for there are other *dhammas* that do not generate future *kamma*, namely, *kiriya-cittas*), or because it is unconscious, but because it defies categorization and undermines the very possibility of conceptualization: to gain insight into *nibbana* is to grasp the inadequacy of conceptual thought and language. Having realized the fiction and imaginative creation inherent to our cognitive apparatus, the awakened mind breaks up the apparently solid world that we normally construct for ourselves. Like the *Upanisads*, as Collins notes, Buddhism describes the ultimate religious goal as transcending time, but within the Abhidhamma framework the sequence of the three times is secondary, generated in and by the process of conditioned and conditioning *dhammas*. If the process is arrested, time will not exist. Since all *dhammas* excepting *nibbana* are 'past', 'present' or 'future', *nibbana* is also liberation from time. Piatigorsky comments in this context that the continuity of the *dhammas* is but a method of naturalization used to apprehend them as 'units of a conscious being', and that the recurring expression 'past, present and future *dhammas*' by no means asserts that there is time where there are the *dhammas:* on the contrary, it is the *dhammas* that we represent as time in our own 'representational' consciousness, or rather, 'time' figures as a secondary consciousness with respect to the *dhammas*.

The canonical Abhidhamma, then, agrees that *nibbana* is a *dhamma* and attempts to specify its nature or individuality as such. This, once again, indicates the tradition's interest in the intension of this *dhamma*'s individuality: the focus is on what the unconditioned element signifies and on its uniqueness; on what it means to occur as the single unconditioned *dhamma*. The *Dhammasaðga~i*'s epistemologically oriented account is representative of the early, formative period of the Abhidhamma and is followed very closely in other canonical Abhidhamma texts, such as the *Vibhaðga*, the *Dhatukatha* and the *Pa tthana*. The subsequent, post-canonical tradition, however, invested this account with a metaphysics from which it drew far-reaching conclusions regarding the ontological status of the unconditioned element.

So far all the *dhammas* we have referred to have been *sabhava*-possessing. But the post-canonical *dhamma* analysis also accommodates *dhammas* that lack *sabhava* (*asabhava-dhamma*): these encompass mentally constructed concepts (*paññatti*), such as space (*akasa)* and time (*kalq*), as well as the attainment of cessation (*nirodha-samapatti*). Interestingly, *nibbana* as the unconditioned *dhamma* is *sabhava*-possessing. For the developed Abhidhamma this means not only that *nibbana* emerges with an own-nature that makes it totally different from any other *dhamma,* but that this quidditative own-nature is also the cause and principle of its occurrence as a distinguishable event in actuality. In its standard discussion of *nibbana* the *Visuddhimagga* refutes the view that *nibbana* is non-existent along with the claims that it is equivalent to mere absence of the aggregates or of the defilements. Instead it proclaims that *nibbana* alone is permanent (*nicca*):

> It is because it is uncreated (*appabhava*) that it is free from ageing and death. It is because of the absence of its creation and of its ageing and death that it is permanent.

The text then quotes the famous verses of the *Itivuttaka* 37 and the *Udana* 80 ('There is an unborn, an unbecome, an unmade, an unconditioned...'), observing that '*Nibbana* is not non-existent as regards *sabhava* in the ultimate sense.' Explicitly this statement admits merely that *nibbana* should not be considered as non-existent, but implicitly it endows *nibbana* with a mode of occurrence of a distinct event that has a referent. *Nibbana* has such a mode of occurrence in virtue of its *sabhava,* which is devoid of everything that belongs to all the conditioned and constructed *dhammas* and which here may be rendered as 'own-essence', for in this context *sabhava* is the principle and determinant of the way *nibbana* eventuates rather than its epistemological individuator. The *Mahatika* to the *Visuddhimagga* comments on this passage:

> The Teacher has demonstrated the existence of *nibbana* in the ultimate sense [...] Just as owing to a complete understanding that from sensual desires and from materiality [i.e., *lokiya dhamma*], which have states superior to them, an escape is made known that is their opposite and whose own-essence is devoid of them, so there must exist an escape that is the opposite of, and whose own-essence is devoid of all conditioned *dhammas,* all of which have the aforesaid own-essence, and it is this escape that is the unconditioned element.

The post-canonical Abhidhamma manifests a remarkable transition towards the articulation of the cause of *nibbana*'s reality and its occurrence as an individual *dhamma*. This doctrinal development culminates in the commentarial finalization of the meta-categorization of the *dhammas* into four broad categories, a fourfold schema that encompasses both the conditioned and the unconditioned: the former under the three categories of *citta, cetasika* and *rupa,* the latter under the eighty-second *dhamma* that is the unconditioned element as a one-membered category. We have already explained that a categorial system highlights the singularity of its members; the fact that each category embraces distinct individuals. A categorization prescribes the different ways of calling up subsistent items for discussion by assigning them categorial designations, but ontologically it makes available to its users the fundamental kinds of being. Collins notes that 'Although nirvana is "wholly other" than all Conditioned Existents, as an item of the Buddhist scholastic classification scheme it can be categorized like any other *dhamma*.' *Nibbana* as a category is a cognizable object of thought that can be referred to, but also a certified actuality, for its inclusion as a *sabhava*-possessing *dhamma* in the *dhamma* meta-categorization establishes not only its mode of being expressed as the subject of a propositional affirmation, but also its mode of occurrence as an actually existing individual.

Focusing on the principle of the *dhammas'* individuality rather than on the mere question of the intension of their individuation, the post-canonical Abhidhammikas sought not only to distinguish *nibbana* as the single unconditioned *dhamma* within the entirety of what occurs in experience, but also to account for its actuality as an individual event in the array of arisen occurrences. The classifications embodied in the extant totality formulas fell short of this objective, for they could not guarantee *nibbana*'s complete exclusivity in thought and in actuality vis-à-vis all other *dhammas*. Hence the Abhidhammikas broached a new categorization in terms of *dhammas*, in which *nibbana* is a single category. In fact, *nibbana* can be placed under the *dhammayatana* and the *dhammadhatu* only when the *ayatana* and *dhatu* formulas are taken separately, not when the *khandhayatanadhatu* threefold scheme is taken as a unified *matika*. The three totality formulas are seen as overlapping with each other, and hence the *dhamma* base in both the twelve *ayatana*s and the eighteen *dhatu*s corresponds to *vedana, sañña* and *saðkhara* in the five *khandhas*. This, however, would have made *nibbana* automatically correspond to either *vedana, sañña* or *saðkhara* – a result that could not be permitted because *nibbana* was said to be wholly different from the *khandha*s. The Abhidhammikas' solution, then, was found in the form of a *dhamma* meta-categorization that subsumes all three totality formulas.

The history of the Theravada Abhidhamma, then, reflects a shift in metaphysical foundation and epistemological approach.

The canonical Abhidhamma framework is concerned with the individuation of one's mind – an endeavour that emphasizes the intension of the *dhammas'* individuality and is, at bottom, epistemological. Conjoined with the Abhidhamma's newly advocated event metaphysics, the analysis of the concept of individuality paved the way for conceptual realism. This led the post-canonical Abhidhamma into pursuing a different question regarding the principle of the *dhammas'* individuality, which had ontological implications. Seeking the foundations of individuality in the *dhammas qua* individuals themselves while incorporating the doctrines of *sabhava* and momentari-ness, the post-canonical Abhidhamma not only attempted to account for the nature of one's mind, but also to establish the indubitable correlates of thought and speech in reality. It was thus gradually drawn into espousing a naturalistic explanation of *dhammas* as actual events that are the fundamental constituents of the phenomenal world. Ye t this explanation supports a metaphysics of mind rather than a comprehensive ontology; if this metaphysics of mind eventually yielded an ontology, then the latter is a sort of psychological ontology.

The Abhidhamma doctrinal evolution is also accompanied by a comprehensive theory of causation, or rather of relationships of causal conditioning (*paccaya*), as explicated in the seventh book of the *Abhidhamma-pitaka,* the *Pa tthana*. We have seen in Chapter 2 that basic to process philosophy is the category of relat-edness (rather than mere relation), and indeed the *Pa tthana* theory of *paccaya* must have been a natural outgrowth of the Abhidhamma event metaphysics that may be subsumed under the category of process philosophy. Now both causes and events, unlike objects and facts, stand in temporal relations to one another, while events are perhaps the most natural items to serve as the terms of causal interre-lations. The *Pa tthana* theory of *paccaya* is also subject to the Abhidhamma's concern with the problem of individuation, attesting to its interest in both the intension and the principle of the *dhammas'* individuality. The next chapter explores this theory as part of a broader investigation into the Theravadin notion of causation.

6

Causation as the Handmaid of Metaphysics

Causation is a salient motif in Indian philosophy: reflections on the topic of causation date back to the Vedic period and, along with a host of derivative questions regarding moral responsibility and human destiny, subsequently come to play a major role in almost every Indian school of thought, orthodox and heterodox alike. The present chapter deals with the development of the Buddhist notion of causation, or rather the early Buddhist principle of conditioning, namely, *idappaccayata*. The later tradition draws explicit connections between causation and the early teaching of dependent co-arising, that is, *paticcasamuppada*, and indeed scholarly investigations of dependent co-arising often emphasize its role as a generalized, logical principle of abstract conditioning applicable to all phenomena.

Nevertheless, as Collett Cox notes, the fact that the later Buddhist tradition examines dependent co-arising in a context determined by the broader topic of causation cannot be taken as an indication of the relative importance or priority of that topic within Buddhist tradition as a whole. Contextual sensitivity thus demands that we examine the role of dependent co-arising from its earliest appearance in Buddhist teaching, as well as its relation to other aspects of later Buddhist doctrine. The first division of this chapter undertakes to examine in what sense dependent co-arising functions as a causal principle and whether the rendering 'causation' is appropriate in this context. The second division investigates the doctrinal transition from the Nikaya view of the principle of conditioning to the canonical Abhidhamma's systematized account of this principle. The Abhidhammikas elaborated on the doctrine of dependent co-arising and supplemented it with a broader theory of relationships of causal conditioning (*paccaya*). Ye t is this theory a theory of causation at all? Underlying this chapter is the argument that the Abhidhamma theory of relations of causal conditioning forms one aspect of the overall intellectual shift from the Nikaya worldview to the Abhidhamma framework, and that since this theory is subject to the Abhidhamma metaphysics as embodied in the *dhamma* theory, it centres on the individuation of the mental rather than on causation as such.

DEPENDENT CO-ARISING AND THE EARLY BUDDHIST NOTION OF CAUSATION: A REASSESSMENT

The Intellectual Backdrop: the Pre-Buddhist Doctrines of Causation

In relation to the general early history of Indian religion, the Buddha and his teaching must be seen against an intellectual and social backdrop composed of two major elements: first, the Brahmanical, orthodox tradition, mainly represented by the central teachings of the several pre-Buddhist *Upanisads* that had been extant at that time; second, the contemporary religious milieu constituted by a vast number of wandering ascetics, loosely grouped around various teachers into heterodox sects. Those Brahmins and ascetics endorsed a variety of conflicting ideas about the nature of worldly phenomena. The present section reviews this doctrinal background against which the Buddha presented his concept of causation.

The Indian theoreticians' concern with causation originated from two main sources: first, the Vedic interest in ritual and in the mechanisms by which certain actions bear fruits; second, the cosmogonic speculations of Vedic thinkers who tried to explain the evolution of the universe. The Vedic outlook was later challenged by a dominant conceptual framework that arose, at least in its part, within the Brahmanical tradition itself and constructed a new symbolic world. Almost all the major intellectual and spiritual movements elaborated their worldviews within this conceptual framework, which is evidenced in the early *Upanisads*. It consists in three fundamental concepts: *saµsara*, the idea that existence is subject to a round of rebirth, which is a state of bondage and suffering; *karma*, the idea that ritual and moral actions fuel and determine this process of rebirth; and *moksa*, the idea that liberation from *saµsara* is possible and is the ultimate goal to which all spiritual effort should be directed. It is this conceptual framework that provides the context for understanding ancient India's concern with causation. Once this framework gained dominance and *moksa* was acknowledged as the highest ideal, the Indian thinkers sought to account for a universe that allows for the possibility of liberation. Such an account must guarantee that events and actions stand in causal relations to each other. The Indian thinkers thus sought to identify the causal relations that are relevant to liberation.

The inseparability of religious concerns and theoretical-doctrinal interests characterizes Indian Buddhism as well as the primary Brahmanical schools. Setting human experience in *saµsara* as the starting point of the philosophical discussion would shape an introspective mindset that closely relates the contents discussed to the interior of human experience, causation being no exception. This is markedly different frcm the line of development of the concept of causation in Western thought that begins with the pre-Socratics, continues with Aristotle and culminates in the works of Hume and Kant. According to this line of thought speculations about the problem of causation are instigated by fascination with the sciences, the paradigm of which is mathematics, rather than with the existential problem of human suffering. Ye t the preoccupation of the main Indian religious-philosophical traditions with experience and soteriology does not necessarily result in psychologism or mysticism. Exactitude, clarity and formal criteria of theoretical investigation can be applied to aformal contents, and Indian philosophy, indeed abounds with analytical discussions of the veridical status and the nature of the scope of the mental.

In the *Nikayas* the Buddha's formulaic descriptions of dependent co-arising and the explanation of the origin of suffering are contrasted with four doctrines of causation: the first is the doctrine of 'done by oneself *(sayamkatam)*, or self-agency, according to which suffering depends upon one's own deeds; the second is the doctrine of 'done by another' *(paramkatam)*, claiming that suffering is determined by factors external to the person; the third is a combination of these two views *(sayamkatañ ca paramkatañ ca)*, arguing that suffering results both from one's own deeds and from external factors; finally there is the doctrine that refuses to admit the notion of causation as an invariable relation altogether *(asayamkdram aparamkdram)*, claiming that suffering arises fortuitously and is created neither by oneself nor by another. Having classified these four positions, the Buddha rejects them all.

The first doctrine, *sayamkatam*, implies the view that the effect is not different from the cause but is somehow inherent in it. Its origins can be traced back to the Rg Vedic period and to the Upanisadic notions of *atman* and evolution. The Rg Vedic hymns do not yet have a clear concept of causality, although they do attest to the fact that the Vedic poets held a belief in the uniformity of nature and that they tried to explain how the ordered universe they witnessed had originated and developed to its present form. Thus various Rg Vedic hymns express the idea that becoming or change is a self-becoming or a self-manifestation of the very same origin in different forms, and so that which changes and that into which it is changed are identical. For example, the hymns that address Agni depict his different births and imply that Agni is a foetus *(garbha)*, a germ or a latent form which already exists in the kindling fire sticks, in plants, in the earth and the sky and in the cosmic order. A further development of the idea of the pre-existence of the effect in its cause is implied by the latest hymns, mainly the cosmogonic hymns of the tenth *mandala*, which introduce the view that the universe is the result of a gradual evolution of one or several primeval substrates and that certain phenomena give rise to certain other phenomena in an orderly sequence by virtue of their inherent power *(svadha)*. For example, *Rg Veda* 10.190 states that 'Order *(rta)* and truth *(satya)* were born from heat *(tapas)* as it blazed up. From that was born night; from that heat was born the billowy ocean. From the billowy ocean was born the year, that arranges days and nights, ruling over all that blinks its eyes.' Another example is the *Purusa Sukta* that introduces the view that the very parts of Purusa's body were actually the original stuff which turned into the four social estates, the sun and moon, the sky and earth, the gods, and so forth. The explicit term *hetu* or 'cause', however, is first found in one of the more personal and psychological Rg Vedic hymns, wherein the poet refers to himself as a gambler who laments his compulsive attraction to the dice.

He confesses that 'because of a losing throw of the dice I have driven away a devoted wife'.

In the *Upanisads* the idea of a self-manifestation of the same origin is further elaborated in terms of an abstract notion of being or existence. A central Upanisadic teaching concerns the cosmic homology or correspondence between the essence or true nature of the microcosm, namely, *dtman,* and the essence or true nature of the macrocosm, that is, *brahman.* The latter was conceived of as the reality underlying the phenomenal world and was characterized as having a permanent, immutable and unchanging nature. In the sixth chapter of the *Chdndogya Upanisad,* one of the most famous Upanisadic passages, Uddalaka Åruni instructs his son on the nature of reality and unfolds the representative Upanisadic teaching of substantial-ism and eternalism. According to this teaching, the world has its origin and unity in existence or being *(sat),* namely, that which exists solely and completely by virtue of its own power of existence; it is the ultimate, irreducible substance in which all entities are a priori contained and with which they are identical. Uddalaka maintains that this primal existence, the root and cause of everything, cannot originate, as some think, in non-existence. Rather, it is something that is alive and has the conscious desire 'to be many' and to emanate powers from itself.

The Buddha, however, refusing to admit any metaphysical principle as a common thread holding the moments of encountered phenomena together, rejects the Upanisadic notion of an immutable substance or principle underlying the world and the person and producing phenomena out of its inherent power, be it 'being', *dtman, brahman* or 'god'. Rather, he declares: 'Kassapa, with reference to what exists from the beginning, [the thought] that "the one who acts is the one who experiences [the result]" amounts to the assertion of eternalism, namely: "suffering is created by oneself".'

The second doctrine of causation, *paramkatam,* suggests that the effect is a completely different entity from the cause. This view groups various teachings promulgated by non-Buddhists and wandering ascetics, which emerged as a revolt against Vedic ritualism and certain elements of the influential Brahmanical metaphysics. That this position was popular mainly among non-

Buddhist religious followers is indicated by the initial verses of the *Svetdsvatara Upanisad,* which mention a set of heretical doctrines of causation:

People who make inquiries about *brahman* say: 'What is the cause of *brahman?* Why were we born? By what do we live? On what are we established? Governed by whom, O you who know *brahman,* do we live in pleasure and in pain, each in our respective situation? Should we regard it as time *(kdla),* as inherent nature *(svabhdva),* as necessity *(niyati),* as chance *(yadrcchd),* as the elements *(bhutdni),* as the source of birth *(yoni),* or as the Person *(purusd)*? Or is it a combination of these?' But that can't be, because there is the self.

The representatives of such teachings are the materialists and the sceptics, generally called Lokayatas. Among them the Carvakas, whose main proponent is identified as Ajita Kesakambali, argued that all phenomena are reducible to transformations of material particles and occur by virtue of matter's inherent nature, *svabhava.* This view, *svabhdva-vdda,* or naturalism, is classified in the *Nikayas* as a *paramkatam* doctrine because that inherent nature was conceived of as a force at work in material phenomena, a purely physical law and in this sense external to the person and so denying the validity of human exertion as a causal factor. Others, mainly the Ajivikas, adhered to determinism *(niyati-vdda),* leaving no room for human volition or chance occurrence. We are told that Makkhali Gosala, for instance, taught that

There is no cause, no condition for the defilement of beings, they become defiled without cause or condition. There is no cause, no condition for the purification of beings, they are purified without cause or condition. [...] All beings, all that lives, all creatures, all living things are without control, powerless and without vigour; they are changed according to fate, species and nature as they experience happiness or suffering in the six classes of being.

Purana Kassapa and Pakudha Kaccayana are said to have arrived at a similar rejection of a moral account of action. The Buddha rebuffs the *paramkatam* doctrine for two main reasons: first, it leads to annihilationism while positing an existence which is annihilated. Second a necessary corollary of this doctrine is the denial of human exertion and moral retribution - an outcome which the Buddha strongly disapproved of. He is recorded as saying: 'Kassapa, with reference to one stricken by feeling, [the thought] that "the one who acts is one, the one who experiences [the result] is another" amounts to the assertion of annihilationism, namely: "suffering is created by another".'

In repudiating the third type of causational doctrine, *sayamkatañ ca paramkatañ ca,* the likelihood is that the Buddha pointed his criticism at the Jain teaching. The *Sutrakrtanga,* one of the oldest parts of the Svetambara texts (dated to the fifth or fourth centuries BCE), contains references to the various non-Buddhist positions mentioned in the opening sentence of the *Svetasvatara Upanisad* cited above. The Jains did not simply dismiss these positions, but rather argued that each of them had overemphasized the role of a certain factor, such as time, inherent nature etc., and that none of them was tenable when taken individually; only when considered as a group or from different standpoints was their causal status admissible. This assimilative view follows from the Jain non-absolutism, or non-categorical theory of truth (literally 'many-pointedness theory', *anekanta-vada),* namely, the view that everything has various aspects and hence conflicting theories may each be true from one point of view but false from another. With reference to causation this implies that cause and effect may be both identical and non-identical. A cause has a potential to produce an effect, and so the effect pre-exists in its cause, but at the same time the effect is a real, new entity different from its cause. In the *Nikayas* this assimilative doctrine is not attributed to any specific school, but the Buddha criticizes it all the same.

Logically this doctrine combines two opposite views both refuted by the Buddha, and a valid view cannot be obtained by conjoining two untenable views.

Finally the Buddha rejects the doctrine of *asayaµkaram aparaµkaraµ*, or rather indeterminism (*yad®ccha*), namely, the view that all events are subject to chance occurrence, which undermines the very notion of causation and amounts to a belief in fortuitous origination (*adhiccasamuppada*). He relates to the adherents of this view thus: 'There are, monks, some ascetics and Brahmins who are "Chance-Originationists", who proclaim that the self and the world are chance-originated.' He then classifies this position under the group of 'wrong views', for it subverts human volition and moral responsibility, and hence is opposed to the Buddhist principles. By using the appellations *sayaµkatam* and *paraµkatam,* thus referring to the cause in terms of a personal agent, the Buddha argues with the Upanisadic notion of *atman.* The term *kataµ,* a passive participle, introduces the idea of agency, which implies moral responsibility – an ethical issue separate from causation. As we shall see below, the Buddha rejects the idea of an agent, though he is committed to human agency and moral responsibility. His earliest teaching is thus concerned more with ethics than with causation *per se.* At some point, however – whether during the lifetime of the Buddha himself or of his immediate followers – what is morally good was regarded as intellectually good, so that moral conduct became interchangeable with knowledge of how things truly are, namely, the way phenomena originate and pass away according to causes and conditions. Both the ethical and the intellectual dimensions of the Buddha's teaching are integrated in the *paticcasamuppada* formula, where they are mainly expressed by the links of craving and ignorance respectively.

In sum, the Buddha's stance regarding causation is empirical, morally oriented and focused on human responsibility. The Buddha dismisses the particular claims of all his contemporary causational doctrines, but in doing so he rejects something deeper than that. Despite their diversity these doctrines rely, to different degrees, on substance metaphysics. As explained in Chapter , substance metaphysics engenders an ontological model on which the phenomenal world is made up of externally real entities endowed with qualities; 'things' that at their basis are immutable substances and that possess certain characteristics. Resultant from such an ontology are the assumptions that the causal relation is a binary function of 'cause' and 'effect', and that it has a sense of production. A cause is that which produces something and in terms of which the product, its effect, can be explained. Causes and effects are thus changes in the states of substances, and causation is an invariable relation between the characteristics of those substances: whenever a substance occurs with the characteristic x, it produces a substance with the characteristic y. Now the metaphysical horizons of a given philosophical system shape and determine its ensuing concepts, causation inclusive. A causal relation between two substances would have a different sense from a causal relation between two processes or events. Drawing on process metaphysics rather than substance metaphysics, the Buddha was led into recasting the concept of causation as a whole. We now turn to the embodiment of this concept in the doctrine of dependent co-arising.

Kamma, Causation and the Paticcasamuppåda Doctrine

The Buddha's experience on the night of his awakening illustrates the fundamentals of early Buddhist teaching as presented by the tradition. Having recollected his own and others' former lives, the Buddha (re)discovers the way to uproot the deepest tendencies (*asava*) that bind one to continued rebirth, and directly sees the four noble truths. He then realizes how and why the arising, maintenance and dissolution of any given individual history, as well as of *saµsaric* experience as a whole, follows a certain orderly pattern. This brings about his insight into the dynamics of the law of *kamma:* how every action has its consequences and that everything occurs in dependence on other conditions. *Saµsaric* existence can thus be seen as a 'mass of karma', any segment of which appears depending on the rise of certain sequences of coordinated factors. The relationship between the patterns of these sequences is called *paticcasamuppada* (Sanskrit *pratityasamutpada*), dependent co-arising, which we may render as 'causal relatedness' or 'condition-ality'. In the sense that all *saµsaric* phenomena are conditioned (*saðkhata*), *paticcasamuppada* is the Buddhist principle of causation. Since *saµsaric* experience is characterized as *dukkha, paticcasamuppada* is particularly an explanation of the nature and origin of *dukkha* – the crux of the four noble truths. By clarifying how one process leads to another, *paticcasamuppada* illustrates what makes up sentient experience: the causal relations between ordered successions of physical and mental processes, not their inherence in some substrate. And this is the way things truly are: to grasp the *paticcasamuppada* principle is therefore to realize *Dhamma*. Indeed, the canonical texts often equate the *Dhamma* with *patic-casamuppada*. Perhaps the most acclaimed occasion is when Sariputta reports the Buddha to have said that 'Whoever sees *paticcasamuppada* sees the *Dhamma,* and whoever sees the *Dhamma* sees *paticcasamuppada.*'

The causational principle is also labelled *idappaccayata* (Sanskrit *idaµpratyay-ata*), 'the state of having this or that as its cause', and is represented by a succinct formula: 'This existing, that comes to be; from the arising of this, that arises; this not existing, that does not come to be; from the cessation of this, that ceases.' One may thus be tempted to conclude that *paticcasamuppada* is but the Buddhist formulation of a law of universal causation. The latter is defined by Bertrand Russell as follows: 'There are such invariable relations between different events at the same or different times that, given the state of the whole universe throughout any finite time, however short, every previous and subsequent event can theoretically be determined as a function of the given events during that time.' *Pa ticcasamuppada,* however, is bound up with the concept of *kamma*. Now the Buddha did not simply take over an extant doctrine of karma. The word *karman* means 'action' or 'activity', but within the Brahmanical context it refers to the Vedic ritual, which is regarded as the paradigmatic action. From this perspective every action produces a fitting result, the quality of which is determined by the quality of the action. By contrast, the Buddha redefined karma and turned it into an intrinsic, psychological process: *kamma* emerged as a particular kind of mentality, one's act of will or intention (*cetana*), which is manifested in physical, speech or mental acts. 'It is intention', the Buddha says, 'that I call *kamma.* Having intended, one performs acts by body, speech and mind.' Recasting karma from 'action' to 'intention', the Buddha ethicized the contemporary conceptual framework and shifted the focus of interest from the Brahmanical outlook of external, ritual action to the arena of one's mind and its intrinsic psychological processes. It is this ethicized sense of *kamma* that is fundamental to the *paticcasamup-pada* doctrine. The Pali texts thus portray *kamma* as the key conditioning factor in the causal chain:

What one intends, plans and inclines to is the basis of the establishing of consciousness. When there is a basis there is support for consciousness. When consciousness has been supported and has grown, there follows the production of future renewed existence. Once there is future renewed existence, future birth, ageing and death, sorrow, lamentation, unsatis-factoriness, grief and unrest come into being. Such is the arising of this whole mass of suffering.

This *Nidana-saµyutta* statement is followed by another similar passage, which explicitly sets *cetana* as the first link in the traditional, twelvefold *paticcasamup-pada* formula, instead of the first two usual links of ignorance and mental formations. The Buddhist construal of causal conditioning, then, is concerned with the workings of the mind rather than with the mechanics of the world: the emphasis is on how certain kinds of mentality that condition the ways in which one thinks, talks and behaves, shape and determine one's course of life and one's relation to the environment.

Now *paticcasamuppada* as centred around *kamma* is not equivalent to a law of universal causation. First, such a law deals with causes and effects regardless of whether they are related to the person, whereas the *paticcasamuppada* principle delineates the relationships between physical and mental processes insofar as they impinge on one's experience in *saµsara*. Second, a law of universal causation does not necessarily entail that like causes produce like effects, while the *paticcasamup-pada* principle implies that like intention conditions like action. The moral character of one's intention – whether it is skilful, unskilful or neutral – determines the quality of the respective acts it motivates. What type of causational principle is it, then?

First a distinction should be made between *paticcasamuppada* as an abstract principle of causation – a metaphysical account of the true nature of things – and the articulation of this principle for the sake of specifying the actual patterned operation of causal conditioning. This is given by succinct formulas listing chains of several factors or links (*nidana*). The most representative formula is that of the twelvefold chain:

Conditioned by (1) ignorance are (2) mental formations, conditioned by mental formations is (3) consciousness, conditioned by consciousness is (4) name-and-form, conditioned by name-and-form are (5) the six senses, conditioned by the six senses is (6) sense contact, conditioned by sense contact is (7) feeling, conditioned by feeling is (8) craving, conditioned by craving is (9) clinging, conditioned by clinging is (10) becoming, conditioned by becoming is (11) birth, conditioned by birth is (12) ageing and death – sorrow, lamentation, unsatisfactoriness, grief and unrest come into being. Such is the arising of this whole mass of suffering.

There are numerous canonical variations on this traditional twelvefold formula, even in its forward order (*anuloma*): some present consciousness and name-and-form as mutually conditioning, or list the twelve links in a different order. Others present the formula in backward order (*patiloma*); some trace the cessation of each link; some omit links to various numbers ranging from eleven down to just two, while others add links. This diversity in the presentation of the *paticcasamup-pada* formula has invoked speculation as to the possible stages of its evolution. Whatever its history, however, the largely shared body of Pali and Chinese material shows that a variety of formulaic descriptions of the *paticcasamuppada* doctrine already existed at an early stage of Buddhist thought, and that the stock twelvefold formula served as a standard schematization of pivotal elements of the Buddha's teaching. The various canonical and commentarial interpretations of the *patic-casamuppada* formula have long been studied by modern scholarship and there is no need to repeat them here. Most pertinent to our present concern, however, is that at the level of metaphysics the formula demonstrates the Buddhist conception of change and continuity as consisting solely in the causal connectedness between impermanent processes, rather than in an immutable substance underlying change in its secondary qualities. It exemplifies that the notions of continuity and identity are meaningful, although they do not imply the existence of any metaphysical principle that makes encountered phenomena continuous and identifiable.

This leads us from the formulaic presentation of the *paticcasamuppada* to the principle it articulates. The Buddha is recorded as saying that he teaches both *paticcasamuppada* and the *dhammas* that arise in dependence on conditions. An adequate examination of the *paticcasamuppada* doctrine, then, must take into account not only the nature of dependent co-arising itself, but also the nature of the arisen *dhammas*. A first hint in that direction is given immediately following the above statement, where, in reply to the question 'What are the dependently co-arisen *dhammas?*' the Buddha depicts each of the twelve factors of the *paticcasamuppada* formula as 'impermanent, conditioned, dependently arisen, subject to decay, subject to waning away, liable to fading away and of a nature to cease.' The point is that all the enumerated phenomena – ageing and death, birth, becoming and the rest of the factors of the twelvefold formula – are processes: dynamic, physical and mental processes that are subject to constant change. The *paticcasamuppada* formula explains why and how the processes that tie one to *saμsara* occur in a non-random order, and since these processes are paradigmatic of all the dependently arisen *dhammas* – all conditioned phenomena – it establishes a comprehensive portrayal of the way things operate. The formula thus embodies the early Buddhist process epistemology, which maintains that processes rather than 'things' best represent encountered phenomena, and that to know how experience in *saμsara* originates and ceases is to comprehend how those phenomena are causally connected. From this one may disentangle a metaphysics that sees temporality and change as fundamental to human experience, and that repudiates the notion of a substance or agent, that is, *atman*, as an underlying self-substantiated reality from which phenomena derive their actuality. William Waldron remarks in this context that 'Instead of asking how independent entities act within or upon an objective world, the view of dependent arising asks "under what conditions does such and such a phenomenon arise?" or, more elaborately, "what complex of conditions operates in what recurrently patterned ways in order to typically give rise to what kind of phenomena?"'

Pa ticcasamuppada as a principle of causal connectedness does not posit that a certain independent substance at some point operates on another independent substance to activate change. Indeed even within the framework of a substance-attribute ontology the causal relation does not necessarily hold between substances: in modern philosophy causation is frequently regarded as a relation between changes or states of substances, or alternatively between events – where 'event' signifies a change or an absence of a change in an object. But the Buddhist position is more radical than that: it not only states that causation is a relation between experiential processes rather than substances, but it also recasts the whole concept of causation in line with its process-oriented epistemology, thus investing it with a novel significance. As part of this conceptual reconstruction the very terms 'cause' and 'effect' are recognized as mere constructs that emerge conditioned by the cognitive process through which we make sense of all the factors of our experience. Sue Hamilton has elucidated the connection between the operation of the *khandhas* as our cognitive process and dependent co-arising: if one links the description of all things in our cyclical experience as conditioned by other things with the way the operation of our cognitive apparatus *is* this very experience, Hamilton says, 'one can see that what all things are *actually* dependently originated in is our cognitive apparatus'. This is demonstrated in a *Majjhima* passage, where repeated examples of *khandha* activity yielding various cognitive processes – such as the six modalities of cognitive awareness (*cakkhuviññã~a* etc.) – are interspersed with the statement: 'Such are the depend-ently originated phenomena, namely, the five aggregates of grasping.' Causation, then, is a relation holding between psycho-physical processes as constructed by the mind, and the *paticcasamuppada* principle reveals how past or present mental formations ripen into present or future courses of action.

Ye t this reconstruction does not amount to an elimination of the concept of causation, for otherwise early Buddhism could not have retained its commitment to moral responsibility. The canonical texts not only emphasize the conditioned co-arising of all phenomena as constructed by our cognitive process, but also stress the regularity, objectivity and universal validity of the causal relation. Thus, having explained what *paticcasamuppada* and what the dependently arisen *dhammas* are, the Buddha states that whether Tathagatas were to arise in this world or not, 'that element still persists: the way things are, the way they work and the fact of conditionality'. He then adds that *paticcasamuppada* is characterized by exactitude (*tathata,* literally 'it is exactly so'), necessity (*avitathata*), invariability or uniformity (*anaññathatã*, 'not otherwise') and the fact of conditional-ity (*idappaccayata*). This is supported by the commentary that explains the characteristics in the above passage as follows:

'Exactitude' etc., are epithets of the mode of conditions. Because on account of such-and-such conditions alone, neither more nor less, there arises such-and-such a *dhamma,* there is said to be 'exactitude'. Once the conditions have combined together there is no obstruction, even for a moment, of the development of the originating *dhammas,* and hence there is said to be 'necessity'. Because no *dhamma* arises on account of the conditions of another *dhamma,* there is said to be 'invariability'. Because there is a condition or a group of conditions of ageing and death etc., as stated, there is said to be 'conditionality'. Another revealing indication of the Buddha's emphasis on the objectivity of the causal relation and its independent status is found in the *Nagara-sutta,* wherein he compares his insight into the *paticcasamuppada* principle to the exposure of an ancient, buried city that has existed independently of anyone knowing of it. The *paticcasamuppada* doctrine centres on the idea of *kamma,* and *kamma* is mainly intention, that is, a certain kind of mentality. This implies that any attempt to evaluate the early Buddhist conception of *paticcasamuppada* as a causational principle must take into account this mental aspect, which Buddhism sees as an integral part of its notion of causation. Moreover, since the formation of concepts about causality is itself part of the way our cognitive apparatus operates, this also means that for early Buddhism the construction of causation by our cognitive process – just as the construction of all encountered phenomena – is not regarded as a representational activity mirroring what is outside the mind, and its analysis is not thought to uncover how the mind constructs mental copies that correspond to an external reality. The causal relation enjoys objectivity and universal validity, but these need not necessarily or exclusively characterize what is externally real.

Once a substance-attribute ontology is replaced by process metaphysics, the analysis of the causal relation in terms of 'cause' and 'effect' becomes inappropriate, for these are not regarded as two distinct entities whose qualities or properties undergo change. The binary idea of causal determination is replaced by the notion of *kammic* conditioning. By placing *kamma-*as-*cetana* at the hub of the *paticcasamup-pada* doctrine the Buddha clarifies that the causal relation is mentally conditioned in various ways. *'Kammic* conditioning' is a notion more flexible than 'causal determination' and suitable for representing the variety of *cetana*'s conditioning powers. Such a deflationary concept of causation avoids determinism (*niyati-vada*) and thus befits the intrinsic mental aspect of causation as seen from the Buddhist perspective. At the same time it also escapes the belief in fortuity (*adhicca-vada*) and is not too loose a concept. Let us examine this relation more closely.

Necessity and Sufficiency in the *Nikåya* Notion of Causal Conditioning

The causal relation exemplified by the *paticcasamuppada* formula is not that of production of a substantial entity out of some other substantial entity or entities, but of the supporting conditions for the arising and ceasing of *dhammas*. In accordance with the Buddhist postulate of impermanence, what is being discussed here is the arising and ceasing of *dhammas qua* physical and mental processes that are subject to change. Such an analysis requires one to distinguish between the diverse supporting conditions that are individually necessary and collectively sufficient for the arising of a given process. This is reminiscent of a model of causation which has gained currency in contemporary Western philosophy, contrary to the fundamental position advocated by Hume.

The most influential contribution to the analysis of causation was made by David Hume (1711–76). In harmony with his empiricist worldview, Hume sought to establish non-demonstrative inferences about empirical matters, that is, justify our reasoning concerning matters of fact beyond the testimony of the senses. He assumed that causation is the fundamental and immediate subject of all such inferences and that our idea of causation combines three elements: succession, contiguity and necessary connection between causes and effects. His specific task was to account for the necessary connection between phenomenal objects. His conclusion, though, was negative: in objects there is no such necessity that could justify our non-demonstrative inferences. Our idea of invariable causation results from those very inferences, which are grounded in the psychology of human custom rather than in reason. Hume's conclusion is summed up in his two definitions of causation: (i) 'A cause is an object precedent and contiguous to another, and where all the objects resembling the former are placed in like relation of priority and contiguity to those objects that resemble the latter.' Here causation is identified with regular succession. (ii) 'A cause is an object precedent and contiguous to another, and so united with it, that the idea of the one determines the mind to form the idea of the other, and the impression of the one to form a more lively idea of the other.' According to this definition the above succession becomes a psychological association.

Hume's idea of causation is at odds with situations where there is a set of factors, each necessary and jointly sufficient for a certain result, which all precede or occur contiguously with that result. Then, had any given factor not occurred the result would not have occurred either, although one would be reluctant to say of each of these factors that it caused the result. Contrary to Hume's conclusion, then, there arose the view that a given event occurs under a set of conditions, both indispensable and contingent. The former are conditions without which the event in question would not have occurred; the latter are conditions of which presence is accidental to the event's occurrence. This model requires one to distinguish the indispensable conditions from the 'proper' cause of a given event.

In his discussion of causation John Stuart Mill (1806-73) claims that the invariable sequence we find in nature between antecedents and consequents of certain sorts consists in the consequent and the sum-total of several antecedents, the occurrence of all of which is requisite to produce the consequent. 'In such cases', Mill claims,

> it is very common to single out only one of the antecedents under the domination of Cause, calling the others merely Conditions. [...] The real Cause is the whole of these antecedents; and we have, philosophically speaking, no right to give the name of cause to one of them exclusively of the others'.

The contemporary reading of this view draws the following distinctions: a given event that is sufficient for the occurrence of another event is the latter's cause; one that is necessary for that matter is the latter's condition; necessitated by the occurrence of a certain event is the effect; contingent upon the occurrence of a certain event is a resultant of that event.

This construal of causation as a relation between events is still grounded in a substance metaphysics, for an event here signifies either a change or an absence of change in the relation of an object to a standard reference during a specified time interval. Events are the having or lacking of properties by particular objects at particular time intervals. Substance metaphysics, however, is not the single type of metaphysics at one's disposal. The early Buddhist *paticcasamuppada* doctrine shows that causation may well be construed within the framework of process metaphysics, as a relation between phenomenal occurrences that do not draw on the notion of a substance. Within this framework the causal relation denotes causal connectedness based on *kammic* conditioning. The *Nikayas* explicate this type of conditionality in terms of necessary and sufficient conditions for the arising and ceasing of physical and mental processes. Consider, for example, the account of visual cognitive awareness *(cakkhuviññana):*

> If the eye is internally intact, but no external visual forms come within its perceptual range and there is no corresponding appropriate act of attention, then there is no manifestation of the corresponding type of cognitive awareness. If the eye is internally intact and external visual forms do come within its perceptual range, but there is no corresponding appropriate act of attention, then there is no manifestation of the corresponding type of cognitive awareness. But once the eye is internally intact, visual forms come within its perceptual range and there is a corresponding appropriate act of attention, then there is, indeed manifestation of the corresponding type of cognitive awareness.

The commentary explains the term 'appropriate act of attention' *(tajjo samannåharo)* as proper attention *(manasikara)* arising conditioned by the eye and visual forms. This, following the Abhidhamma analysis of the consciousness process, is identified as the *kiriya* mind consciousness element that directs the flow of the passive mind *(bhavanga)* towards the initiation of an active process of visual cognitive awareness at the eye door process. When the visual forms fail to come within the eye's perceptual range, or if one is occupied with something else, such an act of attention does not occur. The point is that visual cognitive awareness results from the presence of three conditions: an unimpaired sense organ of sight, external visible forms entering into the field of vision and an appropriate act of attention on the part of the mind. Each of these three conditions is necessary to the occurrence of visual cognitive awareness, and when the three of them are obtained they are collectively sufficient for the manifestation of the particular kind of consciousness in question.

Another canonical indication of the understanding of the causal relation in terms of necessary and sufficient conditions is found in a *Samyutta* passage delineating the supporting conditions for the growth, increase and expansion of five kinds of seeds into sprouts. Therein the process of growth is depicted as resultant from a group of *sine qua non* conditions, each of which is a necessary condition such that had it not been present, the sprout would not have grown: the seeds have to be unbroken, not rotten and undamaged by the wind and sun; they should be fresh; they must be well planted; and they must be supported by earth and water. When all four conditions are collectively satisfied the growth of the seeds comes about.

To sum up, the Nikaya notion of causation is remarkably different from its contemporary doctrines of causation. First, rather than analysing the production of entities it accounts for the arising and ceasing of psycho-physical processes. Second instead of physical causality it centres on the idea of *kammic* connectedness by mental conditioning. Third instead of a binary portrayal of the causal relation as holding between a single cause and a corresponding single effect, it regards this relation as a manifoldness of supporting conditions: a group of interacting factors, individually necessary and jointly sufficient for setting off processes, none of which is *the* cause for the arising of those processes. Finally, it substitutes for the relation of causal determination that of *kammic* implication. This is evidenced in the abovementioned succinct verse formulating the principle of causation: 'This existing, that comes to be; from the arising of this, that arises; this not existing, that does not come to be; from the cessation of this, that ceases.' The formula by no means states that 'a causes b'. Rather, the arising of x implies the presence of y, and by the same token, the cessation of y is implied by the absence of x. The meaning, then, is framed in hypothetical terms: if y arose, then x had necessarily been present, whereas if x had ceased then y was necessarily eliminated. In this context, Sue Hamilton remarks that in order to understand this formula accurately, 'one has to see it not in terms of causation but of origination', which means that 'dependent origination is not stating that a will cause b, but that b occurs because there was a. Further, to grasp the mechanics better one needs to see it in the even looser sense that if there is a b, then there must have been an a.'

My argument is that the *paticcasamuppada* formula is not so much loose as pragmatic. It must be pragmatic if it is to deal with the workings of the mind. From the Buddhist perspective all encountered phenomena that constitute our experience in *samsara* are dependently originated precisely because they are conditioned by our cognitive process. *Paticcasamuppada* as a principle of causation does not depict what things are as given in an external, mind-independent reality, but reveals the mechanics of our cognitive apparatus, and hence it cannot be a deterministic law, although it may be universally valid. For, again, it shows that the structure of the experiential world is correlated with the cognitive process, and hence all the factors of experience are made factors of experience because they invariably and inevitably emerge as constructs of our cognitive apparatus.

At this stage we should appraise the terminology employed in discussing the *paticcasamuppada* doctrine. In the Pali Canon several words denote 'causal relatedness'. Buddhaghosa lists the most conspicuous ones: 'The words *paccaya, hetu, kdrana, nidana, sambhava, pabhava* etc., all have the same meaning, although they are different in the letter.' To this list one may add the words *upanisa, sankhara, mula, arammana, ahara, samutthana* and *samudaya*. Of these, the words *hetu* and *paccaya* are the most commonly used though *paccaya* features in the traditional twelvefold *paticcasamuppada* formula and recurs in the vast majority of its versions. *Paccaya* has a wide range of meaning: it signifies 'support', 'requisite', 'means', 'reason', 'grounds', 'cause'and 'condition'. *Hetu* is less laden a term, primarily denoting 'cause', 'reason' and 'condition'. Modern translations of the canonical texts and the extant scholarly literature show that contemporary Buddhologists normally translate *paccaya* as 'condition' and *hetu* as 'cause'. Nevertheless, in the *suttas* there is no ground for such a distinction: both terms are used interchangeably for rhetorical purposes. Numerous occasions testify to this semantic indiscrimination. For instance, in the *Mahanidana-sutta* the Buddha teaches Ånanda the *paticcasamuppada* doctrine and of each *nidana* of the twelvefold formula he says: 'Therefore, Ånanda, just this is the cause *(hetu)*, the source *(nidana)*, the origin *(samudaya)*, the condition *(paccaya)* for ageing and death, namely, birth... the condition for birth, namely, becoming, etc.' In this context *hetu andpaccaya* are synonyms that, for literary and pragmatic reasons, are juxtaposed with a series of other terms having slightly different meanings. Another example is the oft-repeated question, 'What is the *paccaya*, what is the *hetu*?' Similarly, in the *Mahaparinibbana-sutta* the Buddha relates to Ånanda 'Eight *hetu, eight paccaya* for the appearance of a great earthquake'; yet again, the *Dasuttara-sutta* says that 'There are eight *hetu*, eight *paccaya* for wisdom regarding the holy life.'

In the *suttas,* then, the causal relation is better construed in terms of condi-tionality, and both *hetu* and *paccaya* mean 'condition'. The semantic distinction between them probably mirrors the modern philosophical differentiation between cause and condition respectively. Nevertheless, while there is no ground for assigning the canonical texts the modern distinction between 'causal condition' and a 'proper cause', the texts do entertain a distinction between supporting conditions that are individually necessary for the occurrence of a certain process, and the set of those conditions collectively sufficient for the occurrence of the process in question. The *paticcasamuppada* twelvefold formula supposedly represents a linear succession of processes necessarily conditioned by one another: the arising of any given process implies the operation of another process, either preceding or coexistent with the former; the obliteration of any given process implies the cessation of another process, either subsequent to or coexistent with the former.

Within such a linear chain of couplets related by necessary and sufficient conditions it should have been possible to do away with *dukkha* simply by the cessation of any one of the twelve links, for the cessation of any *nidana* brings to a halt whichever *nidana* is said to follow it, thus obliterating the operation of the entire *dukkha*-process. This, however, works within each *nidana,* but not across the totality of them: the cessation of any one *nidana* is insufficient for the cessation of *dukkha* as a whole, and hence the process of conditioning still continues, for there are interrelations among the twelve *nidanas*. Ye t this is not to say that the *paticcasamuppada* formula represents a network of causally interrelated conditions. We shall see in the next section that such a network model, in which everything is interconnected to everything else, was developed by the Abhidhamma.

Still, the *Nikayas* already describe at least some of the twelve *nidanas* as mutually conditioned and as interrelated by a web of conditions with other processes. First, consciousness (*viñña~a*) and name-and-form (*namarupa*) are, on various occasions, said to be mutually dependent and then form a 'loop' once they have been combined into the twelvefold schema. The *locus classicus* of this view is the *Mahanidana-sutta,* which states that conditioned by consciousness there occurs name-and-form, and conditioned by name-and-form there emerges con-sciousness. This reciprocity is compared to that between two standing sheaves of reeds mutually supporting and leaning against each other so that if one were to remove either of them, the other would fall. The mutual conditioning between consciousness and name-and-form may be highlighted from another angle. As mentioned above, the process of sensory, discriminative cognitive awareness is explained as conditioned by the joint operation of three necessary factors: an intact sense organ, sense data entering the sense sphere, or the perceptual field of the appropriate sense organ, and an appropriate act of attention on the part of the mind. Now what is implied by these three conditions is the operation of a psycho-physical complex equipped with sense faculties, namely, *namarupa*. But this psycho-physical complex is incapable of arousing sensory discriminative, cognitive awareness on its own unless it is supported by consciousness. Hence both *viñña~a* and *namarupa* are mutually dependent and reciprocally condition each other. Hamilton explicates this mutual dependence from another perspective: first, she shows that in the Pali texts *namarupa* is associated with the structure of our cognitive apparatus, and hence that *nama* should be taken to refer to what is conceived of, *rupa* to what is apperceived. Insofar as these two thus cover the range of whatever is cognizable, *namarupa* is equivalent to the four *khandhas* other than *viñña~a.* Since *viñña~a* and *namarupa* represent the most fundamental aspects of one's present life – for they are what actualizes the processes that are the person and are equally necessary for one's subsequent development – they operate together and are mutually dependent.

Other processes within the *paticcasamuppada* formula, too, are mutually conditioned, although this is not explicitly stated. For instance, becoming conditions birth, but birth conditions becoming in a future renewed existence. The same applies to birth and ageing-and-death. Along with the relation of reciprocal conditioning the *paticcasamuppada* also accommodates the relation of concomitance: this is exemplified in the relation between sense contact (*phassa*) and feeling (*vedana*), which is compared to that between fire and its resulting heat. Just as from the friction of two fire sticks both fire and heat are emitted concomitantly, so from a sense contact experienced as pleasant, painful or neither-pleasant-nor-painful a corresponding feeling concomitantly springs up. It turns out that there are interrelations among the *nidanas*, as well as among other processes. Ignorance, for instance, mutually interacts with the defiling tendencies (*asava*), and consciousness is also one of the four nutriments (*ahara*) and as such follows from craving, while the four nutriments condition consciousness and future renewed existence. The *paticcasamuppada* thus hints at the possibility that interrelations of mutual conditioning and reciprocity hold not only among those processes directly tracing the origin of suffering, but also among whatever phenomena may eventuate. The five physical sense faculties (*indriya*), for example, originate in dependence on the life force (*ayu*), but the latter is conditioned by the *kamma*-born heat (*usma*) intrinsic to the living body, which itself is conditioned by the life force.

Accommodating relations such as mutual conditioning or concomitance, the *paticcasamuppada* formula expresses something more intricate than mere one-directional, causal relations between the operation of a single process and the occurrence of a certain other process. This was later on made clear by the commentaries, which advocate the view that 'There is no single or multiple result of any kind from a single condition, nor a single result from multiple conditions, but only multiple results from multiple conditions.' It also invokes the idea that each process conditions and may be conditioned by a set of other processes, to each of which it may stand in a different type of causal relation.

These different relations are treated in the *Nikayas* in a rather perfunctory manner. To judge by the *Nikayas*, the Buddha and his immediate disciples were not too interested in analysing the possible relations among the *sine qua non* conditions that make up a sufficient condition for an arisen process, nor in the variety of possible relations between these conditions and the arisen process. Rather, they were preoccupied with singling out the general mechanism by which processes are related. The motivation of the immediate community was not to reveal the exact nature of the relations by which birth, for example, is connected with numerous other processes, one of which is ageing-and-death, but to uncover which processes are most prominently related to ageing-and-death, so that with their elimination ageing-and-death would cease. The focus is on the cognitive apparatus, which, in turn, determines how and why one's life comes about. To know how and why one's life occurs the way it does is, according to the Buddhist postulate of impermanence, to understand the mechanics of the incessant, dynamic process of arising and ceasing of phenomena. The Buddha offers a cure for an ailment, a prescription of how to bring to a halt this continuous cyclical experience in *saµsara*. For this purpose the most efficient analysis is of how processes operate: how experience as suffering comes about and how it can be ended. In an oft-quoted *Majjhima* passage, the Buddha states that he has always made known only two things, namely, *dukkha* and the cessation of *dukkha*. With such a goal in mind speculations regarding the true nature and status of the constituents of experience become secondary. The Buddha was thus less anxious to account for such questions and dispensed with a theoretical account of reality. The *paticcasamuppada* doctrine is a pragmatic manual of the dynamics of change, rather than a descriptive metaphysics. An analysis of all the possible relations that may hold among the sum-total of conditions, and between those conditions and their conditioned processes, constitutes one such theoretical account or metaphysical explanation of sentient experience. It was the task of the Abhidhamma to offer such a systematic account.

THE ABHIDHAMMA THEORY OF CAUSAL CONDITIONING

Taking into account the Buddha's statement that there are two aspects to his teaching, namely, dependent co-arising and the dependently arisen *dhammas*, I have argued that the *paticcasamuppada* doctrine must be related to the Buddhist notion of what the *dhammas* are. By *dhammas* the Buddha and his immediate followers understood the physical and mental processes that make up sentient experience. Previously we have seen that this construal of *dhammas* yielded a notion of causal conditionality that is better understood in terms of *kammic* conditioning and implication rather than of causal production. Within the Abhidhamma framework, however, the conception of the plurality of *dhammas* changes significantly, and hence to understand the Abhidhamma theory of relations of causal conditioning, its relation to the *paticcasamuppada* doctrine and whether this theory is about causation at all, it must be investigated in the context of the consolidating *dhamma* theory and adjoined with the Abhidhamma metaphysics of mind, which may elucidate how this allegedly scholastic development is concerned with Buddhist soteriology. For the Abhidhammikas *dhammas* are diverse capacities or capabilities of psycho-physical events: short-lived minds and the instantiations of consciousness types that interact with material phenomena, each of which arising and ceasing in sequential series while having its own function and capability. In tandem with the tradition's gradual assimilation of the doctrine of momentariness, those events emerged as momentary: psycho-physical instants that emerge and subside extremely rapidly a large number of times each second, and that are all interrelated in a web of conditions. The Abhidhamma's concern with the systematization and individuation of the *dhammas* had direct implications for its notion of causal conditioning: to individuate one's mind the Abhidhammikas not only had to categorize all possible types of *dhamma* and provide the criteria for individuating any of their possible instances, but also to analyse all the possible conditions by which these discrete events interact and stand in relation to each other in the incessant process of their occurrence and cessation. Thus, the Abhidhamma substitutes for the image of a causal chain the image of a branching network of causal conditions. The *locus classicus* of the Abhidhamma theory of relations of causal conditioning is the *Pa tthana*.

The Patthåna

The *Pa tthana* (also called *Mahapakara~a*, The Great Book), the last and longest of the seven books of the *Abhidhamma-pitaka* is dated roughly to the second century BCE. In the *suttas* the term *patthana* is always found compounded with the word *sati*, forming the term *satipatthana*, which frequently recurs in the context of the meditative practice of observation and awareness of body, feelings, consciousness and *dhammas*. Bhikkhu Bodhi notes that the commentaries offer two derivations of *patthana* in this compound: one from the root *upa-stha* and the other from *pra-stha*, and that although they prefer the latter derivation, the former is supported by the Sanskrit *sm®tyupasthana*. C.A.F. Rhys Davids indeed points out that it is almost always derivatives from the root *upa-stha* rather than *pra-stha* that are associated with *sati* in the *Nikayas*. In the Abhidhamma literature, however, the term *patthana* does seem to derive from *pra-stha*. In classical Sanskrit, *pra-stha* means 'to stand forth, 'to set out' or 'depart from', and hence *prasthana* means 'setting out', 'departure', 'course' and 'method'. In the title of the seventh book of the *Abhidhamma-pitaka, patthana* roughly means point of departure, origin or cause, or alternatively a course of conditions. The term *thana* (literally 'place' or 'station') may be defined as the event by which a result is established, whereas the prefix *pa* signifies 'predominance' or 'pre-eminence'. Hence the *Pa tthana* teaches the principal causal conditions among all conditions.

The *Pa tthana* is concerned with the dependent nature of all encountered phenomena, and therefore represents the Abhidhamma elaboration on the *patic-casamuppada* doctrine, although here the analysis is not arranged according to the twelve *nidanas*, but rather according to twenty-four relations of causal conditioning, namely, *paccayas*. Where did these twenty-four relations originate? The *paticcasamuppada* doctrine, entwined with the Nikaya notion of causal conditioning as an assemblage of *sine qua non* conditions, reflects a sequential temporal model of causal conditioning, in which a certain process serves as the condition for the emergence of a subsequent process over a period of time, while the explanations of the enumerated processes emphasize their role in the operation of *kamma* and rebirth. Ye t the questions of the temporal relation and causal interrelations among the processes is not addressed in the *Nikayas*. The Abhidhamma shifts form a sequential approach to a momentary approach: it describes particular events using the categories which the *Nikayas* rather employ to refer to successive processes. The Abhidhamma thus offers a simultaneous temporal model of causal conditioning, in which all the distinct events partaking in a process function within a single moment. Drawing on this idea, the *Pa tthana* deals with all possible conditions that hold simultaneously among *dhammas* arising together in a given psycho-physical assemblage at a given moment in time. The text analyses each of those conditions in order to determine not only the relationships between successive *dhammas*, but also the interrelationships between simultaneous *dhammas*. It seeks to distinguish all possible ways in which a given psycho-physical event conditions the emergence of other psycho-physical events of its kind as well as of different kinds, that is, events arising both within and outside its own consciousness series. The twenty-four types of relationship of causal conditioning that are found to be holding between *dhammas* over a period of time and among *dham-mas* at a given instant form the scope of the *Pa tthana*. We shall see below that the post-canonical Theravada tradition further elaborates on this analysis by applying the scheme of the twenty-four *paccayas* to each of the twelve *nidanas*, explicating how the twelve *nidanas* operate successively over a period of time and how they function simultaneously within a single consciousness moment.

The structure of the *Pa tthana* is complex and difficult to follow. It consists of several different modes of analysis which interact and converge, forming many levels of divisions and subdivisions. The *Pa tthana* combines the analysis of the twenty-four causal conditions with the triplet-couplet *abhidhamma-matika*. The introductory part consists of a *matika* listing these twenty-four conditions and is followed by their analytical exposition. The main body of the text analyses the *dhammas* by four methods which form the four great divisions of the text. In each division the subject matter consists of six kinds of combination (according to triplets, couplets, couplet-triplet, triplet-couplet, triplet-triplet and couplet-couplet combinations). This gives the twenty-four divisions of the *Pa tthana*. Each of these combinations is treated under seven headings, each of which is divided into four sections according to whether the causal conditions are taken positively or negatively. The contents of each heading are then divided into a Questions Chapter and an Answers Chapter. In the very first Questions Chapter, for instance, the questions regarding the conditioned arising of the *dhammas* are asked (i) taking the conditions singly, by twos, by threes etc., up to the maximum of twenty-four conditions, (ii) by referring to each of the seven ways of taking the triplet skilful/unskilful/undeclared (*kusala, akusala, avyakata*), (iii) and under the seven headings of 'dependent', 'conascent', 'conditioned', 'supported', 'conjoined', 'associated' and 'investigation'. All these combinations are enumerated by means of four divisions, according to the following four methods:

1. *anuloma* or positive method, asking whether a certain *dhamma* may originate while being positively conditioned by another *dhamma* (e.g. 'Dependent on a skilful *dhamma,* may there arise a skilful *dhamma* by root condition?');
2. *paccaniya* or negative method, asking whether a certain *dhamma* may emerge while being negatively conditioned by another *dhamma* (e.g. 'Dependent on a skilful *dhamma,* may there arise a skilful *dhamma* by not-root condition?');
3. *anuloma-paccaniya* or positive-negative method, asking if a certain *dhamma* may occur while being both positively and negatively conditioned by another *dhamma.* Each of the

twenty-four relations of causal conditioning is then taken in its positive form and united with each of the remaining twenty-three relations in their negative form (e.g. 'Dependent on a skilful *dhamma,* may there arise a skilful *dhamma* by root condition, not-object condition?...by root condition, not-predominance condition?' etc.);

4 *paccaniya-anuloma* or negative-positive method, asking whether a certain *dhamma* may eventuate while being both negatively and positively conditioned by another *dhamma.* The difference is that here each of the twenty-four causal conditions is first taken in its negative form and united with each of the remaining twenty-three relations in their positive form (e.g. 'Dependent on a skilful *dhamma,* may there arise a skilful *dhamma* by not-root condition, object condition?...by not-object condition, predominance condition?' etc.).

Each of the Questions Chapters is then followed by a corresponding Answers Chapter. If all the possible combinations had been taken into account, there would have been roughly a billion questions, but not all can be answered: for example, for the forty-nine questions obtained by combining the first condition with dependent heading in the positive, only nine answers are obtained. The text does not specify all the questions and answers, but merely those that are necessary for illustrating the types of questions involved. Only the forty-nine questions for the first condition are fully given, while the others are abbreviated.

Having reviewed the *Pa tthana*'s structure and method, we now turn to the twenty-four types of relationships of causal conditioning and their analysis. While the *Nikayas* use the terms *paccaya* and *hetu* interchangeably, in the Abhidhamma *paccaya* specifically denotes the types of the relationships of causal conditioning, and *hetu* signifies one of these relationships only. Buddhaghosa explains the term *paccaya* as 'that from which [the result] comes about dependent on it'. The commentator emphasizes that *paccaya* is not merely any contingent circumstance invariably connected with the arising result, but that it must be actively helpful in this process of arising; it has to render service to the arisen result or group of results. The definition of *paccaya* is thus extended by saying that 'it has the characteristic of assisting'.

The *Pa tthana* commences with a *matika* listing the twenty-four *paccayas*, the first of which is cause condition (*hetupaccaya*). The analytical explanation merely says that this relation holds between a *dhamma* that conditions a certain other *dhamma* by being its *hetu*. Buddhaghosa glosses this as follows:

The word *hetu* is a designation for the roots that are the reason for the items being referred to [...] Briefly, here *hetu* has the sense of root and *paccaya* has the sense of assistance, so that cause condition is a *dhamma* assisting as a root. The teachers' intention is that it establishes the skil-fulness of the skilful etc., as paddy seeds do for paddy etc., and as the colour of crystal does for the lustre of crystal etc. [...] For *dhammas* that have obtained a cause condition are firm and stable, like trees whose roots have grown, but those without cause are unstable, like moss, sesame seeds etc. Hence the term 'cause condition' is to be understood as an 'assistant in the sense of a root'; an assistant *dhamma* by means of its establishing the state of being stable.

In this context, then, *hetu* is interchangeable with the term *mula*. In the *Nikayas mula* denotes six kinds of mentality or psychological motives: three of these are defiled and unskilful, namely, greed, hatred and delusion (*lobha*, *dosa* and *moha*), and the remaining three are their skilful opposites, namely, non-greed, non-hatred and non-delusion. These six are referred to as roots in the sense of primary types of mentality or predispositions that precipitate the occurrence of either unskilful or skilful bodily, verbal and mental acts respectively. The roots are psychological tendencies that shape human action by deed, speech and thought. Just as the roots are related to a tree as the basis for its growth and development, so the six mental roots induce their associated mental dispositions and keep them firmly fixed together, until the latter ripen into manifest acts. Although this explanation is also applicable to the *Pa tthana*, the latter's conception of *mula* is significantly different from the above psychological outlook. In the *Pa tthana* the term *mula* gains a more technical meaning, testifying to the doctrinal transition typical of the Abhidhamma from the empirical-phenomenal to the metaphysical. Within the Abhidhamma framework 'root' is equated with the term *hetu*, thus turning into an instantiation of an abstract category of metaphysically basic particulars: that of essential causal conditions.

For the cause condition is not merely a requisite supporting condition; rather, it is what individuates its related *dhamma*, establishing its nature and rendering it as this particular event rather than any other event of its kind. Of the twenty-four *paccayas*, cause condition is the one that directly capacitates the *dhammas'* individuation. I shall return to this point in greater detail below.

The second relation of causal condition is object condition (*aramma~apac-caya*). This relation is emblematized in the six object fields – visual forms, sounds, odours, tastes, tangibles and mental data – that are related each to its corresponding modality or element of cognitive awareness (*viñña~adhatu*) as a supporting object. All six object fields can impinge upon the mind-element (*manodhatu*) and are likewise related to it as its supporting object. Moreover, since according to the Buddhist intentional model of consciousness any assemblage of *citta* and *cetasika* is always directed to some object, then the consciousness stream flows contingent upon *dhammas* as its support and basis, or rather, *dhammas* condition consciousness being related to it as its object condition. This relation is likened to a weak man who stands by leaning on a stick for support. Object condition, then, establishes a subject-object relationship. Buddhaghosa maintains that consciousness may originate without paying one's attention *(avajjand)* to an object, but not without objective support, and that there is not a single *dhamma* that cannot function as an object of consciousness. That is, while the five physical sense objects serve as objective support of the five corresponding types of sensory cognitive awareness (visual, auditory etc.), all forms of cognizant data, including the mental data base - that is, whatever concepts may arise plus *nibbdna* – function as objective support of consciousness. This is another indication of the conceptual realism introduced by the Abhidhammikas in their attempt to establish a correspondence between conceptual thought, that is, language, and the 'arising of the world', though this ought to be understood epistemologically only, in the phenomenological sense of one's experiential world as it arises. For the *Patthana,* and even for Buddhaghosa, the intentional model of consciousness is not entwined with an a priori assumption that the intentional object must exist, since this would necessitate the existence of, for instance, the son of a barren woman, which is a cogent object of thought - a result that is impermissible within the Theravadin framework.

The third causal relation is predominance condition *(adhipatipaccayd)*. A *dhamma* that assists the occurrence of another *dhamma* in the sense of being foremost is a predominance condition. This is defined as follows: 'When whatever *dhammas qua* assemblages of *citta* and *cetasika* emerge by giving importance to any *dhammas,* these latter *dhammas* are a predominant condition for those former *dhammas*.' Just as an object like gold enslaves someone desiring it, so *adhipati* is to be understood in the sense of a *dhamma's* potency to dominate whatever other *dhammas* render it as of high regard meaning that *adhipati* is a mental quality that gives one the strength to do something. This conditioning relation specifically applies to the four 'bases of success' or *iddhipddas,* namely, will to act *(chanda),* strength *(viriyd),* consciousness *(citta)* and investigation *(vimamsd)*. The success for which these four factors constitute a basis or foundation is meditational success, and this is seen in the commentarial tradition in terms of either access concentration *(upacdrasamddhi) or jhdna*. According to the *Dhammasangani* either one of the four *iddhipadas* may act as the predominant element in certain *citta* types. It is this notion of predominance that is instantiated in the *Patthdna's* third *paccaya*. The *Patthana* thus asserts that 'Predominance of will to act, of strength, of consciousness and of investigation is a predominance condition for *dhammas* associated with will to act, with strength, with consciousness and with investigation respectively, and for the types of materiality originated thereby' The exegetical tradition distinguishes two sub-types of this condition: object predominance *(drammanddhipati)* and simultaneity dominance *(sahajdtddhipati),* explaining that

The four *dhammas* designated *chanda, viriya, citta* and *vimamsd* should be reckoned as predominance condition, albeit not all at once, for when *citta* occurs having made *chanda* the chief, the foremost, then *chanda* alone is the predominant, not the others. The same method applies to the others. But the *dhamma* by which, having made it the chief, immaterial *dhammas* proceed is their object predominance.

The fourth and fifth relations of causal conditioning may be assessed together: these are the conditions of proximity (*anantara*) and contiguity or immediate antecedent (*samanantara*) that, again, obtain only among immaterial *dhammas,* namely, *vipaka* and *kiriya* types. A *dhamma* that is capable of arousing a succeeding *citta* is related to it as a proximity condition. The same temporal relation is also spoken of as one of immediate contiguity in time, without any pause: 'There is no interval between them, so they are called proximate. They are proximate still further, because there is no interval between the cessation [of the preceding and the arising of the subsequent], thus they are contiguous.' All *citta* categories and their associated mental states that have just ceased in the immediately preceding instant are proximity conditions. Conditioned by them are all types of consciousness and their associated mental states partaking in the immediately succeeding consciousness moment. In every process of thought a preceding consciousness that has just ceased conditions its succeeding consciousness that has immediately sprung by a relation of proximity. This relation continuously prevails throughout one's lifespan excepting an *arahant*'s death-consciousness (*cuticitta*), which does not fuel the occurrence of rebirth-linking consciousness (*patisandhi*), for an *arahant* is entirely free from all defilements. The only difference between the proximity and contiguity conditions is that in the latter there does not exist any intermediacy between each two consecutive groups of consciousness and mental associates. These two relations were probably necessary in order to account for the continuity of phenomena without relying on any metaphysical substance. With the assimilation of the developed theory of momentariness, though, the temporal relation of contiguity became especially important for explaining the continuity of the consciousness process, given the supposition that it consists of momentary mental events. Every preceding thought moment is thus regarded as capable of arousing succeeding states of consciousness similar to it in the immediately following instant.

Next in the list is the sixth condition, that of simultaneity (*sahajatapaccaya*): the relation that holds when 'A *dhamma*, while arising, assists [another *dhamma*] by making it arise with itself, as a lamp is for light.' This relation is exemplified by the process of sensory cognitive awareness: when a visible object is detected, visual cognitive awareness ensues simultaneously with the minimum necessary seven *cetasikas*. The commentary identifies this relation as that which applies to cases where the *suttas* speak of reciprocal dependency, such as that which holds among the four immaterial *khandha*'s, between *nama* and *rupa* at the moment of conception in the womb, or among the four great elements (*mahabhuta*). This condition is the focal axis of the list of the twenty-four *paccaya*s and is second in its importance only to the cause condition. There are no fewer than seven other causal conditions further down the list of the twenty-four which are sub-categories of the simultaneity condition. In fact, all the seven are types of dependence-in-coexistence, which strongly implies interdependence; they all instantiate the abstract category of interrelations. As noted above, although in the *Nikayas* there is, to some extent, evidence that the *paticcasamuppada* accommodates reciprocal conditioning and mutual dependency, and that at least some processes are interrelated, these relations are still latent and treated cursorily. In the Abhidhamma, by contrast, the image of a network of interrelations plays a major role and reshapes the entire conception of causal conditioning.

The seven causal conditions that may be classified as species of the genus of simultaneity are:

(i) The seventh condition, mutuality/reciprocity (*aññamaññapaccaya*). It occurs when 'a *dhamma* assists [another *dhamma*] by means of mutual arousing and consolidating', and is likened to the relation among three sticks mutually supporting each other (invoking the *sutta* simile that explains the interrelation and mutual conditioning of *viñña~a* and *namarwpa*). For the Abhidhamma all states of consciousness and their associated mentalities are, reciprocally, conditioned and conditioning *dhammas*. The difference between the relations of simultaneity and reciprocity is that in the latter the conditioning *dhamma* is not simply simultaneous with its associated, arising *dhammas*, but is also conditioned or assisted by them. Whatever *dhammas* are reciprocally conditioned are also simultaneous, but not vice versa. Consciousness and associated mentalities, for instance, are related to mind-produced matter by simultaneity condition, though not by reciprocity.

(ii) The eighth relation, support condition (*nissayapaccaya*), applies when a conditioning *dhamma* supports its conditioned *dhamma* by arousing other *dhammas*. This relation is likened to that between soil and a tree. Under this causal condition the *Pa tthana* lists again the examples of mutual dependence among the immaterial aggregates, among the four great elements and between *nama* and *rupa* at the time of conception; it then adds a series of other exemplary cases, such as the relations among the sense faculties, their corresponding modalities of sensory cognitive awareness and the *cetasikas* accompanying them on their occurrence.

(iii) The fourteenth condition is fruition (*vipaka*): the relation between a *dhamma* that assists the arising of another *dhamma* without exerting any effort. This relation obtains when a conditioning event is associated with its conditioned events by making them commence simultaneously with it as passive and effortless as itself. For example, in the five-door consciousness process, once the sense object and the sense faculty have coincided, the five modes of cognitive awareness emanate without having to make any effort. Another example is one's consciousness at death (*cuticitta*): when one dies with one's attention fixed on one of the objects of the mind-door consciousness, *kamma* then comes to fruition in the immediately following rebirth. Therefore states of consciousness and their associated mentalities which are the results of volitions (*cetana*) and volitions themselves are called *vipaka*, 'resultants'. Thirty-six types of resultant consciousness are related to their associated mentalities by this condition. They are also mutually related to one another.

(iv–v) The nineteenth and twentieth conditions are association (*sampayutta*) and dissociation (*vippayutta*). Association holds when a conditioning event relates to its conditioned events by causing them to issue associated in a group, so that they are inseparable and cannot be singled out, for they possess the four characteristics of association, namely, simultaneous origination, simultaneous cessation, taking the same object and depending on the same sense faculty. This state is likened to water in the ocean, which cannot be distinguished as originating from different rivers. For example, visual consciousness and the seven necessary *cetasikas* are associated together as an inseparable group. All *citta* types and their mental concomitants are mutually related by association condition. Dissociation, by contrast, obtains when a conditioning *dhamma* relates to its conditioned *dhammas* by making them set in simultaneously with it, though not according to the characteristics of association. This is likened to a mixture of water and mercury which, albeit combined remain separate. When a visual object and the eye faculty coincide to instigate visual cognitive awareness, the latter can be observed distinctly from these visual object and eye faculty, albeit derived from them; it occurs simultaneously with its conditioning factors but not due to association with them. Association is one of the possible relations among the four immaterial *khandha's,* while dissociation holds when material and immaterial *dhammas* condition each other, thus explaining the interaction and synthesis of physical and mental phenomena.

(vi-vii) The twenty-first and twenty-fourth conditions are presence *(atthi)* and non-disappearance *(avigata).* Both these conditions are defined in exactly the same way: they obtain when a *dhamma,* by means of its presence, assists the arising of another *dhamma* of its kind. These conditions hold among the four mental *khandhas,* the four great elements, *namarupa, citta* and *cetasika,* the sense spheres (sense objects and faculties) and their corresponding modalities of cognitive awareness etc. For example, in a sense-door consciousness process, such as eye-door process, there arise in succession several consciousness instances with specific functions: adverting to the eye door *(avajjana),* which is undertaken by the *kiriya* mind element; the act of seeing itself; receiving *(sampaticchana)* of the sense object, which is executed by one of the two resultant mind elements; examining *(santirana)* of the object, which is carried out by one of the three resultant mind-consciousness elements; determining *(votthapana)* of the object's nature, undertaken by the *kiriya* mind-consciousness element; impulsions *(javana),* or the act of actually apperceiving the object, operated by the actively skilful and unskilful *cittas;* and *tadarammana,* or retaining the object of the *javana* mind in the *bhavanga* mind which is performed by eleven types of resultant consciousness. Each of these mental events with its own function conditions its subsequent mental event in the series by its presence at the appropriate moment. The presence and non-disappearance conditions make sense in view of the Buddhist notion of a complex, sufficient condition which is the sum-total of several necessary conditions. Even after the sufficient condition issued its resultant process, the latter may still require the presence of some of the necessary conditions for its maintenance, as the sprout needs earth and water even after it has arisen. A possible difference between the relation of presence and the otherwise identical non-disappearance is that while the former focuses on co-presence, the latter emphasizes that it is not merely a contingent co-presence but also inseparability-in-simultaneity

Having evaluated the central role of interrelatedness and interdependence within the Abhidhamma network model of causal conditioning, we now turn to the remaining *paccaya*s on the list. The ninth relation, decisive support condition (*upanissayapaccaya*), obtains when a *dhamma* is capable of arousing a resultant *dhamma* self-sufficiently. This is how actively skilful and unskilful *dhammas* are related to subsequent actively skilful and unskilful *dhammas* respectively. The difference between this condition and the aforementioned support condition (*nissaya-paccaya*) is that the latter is a primary condition and is necessary specifically at the time of the arising of the conditioned *dhamma*, whereas a decisive support condition is not necessarily the foremost: it lasts longer, has a long-term effect and implies action at a distance. Past *kamma* thus assists the occurrence of sensory cognitive awareness arising at one of the sense-door processes as a decisive support, but the actual emergence of, say, visual cognitive awareness, is primarily dependent at that time on the visual sense sphere, and hence the latter is its support condition. The importance of the decisive support condition seems to lie in its accounting for moral and spiritual progress: virtues like trust or confidence (*saddha*), generosity (*dana*), undertaking the precepts and others, all assist the occurrence of their long term results (the *jhana*s, insight, taking the path etc.) as their decisive support, and these results, in their turn, condition the repeated arising of trust, generosity etc. The commentarial tradition distinguishes three sub-types of this causal conditioning relation: object decisive support, proximate decisive support and natural decisive support (*aramma~upanissaya, anantarupanissaya, pakatupanissaya* respectively).

The tenth and eleventh causal conditions are pre-existence (*purejata*) and post-existence (*pacchajata*). A *dhamma* that assists by its presence, having previously arisen, is a pre-existent condition. This relation is held between the sense faculties and their appropriate sense objects: the consciousness series of any cognitive process cannot commence without the pre-existence of the sense objects and sense faculties. These are not completely antecedent events that have expired before the emergence of their resultant consciousness, for according to the Theravada the operation of a conditioning *dhamma* continues even after its result has occurred. By the same token, an immaterial *dhamma* assisting previously arisen material *dhammas* by supporting their continued function is their post-existing condition. Just as the annual rains support trees that already exist, so every posterior consciousness is related to the matter-resultant qualities that are still active and that are born of the four origins (*kamma*, consciousness, temperature and nutriment) by a post-existence condition, thus assisting them to develop. This is another condition, then, that accounts for the synthesis of physical and mental phenomena.

The twelfth condition, habitual cultivation (*asevana*), holds when a *dhamma* builds up its following *dhamma*, enhancing its proficiency and power by making it predisposed to recurrence. For example, developing a certain skilful thought once facilitates the cultivation of the same thought with a greater degree of efficiency and intensity. This causal conditioning relation, effecting the flow of *citta* series during the process of cognizing, marks the way in which one's habitual tendencies and dispositions are shaped, and the latter, in their turn, condition one's bodily, verbal and mental acts. It therefore underlies the cultivation of right view, right speech and right action.

The thirteenth, *kamma*, condition obtains when a conditioning *dhamma*, through accomplishing its function, enables its conditioned *dhammas* to accomplish their own functions. It is likened to a chief disciple who, by encouraging himself to complete his task, makes the younger disciples complete theirs. *Kamma* here ordinarily denotes *cetana*, volition or intention, and the *Pa tthana*'s formulation reflects upon the renowned Nikaya statement equating *kamma* with *cetana*: 'Intention is related to its associated *dhammas* and to the materiality arising from them by *kamma* condition.' The commentary, however, attests to a further elaboration on this idea: therein two sorts of *kamma* condition are distinguished, namely, simultaneous (*sahajata*) and asynchronous (*nanakha~ika*). A simultaneous condition occurs when an intention determines and fashions its corresponding action that emanates simultaneously with it. An asynchronous condition obtains when a past *kamma* comes into fruition in a manifest corresponding action. Although the volition itself ceases, it leaves in the mind latent traces that take effect and assist the arising of an appropriate action when the necessary conditions are satisfied.

The fifteenth relation, nutriment (*ahara*), obtains when a conditioning *dhamma* enables its conditioned *dhammas* to operate by supporting them in the sense of nourishment. It is likened to a prop supporting a house. This condition is prefigured in the *Nikayas*, where the four nutriments – edible food, sense contact, mental volition and consciousness – are presented as the conditions for maintaining one's life. Sense contact, for example, strongly supports its simultaneous mental states, the chief of which is the feeling experienced with regard to desirable and undesirable objects.

The sixteenth condition, controlling faculty (*indriyapaccaya*), obtains when a conditioning event relates to its conditioned events by controlling them. It is likened to several ministers of state who have freedom of control in each region and who do not interfere with one another. This relation specifically refers to the faculties that determine one's behaviour by exercising control over their associated mental states, capacitating them to appear in consciousness. These include the six sense *indriyas* (the five physical plus the mental one, *manindriya*), but also additional faculties such as the female (*itthindriya*) and male faculties (*purisindriya*), the life faculty (*jivitindriya*), and various other controlling motives, like bodily pleasure faculty (*sukhindriya*), confidence (*saddhindriya*), concentration (*samad-hindriya*), awareness (*satindriya*) and others.

For example, the faculty of confidence controls one's trust in the triple gem, the awareness faculty oversees one's cultivation of the four *satipatthanas*, and the bodily pleasure faculty governs one's experiencing bodily pleasure. The Abhidhamma enumerates twenty-two *indriyas*, and the significance attributed to them in moulding one's behaviour may have led the Abhidhammikas to formulate this causal conditioning relation that is held among the faculties as they facilitate the rise of *dhammas* in consciousness.

The seventeenth condition, *jhana*, obtains when the *jhana* factors cause their conditioned states to fix themselves on an object. Here *jhana* is to be understood in the broad sense of focusing the mind attentively on an object, not with specific reference to the higher consciousness types that arise while in meditation and pertain to the *rupa* sphere. Indeed by means of this causal conditioning relation the five meditative *jhana* factors – that is, initial thought, sustained or exploring thought, joy, happiness and one-pointedness of mind (*vitakka, vicara, piti, sukha, cittass' ekaggata*) – enable the mind to sustain and cultivate the *jhana* practice. Nevertheless, without the *jhana* causal conditioning relation no action that involves concentration and cognitive discrimination would have been possible, and hence in this system the *jhana* factors are seven, adding *somanassa* and *domanassa*, pleasant and painful feelings, which facilitate the focusing of the mind in actively skilful and unskilful sense-sphere *cittas* respectively. *Jhana* is therefore likened to an archer who makes the arrow steady, holds it firmly, directs it towards the target and attentively aims it. The seven *jhana* factors are the rope and the post, as it were, which control the mind and prevent it from wandering away. The *jhana* causal conditioning relations thus hold among all assemblages of *citta* and *cetasika* along with the material phenomena co-arising with them.

The eighteenth relation, path condition (*maggapaccaya*), takes place when a conditioning *dhamma* relates to its conditioned *dhammas* by making them function as a path to happy or sorrowful states. It accounts for the relation between the stages on the path and their associated *dhammas*, as each stage is deemed to act on both mind and body and to determine the attainment of its subsequent stage. The conditioning *dhammas* are the twelve path constituents: the renowned eight factors (right view, right resolve, right speech, right action, right livelihood, right effort, right awareness and right concentration) fix volition firmly on the path to the cessation of *dukkha,* while the four wrong factors (wrong view, wrong resolve, wrong effort and wrong concentration) fix volition on the path to further rebirths in *saµsara.*

Finally, the twenty-second and twenty-third relations, absence (*natthi*) and disappearance (*vigata*) conditions, are the exact opposites of the conditions of presence and non-disappearance respectively. These two relations account for instances where certain mental events must cease in order to induce a resultant event. When they do so by ceasing in contiguity to their resultant event, they are related to it by absence condition. Here the conditioning events already belong to the past when the conditioned event follows, just like a flame that by dying out enables darkness to set in. When the same conditioning mental events induce a conditioned event while having disappeared in complete contiguity to it, they are spoken of as being related to the result by disappearance condition, just as the sunlight, while disappearing, enables darkness to settle in.

Having discussed the twenty-four *paccayas*, we shall now reconsider the theory they constitute, this time focusing on its underlying conceptual scheme and its philosophical implications.

To See the Wood for the Trees: Making Sense of the Twenty-four Paccayas

The *Pa tthana* list of the twenty-four *paccayas* involves a prominent doctrinal issue crucial to the construal of the Abhidhamma notion of causation and necessary for completing our account of the doctrinal transition from the Nikaya worldview to the Abhidhamma. This issue is the semantic distinction between *hetu* and *paccaya.* As previously noted, the Nikaya grasp of a sufficient condition consisting in the sum-total of several *sine qua non* conditions has misled modern scholarship into thinking that early Buddhism distinguishes between *hetu* and *paccaya,* and thus into differentiating between 'cause' and 'condition' respectively. As we shall see in greater detail below, such a distinction was systematically developed by the Sarvastivada. The Sarvastivadin position, too – both because of its dominance within Buddhist circles and also owing to modern scholarship's over-reliance on the *Abhidharmakoça* when dealing with doctrinal matters – is likely to have produced the impression that the distinction between *hetu* and *paccaya/pratyaya* is found in the earliest strata of the Pali Canon. But there is no ground for this distinction in the *Nikayas,* where the two terms are regarded as synonymous and are used interchangeably.

In the *Pa tthana* the meaning of *hetu* is restricted to 'root' (*mula*), but in a narrower, more technical sense than its original intension of basic psychological dispositions that shape one's actions. Rather, *hetu*-as-root consists in a specific category of causal conditions: that of basic or primary causal conditions. While *paccaya* refers to supporting causal conditions in the broadest sense of the relations between dependently co-arising *dhammas, hetu* signifies the pre-eminent condition of this set of conditions. This condition is the most fundamental of all the conditions that are necessary to the rise of a given *dhamma,* for it determines what that *dhamma* is, rendering it as a unique, distinguishable and definable particular. Only after the *dhamma* eventuates as a unique particular whose individuality is established do all the other causal conditions required for its occurrence become relevant. Thus, the distinction between *hetu* and *paccaya* and the identification of *hetu* as a *dhamma*'s cause in the sense of its *sabhava* are subject to the canonical Abhidhamma preoccupation with the intension of the *dhammas'* individuality.

Now outside of the *Pa tthana* there are merely two para-canonical texts that uphold the semantic distinction between *hetu* and *paccaya*. These are the two methodological manuals, namely, the *Nettippakara~a* and the *Pe takopadesa*. Relevant to our present concern are two parallel extracts from both these texts, wherein the distinction in question is presented. In what follows, however, I show that if one applies the way these passages construe *hetu* and *paccaya* to the overall framework of the *Pa tthana,* it emerges that the latter accommodates a different interpretation of *hetu*: one that attests to the Abhidhamma concern with the metaphysical question of the principle of the *dhammas'* individuality.

We have already come across the two relevant extracts from the *Nettippakara~a* and the *Pe takopadesa* as part of our discussion of *sabhava* in Chapter 3. Both these passages deal with causal conditioning and invoke the concept of *sabhava* as directly related to it. The *Pe takopadesa*'s fifteenth category of investigation, 'conveying requisites' (*parikkharo-hara*), states that a *dhamma* that conditions the arising of a certain other *dhamma* is the latter's requisite, and there are two kinds of such requisite *dhammas*: a cause, namely, *hetu*, and a condition, that is, *paccaya*. The text then explains the difference between the two:

> The cause is the own-nature, whereas the condition is the other-nature. Although the other-nature's condition is a cause, too, the condition of any other-nature whatsoever, other than the own-nature's cause, is not called 'cause'; it is called 'condition'. The cause is internal, while the condition is external; the cause is not held in common, whereas the condition is held in common [. ..] the cause is single only, while the condition is diverse; the condition is a support for the cause once the latter has obtained.

The cause of a *dhamma*, then, is its very own-nature, its *sabhava* that individuates it and makes it this particular *dhamma*. Any other of the *dhamma*'s attributes or of the contingencies involved in its arising – albeit requisite for its occurrence – does not constitute the *dhamma*'s individuality, and is therefore regarded merely as a condition necessary for its arising. The cause is intrinsic and unique to a *dhamma*; it is what makes up the *dhamma*'s individuality, thus distinguishing it from any other instant, either of other kinds or of the same kind. The condition, by contrast, can be shared by other *dhammas* and contribute to their occurrence. The cause is the very *sabhava* of a particular *dhamma* instant arising in a certain situation, while the condition is some other *dhamma* or a group of *dhammas* that establish this situation once the *sabhava* has been obtained.

The cause is what makes the *dhamma* in its essence, or in Buddhaghosa's words, 'what establishes the skilful in what is skilful, etc.' This state of affairs is likened to the growth of a sprout: the sprout's own-nature, which determines its individuality as this particular sprout rather than any other, is the sprout's cause. Water and earth, however, are each a condition for the growth of the sprout, just as they are the conditions for the growth of any other sprout and plant. Among a group of *sine qua non* conditions for the occurrence of a *dhamma*, then, there is only one that is the principle and cause of that *dhamma*'s individuality. The remaining conditions are all necessary, though they are regarded as secondary in their importance, as it were; tney become relevant only once the primary cause has fulfilled its operation.

Chapter 4 has shown that the concern with the question of the principle of the *dhammas'* individuality takes centre stage in the post-canonical Abhidhamma. Indeed the term *sabhava* does not feature in the *Pa tthana* and the interpretation of *hetu*-as-*sabhava* in the sense of the cause of a *dhamma*'s individuality probably belongs to a textual layer somewhat later than the earliest parts of the *Abhidhamma-pitaka*. Given the problems associated with the dating of early Buddhist literature, we are unable to establish a straightforward, relative chronology of the *Pe takopadesa, Nettippakara~a* and *Pa tthana,* and the best estimation presently available is that they all date roughly around the second or first centuries BCE. At any rate, these texts predate the quintessential commentaries: they are transitional texts that merge various doctrinal layers, reflecting the formative period of the shift from the beginnings of the Abhidhamma to its later systematization, when growing emphasis was put on the metaphysical question of the principle of the *dhammas'* individuality and on their reification.

We have already seen that in developing the *dhamma* theory along with its related doctrines of *sabhdva* and momentariness the Theravadins were influenced by Sarvastivada metaphysics. There are strong grounds for believing that the distinction between *hetu* and *paccaya,* too, was appropriated by the Theravadins and borrowed from contemporary Sarvastivadin sources. The developed Sarvastivadin theory of causation consists of two related doctrines: the doctrine *of hetus* and the doctrine of *pratyayas.* The Sarvastivadins strive to show that these two doctrines originate from the Sutra literature, though no indication of them is found in the Pali *Nikdyas,* Chinese *Ågamas* or the *Vinaya.* Let us first look into the doctrine of *pratyayas.*

One short discourse held to be authoritative by the (Mula)Sarvastivadins -that is, both by the Sarvastivadin and Mulasarvastivadin schools - but without corresponding Pali versions, is the *Pratyayasutra, or rather, the Sutra on the Four Conditions. This discourse is cited in the *Abhidharmakosabhdsya,* and Vasubandhu asserts that he is citing a *sutra:* 'What are the conditions? Four conditions have been stated. Where? In a *sutra:* "There are four conditions, namely, cause as condition *(hetupratyaya),* immediate antecedent as condition *(samanantarapratyaya),* perceptual object as condition *(alambanapratyaya)* and predominance as condition *(adhipatipratyaya)".'* In his discussion of the *Pratyayasutra, Peter Skilling observes that the same *sutra* is referred to in the *Vibhasa,* that it is cited as a *sutra* in the *Sdrasamuccaya,* and that Vasubandhu's above citation means that he must have extracted the text from one of the Mulasarvastivadin *Ågamas.* On the basis of the *sutra's* style,, and drawing on Samathadeva's references to it in his commentary to the *Abhidharmakosa,* the *Updyikd Tikd* - an anthology of canonical and citations originally composed in Sanskrit but extant only in Tibetan translation - Skilling concludes that the *Pratyayasutra was included in the section of fours in the (Mula)Sarvastivadin *Ekottarikdgama* (noting that the school-affiliation of the Chinese *Ekottarikdgama* is not (Mula)Sarvastivadin). Skilling says: 'The references of the Vibhasa, of Vasubandhu, of Samathadeva, and of the anonymous author of the Sarasamuccaya establish the existence and transmission of the *sutra* from before the time of the compilation of the Vibhasa (1st century CE[?]) up to the time of the latter two authors (6th or 7th century [?]).'

The doctrine of four conditions is a fundamental category of the (Mula)Sarvastivada-Vaibhasika and seems to have been the kernel from which more elaborate theories of causation originated within that tradition. It is presented in the canonical or middle (Mula)Sarvastivadin Abhidharma texts, occurring first in the *Vijñdnakdya* (where it is applied to the six modalities of cognitive awareness), followed by the *Prakaranapdda* and the **Åryavasumitrabod-hisattvasangitisdstra,* and finally by the *Jñdnaprasthdna* - a text generally held to be the latest of the seven Sarvastivada Abhdiharma treatises and dated to the first century BCE. If this dating is correct, the doctrine of four conditions must have evolved by the end of the second century BCE, and hence is contemporary with the *Patthdna.* Supporting a fairly early dating of the doctrine is the *Sdriputrdbhidharmasdstra,* a treatise of unknown school considered to be one of the oldest Sarvastivadin Abhidharma works extant. This text advances an explicit causal model based on a distinctive enumeration of ten *pratyayas.* Of these ten *pratyayas,* four are the exact match of the (Mula)Sarvastivadin *pratyayas:* the first three correspond to *hetu-, samanantara-* and *dlambanapratyayas,* the last to *adhipatipratyaya.* Foremost for our present concern, though, is the fact that the remaining *pratyayas* are similar to others of the *Patthdna* list of *paccayas*. Edward Conze thus notes that the Sarvastivadin and the Theravadin enumerations of conditions show sufficient resemblance to make it likely that the two schemes originally evolved before the two schools separated and sufficient dissimilarity to suggest that the developed schemes were thought out after their separation.

As for an exposition of the four *pratyayas,* cause as condition is reckoned the foremost in inciting the process of fruition and origination; the immediate antecedent conditioning relation holds between a consciousness moment and its immediately preceding moment in that consciousness series; perceptual object condition applies to all *dharmas* insofar as they are referents or intentional objects of consciousness, and the predominance condition settles the sensual discriminative quality of fruition, as, for example, the faculty of sight's sovereignty on visual, discriminative cognitive awareness.

It now emerges that the Sarvastivadin four *pratyayas* exactly correspond to the *Patthana's* first five *paccayas* (counting *anan-tara* and *samanantara* as one). There are other parallel interests and points of resemblance between the remaining *paccayas* and the Sarvastivadin causational theory: Kalupahana shows that nearly eighteen of the twenty-four *paccayas* have counterparts in the Sarvastivada and Yogacara theories.

In the most recent of the canonical Sarvastivadin Abhidharma texts, the *Jñanaprasthana* of Katyayaniputra, conditioning relations are examined in the context of a newly elaborated theory of six causes. Thus, by the time of the *Jñanaprasthana* the Sarvastivadin development of a theory of causal relations was extended through the theory of six causes, which, from the *Mahdvibhdsd* onward was interwoven with the theory of four conditions to form the two major components of the Sarvastivadin causal model. The six *hetus,* as they are documented in the *Abhidharmakosabhdsya,* are: (i) *kdranahetu,* the primary *(pradhdna)* cause, or the leading factor in the production of a result; (ii) *sahabhuhetu,* a simultaneous or coexistent cause that connects phenomena arising simultaneously (e.g. the primary and secondary elements of matter);

(iii) *sabhagahetu,* a homogenous cause, explains the homogenous flow of *dharmas,* which evokes our impression of the continuity of phenomena; (iv) *samprayuktakahetu,* or associated cause, operates only between immaterial *dharmas* and explains why the elements of consciousness never appear alone but always accompanied by other mental factors; (v) *sarvatragahetu,* a dominant or pervasive cause, is the origin of defiled *dharmas* (lust, hatred etc.) which form one's habitual cognitive and behaviouristic dispositions; (vi) lastly *vipakahetu,* a cause of retribution or maturation, refers to whatever is the result of actively skilful or unskilful *dharma.*

The two doctrines of six causes and four conditions interact with each other in explaining phenomenal experience: for example, each moment of thought acts both as the homogenous cause as well as the immediate antecedent condition of the rise of thought and its concomitants in a subsequent moment.

Moreover, the two doctrines overlap with one another: the category of cause as condition, *hetupratyaya,* is constituted by the five *hetu* excepting the basic *kara~ahetu*. Note that the *Bhasya* explains *kara~ahetu* as the primary cause or the cause *par excellence,* the generating cause of the origination and fruition of a phenomenon. It is compared to what the eye and visual forms are for visual cognitive awareness, to food for the body and to seeds for the sprout. The *Pa tthana* commentary's exegesis of *hetupaccaya,* as well as the *Nettipakara~a*'s and the *Pe takopadesa*'s explanation of *hetu,* clearly bear resemblance to the Sarvastivadin formulation of *kara~ahetu*. The likelihood, then, is that the Theravadin *Pa tthana* theory of *paccaya,* and the very distinction between *hetu* and *paccaya,* were the result of the contemporary intellectual milieu determined by the Abhidhamma and Northern Abhidharma philosophical and doctrinal discussions before and after the two traditions were finalized.

The Sarvastivadin distinction between *hetu* and *pratyaya,* though, is tied in with its metaphysics and ontological conception of a *dharma*. Within the Sarvastivadin framework *dharmas* are primary existents (*dravyasat*): albeit not permanent, they do have continued, certain and independent existence – a primary ontological status that is indicated by their *svabhava*. Accordingly, the encountered world is seen as constructed from the interaction of *dharmas*, each of which is causally efficacious. On this line of thought a *dharma* is a substantial element endowed with a defining characteristic (*svalaksa~a*), with its *svabhava* (which here may be rendered 'self-essence'), and with secondary attributes. Hence each *dharma* has a certain cause that accounts for what it is in essence, while its accidental attributes are the conditions of the various phases and transformations it undergoes.

The Theravadins, however, as we have seen throughout the present study, do not subscribe to the Sarvastivada metaphysics: first and foremost they do not hold that a *dhamma* is a *dravyasat* and do not use the category of *sabhava* as an ontological determinant of primary existence – at least not until late into the post-canonical period. Therefore, the *P a tthana*' s *hetupaccaya* primarily answers the question what a *dhamma* is, namely, the question of the intension of a *dhamma*'s individuality. Even when this causal condition is equated with a *dhamma*' s *sabhava*, it answers the question of what makes a *dhamma* the very particular it is, namely, the question of the principle of a *dhamma*'s individuality. By contrast to the Sarvastivada ontology and its subordinate construal of causation, *hetupaccaya* as a reply to the question *what* a *dhamma* is does not necessarily imply *that* it is.

The distinction between cause and condition is merely part of an intricate solution to a broader problem that resulted from the Abhidharma/Abhidhamma tendency towards doctrinal systematization. The Buddhist postulate of impermanence sets up the ground for the assumption that our experience is reducible to clusters of basic, ever-changing constituents and is not unified by any underlying substance or enduring self.

This assumption requires one to account for the experience of the connection between and the continuity of those constituents. In the early period of Buddhist thought the answer to this challenge was found in the principle of conditioning as embodied in the *paticcasamuppada* doctrine: the processes that make up one's experience were deemed as connected by necessary and sufficient conditions, such that certain processes necessarily arouse subsequent processes that share their qualities. Later on, however, along with the doctrinal systematization of the early tradition, both the Sarvastivada-Vaibhasika and the Theravada Abhidhamma came to adopt, with certain modifications, the theory of momentariness, which portrayed the *dharmas/dhammas* as discrete, individual and radically momentary constituents of experience, whether primary existents or psycho-physical events.

Such a radical construal of experience as basically momentary is not only a move away from the early Buddhist experientially oriented teaching, but it also raises a vexing difficulty: to account for the experience of the connection between and the continuity of discrete, momentary items seems to be logically impossible. Moreover, the theory of momentariness allegedly has destructive repercussions for the notion of causation: supposing that causes, conditions and their results are momentary existents or events, how can an existent or event which has ended and disappeared bring about a result? How can an event that undergoes distinct stages of origination, endurance and cessation in a brief moment have causal efficacy? Notwithstanding their disputes and doctrinal differences, both the Sarvastivada-Vaibhasika and the Theravada Abhidhamma had to confront this problem, and they both did so by formulating a theory of immediate contiguity that grants causal efficacy.

The Sarvastivada thus developed a complex analysis of causal conditionality in terms of intricate interrelations among six types of cause, four kinds of condition and five sorts of effect. At the hub of this analysis lie the principles of action and conditioning. In the early Sarvastivada, as represented by the doctrines of the *Vibhasa*, a *dharma* enjoys primary existential status by virtue of its *svabhava*, but the *svabhava* is an atemporal determinant of such an ontological status and does not concern the temporal status of its possessing *dharma*. Rather, a *dharma'* s temporal status is determined by the presence or absence of function. Given an appropriate assemblage of causes and conditions, the existent *dharmas* manifest a particular momentary function or activity (*karitra*). It is the arising and passing away of this activity that defines the present moment and determines the *dharma*'s momentariness. Collett Cox expounds this idea as follows:

If factors exist as real entities characterized by intrinsic nature in the three time periods, momentariness refers only to the transitory character of a factor's activity, specifically, to the arising and passing away of a factor's activity that defines the limits of each present moment. Even though a factor's activity passes away and the factor is thereby said to become past, the factor continues to exist and can still be said to have the capability of acting as a cause in the production of presently arising factors. Among the infinite number of factors whose impermanent activities constitute the total array of sentient and insentient phenomena, those that occur within the streams of sentient beings arise together with a separate factor, possession (*prapti*). When the present factor and its possession pass away, that possession serves as the homogenous cause for the recurrent arising of subsequent factors.

This doctrine was criticized Vasubandhu who, in the *Abhidharmakoçabhasya,* denies the distinction between a *dharma*'s activity and its own-nature, asserting that the *dharma*'s primary existence itself subsists in its activity that occurs only in the present. Causal interaction can thus become meaningful as a relation between the present moment and its immediately preceding moment: it resides in a stream of contiguous conditioning lacking any mediation such as possession.

To explain the direct conditioning between contiguous causes and effects Vasubandhu relies on the theory of seeds (*bija*), but this lies beyond the scope of this study. The early *Vibhasa*'s doctrine of *prapti,* though, was also criticized by the established Sarvastivada, which provided alternative models in order to account for causal efficacy. Pertinent to our present concern is Saðghabhadra's modification of the early Sarvastivada position in his *Nyayanusara*.

Saðghabhadra, who represents the orthodox Kaçmira Sarvastivadins, argues that causal interaction, even between two contiguous moments, is untenable. For any given moment, the preceding moment is past and no longer exists, whereas the succeeding moment is future and does not yet exist. Hence causal interaction is defensible only if the *dharmas* are admitted to exist in the three time periods. Saðghabhadra's solution is to distinguish between two modes of a *dharma*'s operation: a *dharma*'s specific operation in the present is referred to as function or activity (*karitra*), whereas its more general efficacy, which can occur in all the three time periods, is called capability (*samarthya*). These two differ in their locus of operation relative to the consciousness series (*santana*) constituted by the functional *dharma* in question: activity is an internal causal efficacy that assists in the production of an effect within a *dharma*'s own series. Capability, by contrast, is an external conditioning efficacy directed towards the consiousness series of another *dharma;* it constitutes a condition that assists another *dharma* in the production of its own effect. A present *dharma* must fulfil its function in the production of its own series; past and future *dharmas* can operate only as capabilities conditioning a *dharma* of another series. According to this view, a momentary *dharma* may have two causal operations, only one of which, its *karitra,* is necessary to its spatio-temporal primary existence. Paul Williams clarifies:

Within a series of momentary entities each moment has to engender the next, but it can also act as a contributory condition towards producing a different sort of effect. We might speak of this as 'horizontal' and 'vertical' causality, within the series and transcending it respectively. A momentary instant of visual power horizontally produces the next moment of visual power and may or may not, depending on other factors such as light and so on, vertically produce vision of the object [. ..]

It is ability which gives rise to an entity of a completely different sort, and so it is ability which has the efficacy in the case of a past *dharma* exerting causal activity. The past *dharma* is thus without function and therefore not present, although still causally efficacious. It follows that to be present is to have horizontal causality, which may or may not include vertical causality – a fact which serves to remind us that we are dealing here with primary existents which are frequently positioned within the system in terms of what they do.

Returning to our present interest in the Theravadin Abhidhamma theory of causal conditioning, it should be noted that the Sarvastivadin doctrines mentioned above are much later than the Abhidhamma texts we are dealing with (the Vasubandhu-Saðghabhadra dispute dates to the fifth century CE). Ye t Saðghabhdra's distinction between activity and capability has much in common with the Theravadin distinction between *hetu* and *paccaya* as advocated in the *Nettippakara~a* and the *Pe takopadesa*. In these treatises *hetu* is identified as a *dhamma*'s horizontal causality in the sense of its own-nature – its mode of operation within its consciousness series, which determines its individuality as that particular *dhamma*. On a stronger metaphysical interpretation *hetu* is the proper cause of a *dhamma*'s individuality, but as such is equivalent with *sabhava* in the sense of an individuator and not of an ontological determinant of primary existential status. *Paccaya* is a condition in the sense of other-nature – a *dhamma* that operates as a contributory condition towards producing another *dhamma* outside its own consciousness series, thus resembling the Sarvastivadin idea of vertical causality.

This Sarvastivadin distinction between horizontal and vertical causality is helpful in understanding the *Pa tthana* theory of the twenty-four *paccayas*, the distinction between *hetu* and *paccaya* specifically, and the affinity of the two conceptual frameworks may indicate that they belong to the same complex of ideas within the early history of Buddhist thought. Nevertheless, the application of the Sarvastivadin scheme to the Theravadin context must be qualified: first, within the Theravadin context a *dhamma* is a psycho-physical event; 'a rise of thought' in one's consciousness, not a primary existent. Second, insofar as the *Pa tthana* theory of *paccaya* accommodates horizontal and vertical causality, these two modes of causal operation are not intended to account for the *dhammas'* temporal existence but for their individuality.

Saðghabhadra's notion of a *dharma*'s function as horizontal causality clarifies the meaning of the f irst *paccaya* on the *P a tthana* list, namely, *hetupaccaya*. This causal condition is exactly what defines a *dhamma* as that particular event, thus answering the question of the intension of the *dhamma*'s individuality.

A *dhamma*'s activity within its consciousness series in precipitating the next moment of this series is its very individuality. Alternatively, *hetupaccaya* could be interpreted metaphysically, as a mode of operation within the *dhamma*'s series which constitutes the *dhamma*'s own-nature or quidditative essence; as what makes the *dhamma* the particular event it is, thus answering the question of the principle of the *dhamma*'s individuality. This is evinced in the commentarial statement 'There is no such thing called "activity" (*kiriya*) apart from the *dhamma' s sabhava*.' We have already explained that the *dhammas* are diverse capacities of mental events, and that each particular *dhamma* instant is distinguishable from any other instant by virtue of its unique *kammic* operation within and outside of its series. The first *paccaya* on the list of the twenty-four specifically defines what each and every *dhamma* is and what makes it so, while the remaining twenty-three *paccayas* further explicate this account by revealing the *kammic* quality and intensity of operation unique to each *dhamma*, that is, its capability of 'vertical' conditioning by which it facilitates the occurrence of other *dhammas* outside its consciousness series.

On the Sarvastivadin theory of causation the horizontal and vertical modes of operation account for the *dharmas'* temporal existence: a present *dharma* has both horizontal and vertical causal efficacy, while past and future *dharmas* have only vertical causal efficacy.Within the *Pa tthana* framework, however, these two modes of operation are intended to account not for the *dhammas'* temporal existence but for their individuality. In fact, the Sarvastivadin surmise that present existence may be explained in terms of causal efficacy is circular, for it is untenable to define the present in terms of causal efficacy and then to use this as the basis of an account of existence-in-time.

For the Theravadins *hetupaccaya* directly accounts for what any given individual *dhamma* is and for why it is so, whereas the remaining *paccayas* further establish this explanation by locating the *dhamma* within the web of interrelations by which it is connected with the incessant rise and fall of all other *dhammas*. It is here that the image of the network model of causal conditioning takes over from the earlier image of the causal chain. The relative positioning of each *dhamma* within this network of vertical causal conditioning is, first and foremost, a means for its individuation. Only in an indirect, subsidiary sense may this vertical causal conditioning be regarded as an analysis of causal production.

It thus turns out that the *Pa tthana* theory of *paccaya* is not about causation at all, at least not if causation is taken in its customarily accepted meaning. Causation here has the sense of *kammic* conditioning and it is subordinate to the Abhidhamma metaphysical endeavour of the *dhammas'* individuation. In fact, the whole idea of an analysis of causation in terms of causal conditioning is circular: such an analysis would first define causation as a functional dependence between events, only to find out that this dependence is but a causal one. The Abhidhamma theory of *paccaya,* however, is intended to account neither for causal production, nor for the *dhammas'* primary existential status, nor for their temporal existential status, but for the individuality of each and every *dhamma* as a capacity of a certain mental event that occurs within a network of interrelations of causal conditioning.

Within the context of the *Pa tthana* the distinction between horizontal and vertical causality is not clear-cut: the application of these two modes of operation to the *paccaya*s does not amount to saying that *hetupaccaya* alone demonstrates horizontal causality while the remaining twenty-three *paccaya*s embody only vertical causal conditioning. We have seen that no fewer than eight of these twenty-three *paccaya*s instantiate interrelations of simultaneity and mutuality among the operating *dhammas*.

To clarify the issue in question one of these eight relations is particularly significant, namely, *aññamaññapaccaya*. A corresponding concept of a mutually simultaneous cause is found in the Sarvastivadin category of *sahabhuhetu*. The latter has been analysed by Kenneth Tanaka in a paper called 'Simultaneous relation: (*Sahabhu-hetu*): a study in Buddhist theory of causation'. I suggest that this analysis may shed light on the Theravadin notion of *aññamaññapaccaya* and on its implications for the attribution of the distinction between horizontal and vertical causality to the *Pa tthana*.

Tanaka's argument begins by noting that in the *Koça* Vasubandhu documents a definition of *sahabhuhetu*s as 'those *dharmas* that become together', equating 'together' with 'mutuality': '*Dharmas* which are mutual effects are mutually *sahabhu-hetu.*' This definition is criticized by the opponent, who sees in it an abrogation of the temporal sequence of cause and effect, for it is incoherent to hold that *dharmas* that are produced simultaneously can be both cause and effect. The response is that 'Among the coexistent *dharmas,* when one exists then all exist, and when one does not exist then all do not exist; therefore, they do constitute cause and effect.' This statement shows that *sahabhuhetu* has two distinct aspects: one is simultaneity and the other is mutuality. It further indicates that what is at stake here is not the simultaneity of the arising *dharmas,* but rather their alleged mutuality. This is because mutuality, as claimed by the Sautrantika, implies the lack of criteria for determining which of the simultaneously produced *dharmas* constitute the cause and which the effect. It is Saðghabhadra who clarifies what stands behind the relation of *sahabhuhetu*. He argues that this relation does not at all signify a *dharma*'s capability of causally producing other *dharmas*.

The opponent's mistake, Saðghabhadra claims, lies in the attempt to find in the simultaneously produced *hetu* 'sequential' causation – that is, what has been referred to above as 'vertical' causation – while it has no such function. Instead, this *hetu* is concerned with the spatial (as opposed to the temporal) interrelation among the coexistent *dharmas*, emphasizing their inseparability.

To clarify this idea Saðghabhadra proposes the metaphor of the lamp and its inevitably conjoined light: these are not two discrete entities existing independently of each other at any time, but rather two phenomena that constitute a unified whole in which they both support each other.

'What is clearly shown here', Tanaka concludes, is that 'to be mutually cause and effect' does not refer to causation. It, instead, points to the relationship in which one is inextricably related to the rest and vice versa. [...] *Sahabhu-hetu* is the force that coordinates the *dharmas* for a common effect. Its main concern lies with the 'horizontal' relationship among the *dharmas*, not with the direct production of a common effect.

I suggest that this is also the right way to interpret the relation of *aññamaññapaccaya* posited by the Theravadin Abhidhamma. Obviously the Sarvastivadin ontology should not be attributed to the Theravadin mindset, and for this reason the employment of the terms 'cause' and 'effect' is not as directly applicable to the Pali Abhidhamma as it is to the Sarvastivadin framework.

Notwithstanding the doctrinal differences between the two schools, what lies at the core of both *aññamaññapaccaya* and *sahabhuhetu* is not vertical causal production – in fact, not the general idea of causation at all – but rather an attempt to account for the nature of the *dhammas*/*dharmas* in terms of causal efficacy.

Despite the fact that simultaneity and mutuality are indicators of time, in the analysis of the relation of simultaneous causal conditioning temporal considerations are relegated to the background.

This relation does not refer to causation at all, and hence it does not involve time. Rather, it is an atemporal category that contributes to the systematization of the *dharmas* by means of a tenseless use of language.

The Sarvastivadins similarly use the category of *svabhava* as an atemporal determinant of primary ontological status. Just as a *dharma* possesses its primary existential status irrespective of time, the relation of mutually simultaneous causation indicates the *dharma*'s existence as spatially interrelated, and hence it transcends time.

The Theravadins, though, use *sabhava* as an atemporal determinant of individuality. Bear in mind that this notion of *sabhava* as an indi-viduator, and hence as an individual itself, implies that any attempt to individuate a *sabhava* must transcend its possessing *dhamma* and use something else, such as the *dhamma*'s spatio-temporal relations to at least one other individual *dhamma*.

I have shown that the post-canonical Abhidhamma confronts this problem by entwining the notion of *sabhava* with the developed theory of momentariness. The *Pa tthana* theory of *paccaya* embodies another, earlier attempt to offer a solution to this problem. Here the Theravadins use *aññamaññapaccaya* as an indicator of the spatial interrelations among the *dhammas* for the sake of their individuation.

The Abhidhamma systematized analysis of all possible relations of causal conditioning, then, is subordinate to the *dhamma* theory and its associated metaphysical vision of the individuation of one's mind.

It forms part of the Theravadins' broader metaphysical account of the nature of sentient experience, meditative experience in particular, and of how it is constructed; it is one facet of a comprehensive method of explaining what every possible event that appears in one's consciousness is, rather than a theory of causation *per se*.

The following and concluding section expounds this claim, situating the *Pa tthana* theory within the broader context of the doctrinal transition from the Nikaya mindset to the Abhidhamma.

Causation and Individuation: how Twelve Nidånas become Twenty-four Paccayas

The *Pa tthana* analysis of causal conditioning is subsidiary to the Abhidhamma metaphysics of mind as this is represented by the *dhamma* theory. In contradistinction to the earliest stratum of Buddhist thought, the Abhidhamma analysis of causal conditioning is primarily intended to account for the true nature of the dependently co-arisen *dhammas,* and only secondarily for the principle of dependent co-arising itself.

The Abhidhamma theory of *paccaya* explains what it is to be an individual *dhamma* in terms of causal efficacy. We have seen that the doctrinal shift from the Nikaya mindset to the Abhidhamma consists in a transition from a process-oriented to an event-oriented conception of sentient experience.

Having portrayed the *dham-mas* as events, and subsequently as momentary events of which dimensions are fixed, the Abhidhamma shifts its doctrinal focus from describing the dependent co-origination of all encountered phenomena to establishing a metaphysical theory of mental events. Providing a theory of events involves settling the question of what events are, and this necessitates methods of their identification as well as criteria for their individuation.

I have already noted that modern philosophical scholarship, especially that interested in philosophy of mind, has put forward various theories of events. To get a clearer idea of the Abhidhamma theory of events as embodied in the *Pa tthana* it would be helpful to address one of the most influential theories of events in twentieth-century philosophy, namely, Donald Davidson's theory that accounts for events in terms of causation.

Davidson argues for the existence of events either directly, or by proving first that there are actions and then showing that actions are but events. Davidson's preliminary step in offering a theory of events is to point to the fact that many of the terms that purport to describe events do so in terms of the causes and effects of those events. He claims that all causes and effects are events, and that only events can be causes and effects. This leads to his theory about what it is to be an event: the properties of being a cause and being an effect, which are unique to events, make it possible to express the very idea of an event.

According to this view, to be an event is to have a place in a series of causes and effects. This implies that identical events must fit into the framework of causal relations in the same way; that is, events are identical if, and only if, they have exactly the same causes and effects. Sameness of causes and effects is a condition of identity for events. Davidson's nexus of causal relations provides a framework for the identification and description of events, analogous in many respects to the way the space-time coordinate system enables one to identify and describe material objects.

In the light of Davidson's theory of events, the *Pa tthana* network of *paccaya* may be seen as a space-time coordinate system that enables one to locate within it any given *dhamma* in relation to all other events.

This not only makes it possible to identify the *dhamma*, but also to render it in its exclusiveness as a unique particular, namely, to individuate it. Two *dhammic* instances of the same type would fit into the web of causal conditions in exactly the same way, but would then be distinguished as discrete, individual instances on the grounds of their unique degrees of causal efficacy. The *paccaya* web of interrelations, then, provides a method of the *dhammas'* individuation, by which any given *dhamma* may be identified and distinguished from any other *dhammic* instance.

The Abhidhammikas sought to offer a metaphysical account of the structure of one's experience. This required them to explain the exact nature of the *dhammas* constituting that experience. Since they portrayed the *dhammas* as events, they had to provide a theory of what it means to be an event and what makes an individual event the particular it is. In accordance with the fundamentals of Buddhist thought, the natural place in which to search for such a theory must have been the principle of causal conditioning and the *paticcasamuppada* doctrine. But the treatment of these was then subject to the requirements imposed by a broader interest in the *dhamma*'s nature. A metaphysical theory of events in terms of causal conditioning was then provided and formulated in line with the systematic methods of the Abhidhamma and its specific doctrinal concerns.

To reconstruct the shift from the Buddha's teaching to the Abhidhamma as a doctrinal transition from explaining human experience in terms of processes to its explanation in terms of events may particularly elucidate the nature of the connection between the early *paticcasamuppada* doctrine and the Abhidhamma theory of the twenty-four *paccayas*.

Within the Nikaya conceptual framework *dhammas* are physical and mental processes, and processes *ipso facto* take place over a period of time. Accordingly, the *paticcasamuppada* formula has traditionally been interpreted as depicting a process – the process that makes up a person – as it stretches over three cycles of lives in the three time periods.

The twelvefold formula was thus divided into three sections: the first, comprised by the first two *nidanas* of ignorance and mental formations, represents one's past life; the second, from consciousness up to the tenth *nidana* of becoming, depicts one's present life; and the third, which includes the last two *nidana*s of birth plus age-ing-and-death, portrays one's future life.

The twelvefold chain was further divided by placing within it three transition points: first, between mental formations and consciousness; second, between feeling and craving; third, between becoming and birth. This division results in four sections: (i) past ignorance and formations are the sufficient condition of (ii) the present fruit (consciousness up to feeling); the present fruit conditions (iii) the set of necessary conditions (craving up to becoming) that will bear fruit in (iv) a future cycle of birth, ageing and death.

In the Abhidhamma the twelvefold formula is viewed differently. Led by their interest in accounting for meditative experience, as well as by their espoused event-oriented metaphysics and the theory of momentariness, the Abhidhamma points out that the *paticcasamuppada* formula applies not only to one's past, present and future lives, but also to each and every single moment of consciousness. Although the *Pa tthana* does not yet contain the full-fledged theory of the momentary consciousness process, the basics of this theory are well established in it and it specifies almost all the stages of the consciousness process.

The theory of the consciousness process can thus be attributed to the canonical Abhidhamma, if not to the earlier Abhidhamma. According to this theory every *dhamma*, every momentary event, emerges in one's consciousness in accordance with the twelvefold chain.

This means that in every consciousness moment the twelve *nidanas* arise simultaneously as a unified whole of which constitutive causal conditions are all interrelated. The principle of *paticcasamuppada* reveals the mechanism underlying experience in *saµsara*. It shows that the latter is a cyclic process encapsulated in the repetitive movement from becoming to birth, which in turn leads to ageing and death, then to a renewed birth that will end, again and again. This means that the chain cannot be broken at any of its links; it can only be demolished as a whole. Hence it is not only necessary to analyse how each two links stand in relation to one another, but also what possible interrelations may obtain among the twelve links in their entirety at any given consciousness moment.

This task is facilitated by analysing the twelve *nidanas* in terms of the twenty-four *paccayas*, and accomplished by Buddhaghosa in the *Visuddhimagga*'s chapter on the *paticcasamuppada* doctrine as well as by the author of the *Sammohavinodani* in commenting on the *Vibhaðga*' s *paticcasamuppadavibhaðga*.

For instance, the investigation of the relation between the first two *nidanas*, ignorance and mental formations, reveals that ignorance is conditionally related to mental formations in many ways: as object condition on the occurrence of the three roots of greed etc.; as a decisive support condition in one whose moral conduct is flawed; or as cause condition, simultaneity, mutuality, support, association, presence and non-disappearance conditions in one while performing anything unskilful. Another example is the inquiry into the sequence from the six sense faculties to sense contact which discloses the following web of conditioning relations:

the five physical sense faculties are conditionally related to their corresponding types of sense contact (eye contact etc.) in six ways, namely, as support, pre-existence, controlling faculty, dissociation, presence and non-disappearance conditions. Subsequently, the mental sense faculty is conditionally related to its corresponding mind contact in nine ways: as simultaneity, mutuality, support, fruition, nutriment, controlling faculty, association, presence and non-disappearance conditions.

Likewise, the five physical sense objects are conditionally related to their corresponding types of sense contact in four ways: as object, pre-existence, presence and non-disappearance conditions. But all these also operate as object condition in relation to mind contact, and hence mind contact has all the five physical sense objects plus mental objects as object conditions.

The *paticcasamuppada* formula and the twenty-four *paccaya*s are thus two different methods of analysing the processes that make up the person. Ye t once it is acknowledged that all sentient and insentient phenomena are impermanent, and that our construction of these phenomena is a dynamic process that may be examined on a number of different scales, it turns out that the two methods in fact converge. When they are applied to the smallest scale of each and every single moment of consciousness, they turn out to be two aspects of an attempted theoretical reconstruction of one's conscious world. Gethin comments on this:

The list of twenty-four *paccayas* can be considered by way of two basic aspects. The first concerns those *paccayas* that illustrate the various relationships that exist simultaneously between *dhammas* that arise together in a given assemblage or complex at a given moment in time. The second concerns those *paccayas* that focus on the relationships that exist between *dhammas* over a period of time, that is to say, the way in which a *dhamma* that arises at one moment can be related to a *dhamma* that arises at another time.

From the Abhidhamma viewpoint what determines the process that makes up the person is his or her consciousness process, and this is understood as a dynamic stream of consciousness moments. The Abhidhamma seeks to cultivate one's mind and wisdom by drawing one's attention to the ways in which one's process of life occurs at each and every single moment of thought. To grasp the mechanism that conditions one's consciousness in its entirety is seen as a requisite part of the spiritual path to awakening.

Just as the process of *samsaric* experience is an interrelated network of conditions encapsulated in every single consciousness moment, so the path factors leading to the cessation of this *samsaric* process are contained in every single consciousness moment that contributes to awakening. Any one of the path factors embraces all the factors, and hence, by the principle of simultaneity and reciprocity, to cultivate any one of the *dhammas* that contribute to awakening is to develop them all. The awakening moment is that at which all the path factors follow simultaneously as a unified whole. At this moment the chain of dependent co-arising is demolished in its entirety and liberation emerges from wisdom. This is where the Abhidhamma systematic and allegedly divergent method is at home with early Buddhist soteriology.

Bibliography

Aronson, Harvey B.: *Love and Sympathy in Theravada Buddhism,* Motilal Banarsidass, Delhi, 1980.

Behl, Benoy K.: *The Ajanta Caves: Artistic Wonder of Ancient Buddhist India,* Harry N. Abrams, New York, 1998.

Buddhadasa, Bhikkhu: *Teaching Dhamma by Pictures,* Social Science Association Press of Thailand, Bangkok, 1968.

Cummings, Mary: *The Lives of the Buddha in the Art and Literature of Asia,* University of Michigan, Ann Arbor, 1982.

Haldar, J. R.: *Early Buddhist Mythology,* Manohar, New Delhi, 1977.

Ireland, John D.: *The Udana: Inspired Utterances of the Buddha,* Buddhist Publication Society, Kandy, 1990.

John Powers: *The Yogacara School of Buddhism: A Bibliography,* Scarecrow Press, Lanham, 1991.

Miksic, John: *Borobudur: Golden Tales of the Buddha,* Shambala, Boston, 1990.

Pal, Pratapaditya: *Light of Asia: Buddha Sakyamuni in Asian Art,* County Museum of Art, Los Angeles, 1984.

Seneviratna, Anuradha: *King Ashoka and Buddhism,* Buddhist Publication Society, Kandy, 1994.

Wagle, Narendra: *Society at the Time of Buddha,* Humanities Press, New York, 1967.

Yang, C. K.: *Religion in Chinese Society,* University of California Press, Berkeley, 1961.

Yushin Yoo: *Books on Buddhism: An Annotated Subject Guide,* Scarecrow Press, Metuchen, 1976).

Zwalf, W.: *Buddhism: Art and Faith,* British Museum Publications, London, 1985.

Index

A

Abhidhamma, 1, 2, 6, 7, 8, 9, 11, 12, 17, 18, 19, 20, 21, 40, 41, 45, 46, 48, 50, 65, 69, 71, 73, 74, 76, 89, 90, 94, 95, 96, 97, 98, 99, 100, 101, 102, 103, 118, 129, 130, 131, 133, 146, 147, 149, 150, 153, 162, 163, 164, 165, 166, 176, 177, 178, 179, 182, 201, 203, 204, 205, 206, 214, 215, 216, 217, 218, 243, 245, 246, 249, 250, 252, 255, 257, 258, 259, 263, 264, 267, 269, 271, 272, 273, 274, 275, 277.

Approach, 16, 38, 58, 80, 93, 107, 112, 113, 114, 116, 117, 202, 211, 212, 215, 216, 220, 243, 246, 274.

Atthakatha, 12, 21, 28, 101, 104, 106, 107, 110, 112, 126, 134.

B

Buddha, 6, 8, 16, 18, 19, 20, 21, 24, 30, 40, 41, 42, 43, 44, 51, 56, 76, 81, 82, 85, 95, 98, 100, 101, 103, 108, 110, 123, 125, 126, 128, 142, 158, 207, 208, 209, 210, 218, 220, 221, 222, 223, 224, 225, 226, 228, 230, 231, 236, 239, 240.

Buddhism, 2, 5, 7, 8, 9, 13, 14, 15, 20, 21, 23, 28, 29, 30, 41, 52, 82, 83, 89, 94, 95, 99, 147, 158, 219, 222, 228, 239, 240, 266.

Buddhist Schools, 13, 23, 27, 37, 74, 78, 79, 81, 107.

C

Conditions, 5, 6, 7, 15, 16, 49, 50, 51, 70, 74, 97, 103, 109, 134, 135, 136, 137, 145, 173, 176, 179, 198, 201, 224, 225, 227, 228, 229, 237, 238, 239, 240, 241, 248, 249, 250, 251, 252, 259, 260, 261, 262, 263, 264, 273, 274, 275, 276, 277.

Construction, 18, 57, 59, 75, 85, 89, 96, 131, 204, 231, 276.

D

Developments, 129, 147, 149, 185, 200.

Dhamma, 1, 2, 6, 7, 12, 19, 20, 21, 22, 33, 34, 35, 36, 37, 39, 40, 41, 42,

43, 44, 45, 47, 49, 50, 51, 53, 81, 82, 83, 84, 85, 86, 94, 96, 98, 99, 100, 101, 113, 115, 116, 117, 118, 119, 120, 121, 122, 124, 131, 133, 134, 135, 136, 142, 143, 144, 145, 146, 158, 159, 160, 164, 165, 171, 172, 173, 174, 175, 185, 186, 188, 197, 200, 201, 204, 205, 206, 207, 212, 213, 214, 215, 218, 225, 230, 240, 241, 243, 244, 245, 246, 247, 248, 249, 250, 251, 252, 253, 254, 255, 257, 258, 259, 263, 267, 268, 269, 271, 272, 273, 275, 276.

I

Idealism, 4, 19, 208.

K

Kamma, 17, 22, 163, 164, 172, 173, 212, 225, 226, 227, 231, 239, 242, 250, 252, 253, 254.

M

Majority, 37, 126, 177, 189, 236.

Metaphysics, 3, 4, 5, 17, 21, 41, 50, 61, 62, 64, 65, 66, 67, 69, 74, 76, 80, 87, 90, 91, 94, 95, 96, 97, 98, 100, 111, 117, 119, 131, 133, 141, 149, 150, 155, 156, 158, 168, 179, 180, 182, 185, 186, 189, 196, 197, 198, 200, 202, 203, 204, 213, 216, 217, 218, 221, 224, 228, 229, 231, 233, 240, 259, 262, 263, 272, 274.

Milindapañha, 12, 36, 101, 126, 127, 128, 129, 143.

N

Nettippakarana, 12, 113, 114, 115, 117, 120, 121, 122.

P

Philosophy, 2, 3, 5, 9, 10, 11, 14, 15, 16, 17, 18, 64, 65, 66, 68, 86, 90, 91, 92, 93, 94, 95, 96, 97, 98, 101, 139, 148, 149, 158, 181, 182, 216, 217, 219, 229, 232, 272.

Powers, 66, 92, 93, 102, 171, 172, 175, 221, 231.

Production, 119, 224, 226, 231, 235, 240, 261, 277.

Products, 25, 143.

R

Relationship, 19, 30, 31, 32, 34, 37, 38, 94, 106, 185, 225, 242, 246, 270.

Religious, 8, 9, 10, 11, 15, 24, 41, 42, 208, 213, 218, 219, 222.

Research, 16, 74.

S

Substance Metaphysics, 64, 65, 69, 74, 90, 98, 131, 141, 156, 158, 185, 189, 196, 224, 233.

□□□